PRAGUE & CZECHIA

North & East Bohemia
p143

⭐ PRAGUE, p42

South & West Bohemia
p115

Moravia
p173

Mark Baker, Marc Di Duca

CONTENTS

Plan Your Trip

The Journey Begins................4
Prague & Czechia Map...........6
Our Picks.............................8
Regions & Cities...................20
Itineraries............................22
When to Go.........................28
Get Prepared......................30
The Food Scene...................32
The Outdoors......................36

The Guide

Prague & Around..................42
Find Your Way.....................44
Plan Your Days...................46
Prague Castle
& Hradčany........................48

Malá Strana........................54
Staré Město........................62
Nové Město........................72
Žižkov & Karlín....................80
Vinohrady & Vršovice.....84
Holešovice.........................88
Bubeneč & Dejvice..........92
Smíchov.............................96
Vyšehrad...........................100
Beyond Prague.................104

South &
West Bohemia..................115
Find Your way....................116
Plan Your Time..................118
Karlovy Vary......................120
Beyond
Karlovy Vary.....................124
Mariánské Lázně..............127
Beyond Mariánské
Lázně................................130
Plzeň.................................132
Beyond Plzeň....................134
Český Krumlov..................136
České Budějovice............140

North &
East Bohemia..................143
Find Your Way...................144
Plan Your Time..................146
Liberec..............................148
Beyond Liberec.................152
The Czech
Switzerland.......................156
Beyond the Czech
Switzerland.......................160
Kutná Hora........................163
Beyond Kutná Hora.........166
Litomyšl............................168

Moravia..........................173
Find Your Way...................174
Plan Your Time..................176
Brno..................................178
Beyond Brno.....................182
Mikulov.............................185
Beyond Mikulov................189
Olomouc...........................192
Telč...................................194
Kroměříž...........................196

St Nicholas Church (p55), Prague

RIGHT: ROMAN KYBUS/SHUTTERSTOCK ©. BELOW: SERGII FIGURNYI/SHUTTERSTOCK ©

Old Town Square (p62), Prague

Toolkit

Arriving 200

Getting Around 201

Money 202

Accommodation 203

Family Travel 204

Health & Safe Travel 205

Food, Drink
& Nightlife 206

Responsible Travel 208

LGBTIQ+ Travellers 210

Accessible Travel 211

How to Enjoy Winter
Sports in Czechia 212

Nuts & Bolts 213

Language 214

Storybook

A History of Prague
& Czechia in 15 Places 218

Meet the Czechs 222

Architecture:
The Battle over
Communist Buildings 224

Czech Humour:
A Penchant For
the Absurd 228

Sports:
Natural-Born
Athletes 232

Statue on Charles
Bridge (p54), Prague

ANGELINA DIMITROVA/SHUTTERSTOCK ©

Old Town Square (p62), Prague

PRAGUE & CZECHIA
THE JOURNEY BEGINS HERE

I'm a wanderer by nature, and there's nothing I enjoy more than meandering around the alleyways and hidden lanes of Prague's Old Town or Malá Strana. Although I've lived here for the better part of 30 years, the experience never gets old. Maybe it's the notion that I'm retracing steps that people have walked for centuries, or maybe it's simply the city's undeniable beauty. Every building, every bridge, every bend in the road feels purposefully placed by a set designer in a lush, historic drama, and for this moment in time, at least, I'm the actor. Life in Prague – and Czechia generally – feels somehow easy. Not in sorting out the nuances of the language, perhaps, or in the ways of the culture, but in the local appreciation of simple pleasures: activities like strolling or sitting down for a coffee or beer in the shadow of 1000 years of history.

My favourite experience is walking across Charles Bridge to feel the breeze and enjoy the sensation of space after wandering the city's closed-in, cobblestoned streets.

Mark Baker

@markbakerprague

WHO GOES WHERE

Our writers and experts choose the places which, for them, define Prague & Czechia

The **Karlovy Vary (Carlsbad) region** is a magical place of low mountains, lonely villages, dark forests and a million stories. One of central Europe's most sparsely populated areas, the snow falls deep on the Krušné Mountains and the Slavkovský Forest, winter's fiery sunsets setting the ice ablaze. Later, the temperature plummets, meaning it's time to find a log burner in a snug tavern for a plate of goulash and a tankard of beer.

Marc Di Duca
Marc is a travel author, translator, guide and outdoor enthusiast based in the Czech Republic.

Stromovka Park in Prague is not just a pretty piece of nature; it also says something about the city's resilience. The park was badly damaged by the tragic flood of 2002. Instead of allowing Stromovka to languish, officials poured millions into rebuilding the area, transforming it into the hidden oasis that residents love today.

Mark Baker
Mark is based in Prague and the author of Čas proměn (Time of Changes), a personal, Czech-language account of the period around the 1989 Velvet Revolution.

5

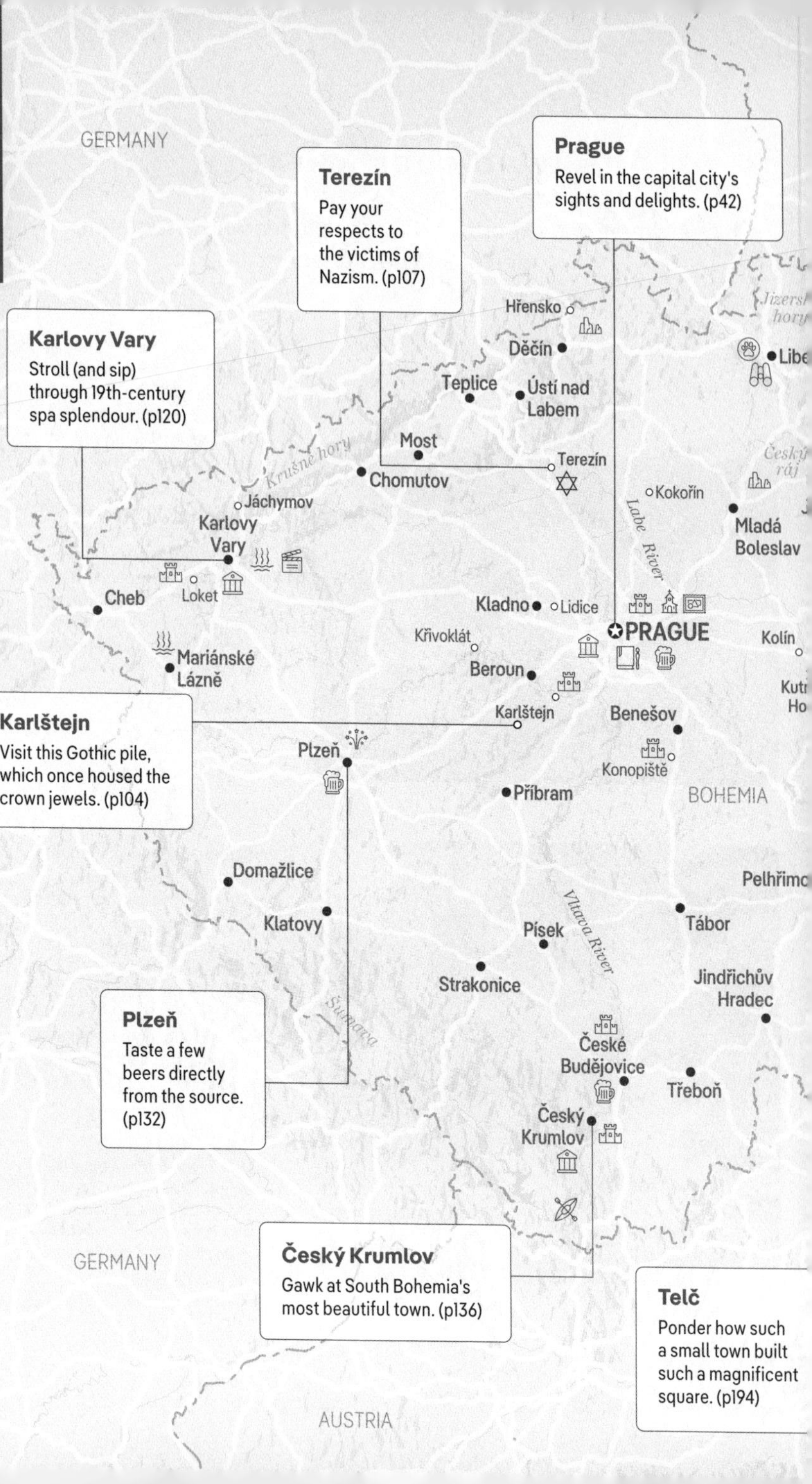

GERMANY

Terezín
Pay your respects to the victims of Nazism. (p107)

Prague
Revel in the capital city's sights and delights. (p42)

Hřensko ○

Jizersk horv

Karlovy Vary
Stroll (and sip) through 19th-century spa splendour. (p120)

Děčín ●

● Libe

Teplice ● Ústí nad Labem

Most ●

Český ráj

Terezín

○ Kokořín

Krušné hory

○ Jáchymov

Chomutov ●

Labe River

Mladá Boleslav

Karlovy Vary

Cheb ● ○ Loket

Kladno ● ○ Lidice

○ PRAGUE

Kolín ○

Křivoklát ○

Mariánské Lázně

Beroun ●

Karlštejn
Visit this Gothic pile, which once housed the crown jewels. (p104)

Karlštejn ○

Kutr Ho

Plzeň ●

Benešov ●

Konopiště

BOHEMIA

● Příbram

Domažlice ●

Pelhřimo

Klatovy ●

Písek ●

Tábor ●

Plzeň
Taste a few beers directly from the source. (p132)

Jindřichův Hradec ●

Strakonice ●

Vltava River

Šumava

České Budějovice

Třeboň ●

Český Krumlov

Český Krumlov
Gawk at South Bohemia's most beautiful town. (p136)

GERMANY

Telč
Ponder how such a small town built such a magnificent square. (p194)

AUSTRIA

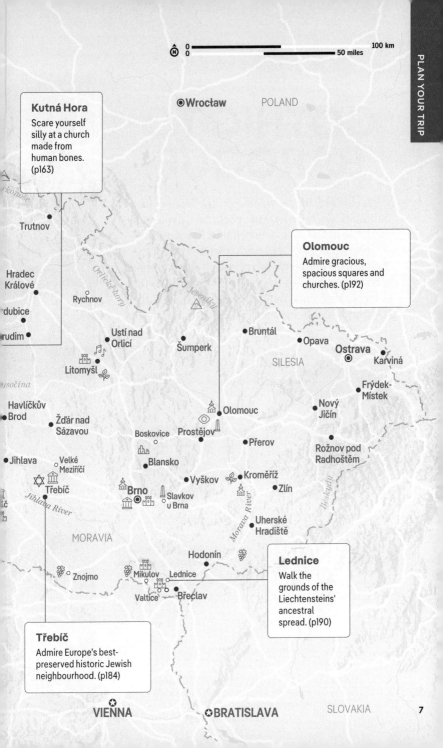

0   100 km
0   50 miles

POLAND

Kutná Hora
Scare yourself silly at a church made from human bones. (p163)

Olomouc
Admire gracious, spacious squares and churches. (p192)

Wrocław

Trutnov

Hradec Králové

dubice

rudim

Rychnov

Orlické hory

Jeseníky

Bruntál

Opava

Ostrava

Karviná

Ústí nad Orlicí

Šumperk

SILESIA

Frýdek-Místek

Litomyšl

sočina

Nový Jičín

Havlíčkův Brod

Žďár nad Sázavou

Olomouc

Boskovice

Prostějov

Přerov

Rožnov pod Radhoštěm

Jihlava

Velké Meziříčí

Blansko

Vyškov

Kroměříž

Zlín

Třebíč

Jihlava River

Brno

Slavkov u Brna

Uherské Hradiště

Morava River

MORAVA

Beskydy

MORAVIA

Hodonín

Lednice
Walk the grounds of the Liechtensteins' ancestral spread. (p190)

Znojmo

Mikulov

Lednice

Valtice

Břeclav

Třebíč
Admire Europe's best-preserved historic Jewish neighbourhood. (p184)

VIENNA

BRATISLAVA

SLOVAKIA

7

GOTHIC TO BAROQUE

Czechia's history is written on the faces of its buildings. Each important epoch, new dynasty or wrinkle in technology ushered in a new type of architecture. The story begins at the turn of the first millennium with heavy, round Romanesque and moves forward through the centuries to the stately Gothic town halls and cathedrals, and then to symmetrical Renaissance, dazzling baroque and beyond.

Everyone loves Gothic

Somber Gothic buildings recall the heady 14th century, when Emperor Charles IV was on the throne and Prague was the capital of the Holy Roman Empire.

Renaissance Symmetry

Italian-influenced Renaissance, with its emphasis on proportion and beauty, came to Czechia in the 16th century and is strongly connected to the Reformation.

Razzle-Dazzle Baroque

The statues on Charles Bridge and the swirling gold and marble interiors of many churches ushered in an era of Catholic-Habsburg supremacy in the 17th century.

BEST ARCHITECTURE EXPERIENCES

Stroll across **Charles Bridge ❶**, a Gothic masterpiece which dates from 1357. The evocative statues were added a few centuries later. (p54)

Take in Prague's beautiful **Old Town Hall ❷**, with its tall tower and Astronomical Clock. This is a textbook example of Gothic architecture. (p63)

Admire **Český Krumlov's castle ❸**, which gained its Renaissance exterior in the 16th century under the noble Rožmberk family. (p136)

Stand before Olomouc's moving **Holy Trinity Column ❹**. It was built during the 18th century and is allegedly the biggest baroque sculpture in Central Europe. (p192)

Walk and gawk at the gorgeous 19th-century **spa architecture** at a timeless resort like **Karlovy Vary ❺**. (p120)

CHILLED TO THE BONE

Czechia is sneakily underrated as a spooky, downright macabre destination. Where else on earth will you find a church with an interior built entirely of human bones? If mummies are more your thing, a monastery in Brno has them splayed out on the basement floor – and the city has its own collection of human bones just down the street. The back alleys of Prague's former Jewish Quarter, Josefov, are haunted by a legendary creature called the Golem.

Sanctuary of Skeletons

Kutná Hora's Sedlec Ossuary is home to Czechia's creepiest creation. František Rint sculpted the church interior from the bones of around 40,000 people.

Blood-Curdling Brno

Brno places first for eye-popping oddities. The Capuchin Monastery houses several mummies, and a nearby church is stuffed with thousands of human bones.

Prague's Jewish Quarter

Prague's former Jewish Quarter is filled with legends going back centuries. These clearly inspired a young Franz Kafka, who considered the neighbourhood his early stomping ground.

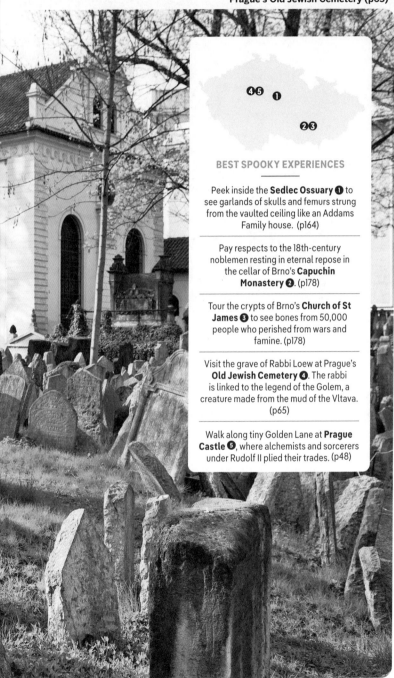

BEST SPOOKY EXPERIENCES

Peek inside the **Sedlec Ossuary ①** to see garlands of skulls and femurs strung from the vaulted ceiling like an Addams Family house. (p164)

Pay respects to the 18th-century noblemen resting in eternal repose in the cellar of Brno's **Capuchin Monastery ②**. (p178)

Tour the crypts of Brno's **Church of St James ③** to see bones from 50,000 people who perished from wars and famine. (p178)

Visit the grave of Rabbi Loew at Prague's **Old Jewish Cemetery ④**. The rabbi is linked to the legend of the Golem, a creature made from the mud of the Vltava. (p65)

Walk along tiny Golden Lane at **Prague Castle ⑤**, where alchemists and sorcerers under Rudolf II plied their trades. (p48)

LEFT TO RIGHT: ALBERTEM/GETTY IMAGES ©, MARCOBRIVIO.PHOTO/SHUTTERSTOCK ©, GIORGIO BIANCHI/SHUTTERSTOCK ©

The National Cemetery at Terezín (p107)

JEWISH LIFE

For centuries, both Bohemia and Moravia were relative safe havens for Jews. Prague, in particular, evolved into an important centre of Jewish life and scholarship, but towns like Mikulov and Třebíč in Moravia also developed into influential Jewish settlements. This came to a brutal end with the German Nazi occupation during WWII.

16th-Century Splendour

The vibrancy of the community, can be seen at Prague's Jewish Quarter, where the main synagogues and Old Jewish Cemetery have been preserved.

Remembering the Holocaust

The German occupation of World War II led to the destruction of this community. Many Jews were held at Terezín before being sent to Auschwitz-Birkenau.

BEST JEWISH HERITAGE EXPERIENCES

Learn the history, of Prague's Jews by touring the city's **Jewish Museum ❶**. (p65)

View the tombstones that push through the ground at the **Old Jewish Cemetery ❷**. (p65)

Visit the city of **Třebíč** to see Europe's best-preserved Jewish neighbourhood ❸. (p184)

Pay your respects to the victims of Nazism at **Terezín**, a transit camp to Auschwitz ❹. (p107)

Marvel at Plzeň's gigantic **synagogue**, the world's third-biggest Jewish place of worship ❺. (p132)

BEHIND THE IRON CURTAIN

Not long ago, Czechia (as Czechoslovakia) was firmly locked into the Soviet-led Eastern bloc. The 1989 Velvet Revolution that overthrew communist rule and brought in playwright Václav Havel as president inspired the world. The changes since then have been profound, but here and there you can still see remains of the former authoritarian dictatorship.

A Coup Declared

Communist rule came to Czechoslovakia in February 1948, when communist leader Klement Gottwald declared a takeover from the balcony of Prague's Kinský Palace on Old Town Square.

Soviet-Led Invasion

Warsaw Pact forces, led by the Soviet Union, invaded a brotherly country in August 1968 to put down the democratic reforms known as the Prague Spring.

A 'Velvet' Revolution

On 17 November 1989, thousands rallied on Prague's central avenue, Národní, to call on communists to step down. Within a month, the regime collapsed.

BEST 'VELVET' EXPERIENCES

Descend to the cellar of **Vítkov Monument ❶** to see the ghoulish laboratory where scientists tried to preserve Gottwald's remains. (p80)

Peak inside the nuclear bunker below Prague's **Hotel Jalta ❷** to see the surveillance equipment used to spy on guests. (p73)

Admire the retro kitsch at Brno's **Retro Muzeum Na Statku ❸**. (p181)

Walk along Prague's **Národní třída ❹**, where the Velvet Revolution began. (p72)

Feel history on Prague's **Wenceslas Square ❺** where hundreds of thousands gathered to call on the communists to step down. (p72)

STORYBOOK CASTLES

The Czechs' homeland in the middle of Europe has seen a long history of raiding tribes, conquering armies and triumphant dynasties. This turbulent past left a legacy of hundreds of castles and chateaux – everywhere there seems to be a many-turreted fortress perched above a town, or a romantic summer palace lazing amid manicured parkland. The number and variety of Czech castles is simply awe-inspiring – everything from grim Gothic ruins to majestic, baroque mansions.

The Bohemian Kingdom

Prague's enormous castle complex has served as the ruling centre of Bohemia, and a model for castles around the country, since around the first millennium.

Fortress Prison

Brno's ancient, foreboding Špilberk Castle dates from the mid-13th century, but it's best known for its later role as the cruellest prison of the Habsburg Empire.

19th-century bling

Many of Czechia's flashiest chateaux, particularly in South Bohemia and Moravia, were built in the 19th century by aristocratic families allied with the ruling Habsburg monarchy.

BEST CASTLE EXPERIENCES

Tour magnificent **Prague Castle** ❶, the world's largest by area. The grounds are breathtaking and surrounded by parks and gardens. (p48)

Let yourself be dazzled by **Karlštejn** ❷, once used to store the Bohemian crown jewels during the 15th century Hussite religious wars. (p104)

Enjoy the Renaissance spectacle of **Litomyšl** ❸, which boasts one of the country's most exquisite chateaux. (p168)

Walk the grounds of **Lednice Chateau** ❹. The Liechtenstein family's ancestral spread includes a lavish greenhouse and minaret. (p190)

Delight your senses at **Hluboká** ❺, an over-the-top confection of neo-Gothic frivolity modelled on England's Windsor Castle. (p141)

LEFT TO RIGHT: ROMAN SIGAEV/SHUTTERSTOCK ©, ATLANTIDE PHOTOTRAVEL/GETTY IMAGES ©, KIRILL RUDENKO/GETTY IMAGES ©

Telč (p194)

UNDERFOOT

A pretty, cobblestoned public square stands at the heart of just about every town and city in the country. Indeed, the Czech word for a plaza or open square – náměstí – literally means 'at the town'. Back in the Middle Ages, towns were ranked in importance by the size of their squares, and Czechia has some very big – and beautiful – ones.

Architecture on Parade

Head straight to the central square to see a town's best historic architecture. It might be a Gothic town hall or a pretty row of Renaissance or Baroque houses.

Main Market Square

Town squares started out as marketplaces. They remain at the heart of town life, and typically serve as scenic backdrops for festivals and holiday celebrations.

BEST COBBLESTONE EXPERIENCES

Enjoy Prague's **Old Town Square** ❶, one of Central Europe's main marketplaces. (p63)

Take in tiny **Telč's** ❷ main square. This Unesco-protected space is one of Czechia's prettiest. (p194)

Walk through České Budějovice's **Náměstí Přemysla Otakara** ❸. It's one of the country's biggest squares. (p140)

Admire **Olomouc's** ❹ majestic squares, with a Unesco-protected Holy Trinity Column. (p192)

See Mikulov's evocative **Náměstí** ❺, to realise squares don't always need to be big. (p185)

NIGHT AT THE PUB

Spending an evening in the pub may just be Czechia's quintessential experience. The pub is more than a bar and means more than the beer. It functions as the country's collective living room. On several nights of the week, people gather to meet friends, catch up on news and enjoy a meal. Oh yeah, the beer's good too.

❶
❷
❺
❹
❸

Beers to the Table

In traditional pubs, waiters may bring beers to the table without the need to order – and stop bringing them only when you say you've had enough.

Local Food

Most pubs serve food and are excellent spots to try traditional cooking. Even if a pub doesn't have a kitchen, they'll always offer beer snacks.

Literary Aspirations

Czech writer Jaroslav Hašek, author of *The Good Soldier Švejk*, wrote many books in the pub. *Švejk* practically begins with the main character swilling beers in the local saloon.

BEST PUB EXPERIENCES

Pair a visit to Prague Castle with a Pilsner-Urquell at the delightfully old-school **U Černého Vola** ❶. (p53)

In Plzeň, finish off the Pilsner Urquell brewery tour with a couple of more cold ones at **Na Spilce** ❷. (p133)

While in Český Krumlov, visit **Hospoda Na Louži** ❸, an intimate tavern with very good food, and the town's own Eggenberg beer. (p138)

A České Budějovice institution, **Masné Krámy** ❹ is one of the best places around to sample the city's own Budvar beer. (p141)

In Olomouc, **Svatováclavský Pivovar** ❺ serves home-brewed beers and plates piled with Moravian specialities. (p192)

17

TOP OF THE HOPS

Few would disagree that Czech beer is some of the world's best. Since the invention of modern-style lager here in 1842, the Czechs have been famous for producing some of the finest beers you can find anywhere. These days, internationally famous local brands – like Pilsner Urquell, Staropramen and Budvar (Czech Budweiser) – have been equalled, and even surpassed, by a bunch of regional Czech beers, microbrews and craft beers.

Inventors of Modern Lager

Plzeň (the Czech word for Pilsen) is famed among beer fans worldwide as the mother of all lagers. Pilsner-style beer was invented here in 1842.

Budvar vs 'Budweiser'

Czech Budvar and US Budweiser share a name and have been embroiled in copyright disputes for decades, but they don't remotely taste the same.

Craft-Beer Revolution

The global craft-beer trend has reached Czechia and is most pronounced in Prague, which boasts several pubs that brew their own creations.

BEST BEER EXPERIENCES

Tour the temple itself. The **Pilsner Urquell Brewery ❶** was where it all began and the highlight of the tour is a sip of the golden nectar itself. (p132)

Stop by at the excellent **Plzeň Brewery Museum ❷** to learn how beer was made in the days before Pilsner Urquell was founded. (p132)

See where the original 'Budweiser' beer was born. The brewers at the **Budweiser Budvar Brewery ❸** continue ther long tradition of brewing excellence. (p140)

Visit Prague's only surviving large-scale brewery, **Staropramen ❹,** and discover a century of brewing that's still going strong. (p96)

Indulge in some home-brewed dark at **U Fleků ❺**, a Prague institution that's been serving its own since 1499. (p78)

REGIONS & CITIES

Find the places that tick all your boxes.

Prague

**MEDIEVAL METROPOLIS
MEETS MODERN VIBE**

Czechia's world-class capital has it all. Whole blocks of breath-taking Gothic, Renaissance, baroque and art nouveau architecture, topped by the world's largest castle complex, dazzle the senses, but don't be deceived. Prague also offers the culture and energy – the restaurants, pubs, clubs, parks and museums – of a dynamic 21st-century city.

p42

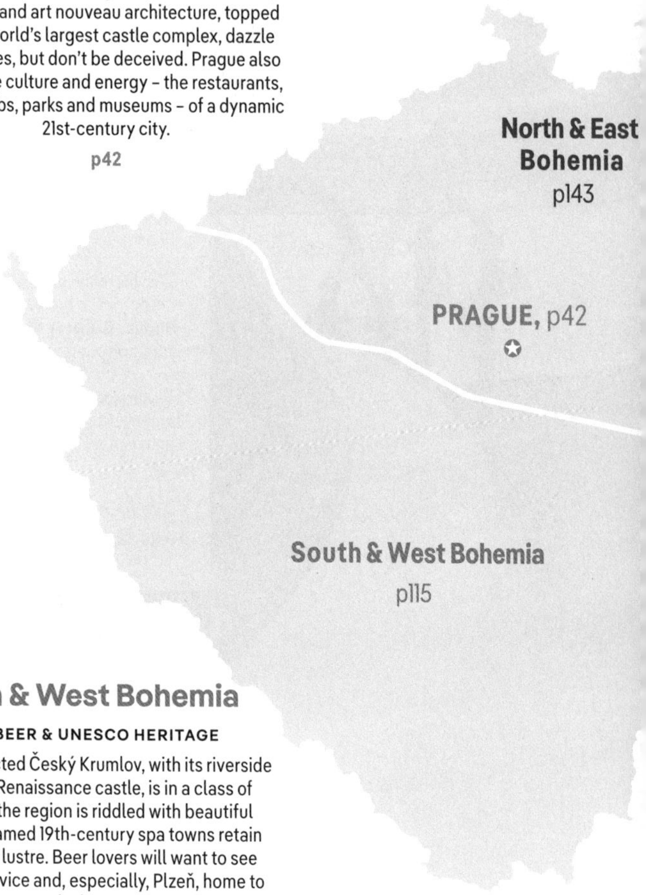

North & East Bohemia
p143

PRAGUE, p42
✪

South & West Bohemia
p115

South & West Bohemia

SPAS, BEER & UNESCO HERITAGE

Unesco-protected Český Krumlov, with its riverside setting and Renaissance castle, is in a class of its own, but the region is riddled with beautiful places. The famed 19th-century spa towns retain an old-world lustre. Beer lovers will want to see České Budějovice and, especially, Plzeň, home to Czechia's renowned Pilsner-Urquell brewery.

p115

Beyond Prague

BEAUTIFUL CASTLES, CONTEMPORARY HISTORY

Use Prague as a base to explore the eye-catching castles and chateaux that surround the capital. Storybook Karlštejn Castle wouldn't look out of place on Disney World's Main Street. The Nazis infamously transformed the remote, former-Habsburg garrison at Terezín into a showcase ghetto for Jewish prisoners during World War II.

p104

North & East Bohemia

SANDSTONE ROCKS & BONE CHURCHES

The quieter lands north of Prague are popular with Czechs but don't see many international visitors. The Czech Switzerland National Park features stunning sandstone-rock formations. The perfectly preserved silver-mining town of Kutná Hora boasts architectural splendours and a freakish church - the interior of which is hewed entirely from human bones.

p143

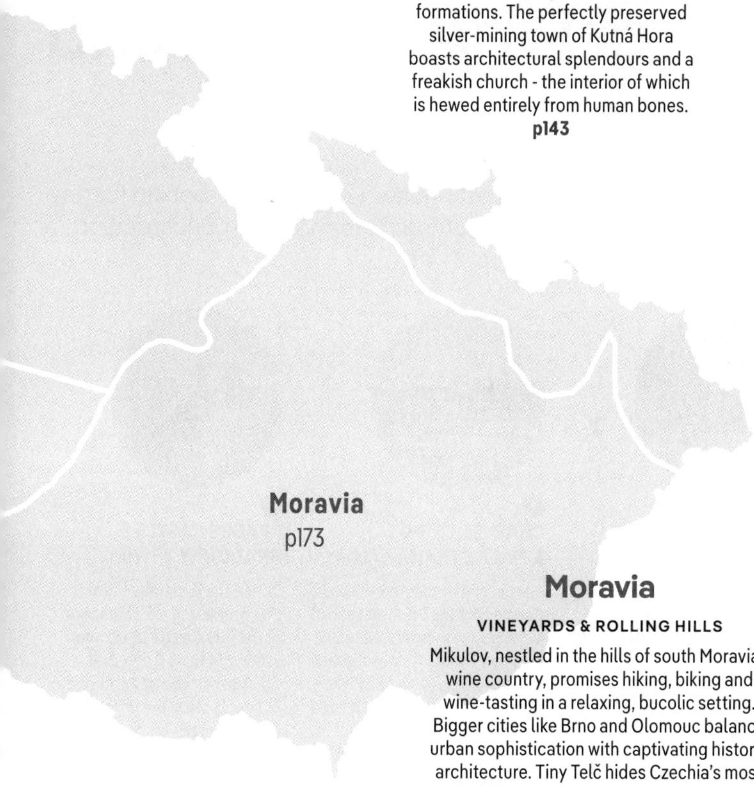

Moravia

p173

Moravia

VINEYARDS & ROLLING HILLS

Mikulov, nestled in the hills of south Moravian wine country, promises hiking, biking and wine-tasting in a relaxing, bucolic setting. Bigger cities like Brno and Olomouc balance urban sophistication with captivating historic architecture. Tiny Telč hides Czechia's most wonderfully preserved town square, lined on all sides by Renaissance and Baroque houses.

p173

WIRESTOCK CREATORS/SHUTTERSTOCK ©

6 Terezín

☆ PRAGUE

5 Karlštejn

Karlštejn Castle (p104)

ITINERARIES

Best of Prague & Around

Allow: 6 Days **Distance:** 200km

From one breathtaking sight to the next, follow this leisurely exploration of Europe's prettiest capital. Leave the city behind for day trips to majestic Karlštejn and somber Terezín, a Nazi concentration camp and weigh station to Auschwitz.

❶ STARÉ MĚSTO ⏱1 DAY

Walk the back alleyways of the Old Town (p62) and catch the hourly spectacle of the Astronomical Clock, then climb the tower of the Old Town Hall for a breathtaking view of Old Town Square.

*🐾 Detour: Tour the magnificent synagogues of the **Prague Jewish Museum** (p65). Don't miss the adjacent **Old Jewish Cemetery**.*

❷ CHARLES BRIDGE & MALÁ STRANA ⏱1 DAY

Plan an early-morning crossing of **Charles Bridge** (p54) and pause to take in the evocative statuary. Meander the quiet lanes of **Malá Strana** (p54) and Kampa Park. Admire the baroque beauty of St Nicholas Church.

*🐾 Detour: Hike (or take the funicular) up to **Petřín Hill** for more magnificent views and fun stuff for the kids.*

❸ PRAGUE CASTLE & HRADČANY ⏱1 DAY

Spend the first half of the day wandering the chambers of **Prague Castle** (p48) and visiting St Vitus Cathedral. Splurge on the pricey admission or simply stroll the grounds (free to enter).

🐾 Detour: Walk around the castle gardens or take a tour of nearby Strahov Library, a medieval masterpiece.

CATARINA BELOVA/SHUTTERSTOCK ©, S-F/SHUTTERSTOCK ©, RASTO SK/SHUTTERSTOCK ©

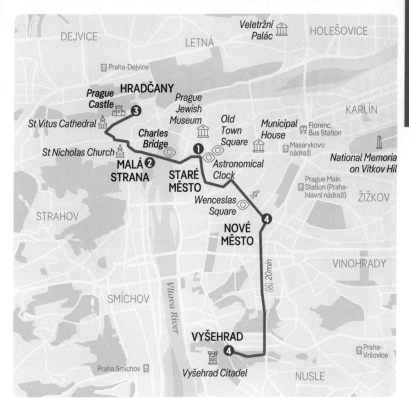

DEJVICE

LETNÁ

Veletržní Palác

HOLEŠOVICE

Praha-Dejvice

HRADČANY

Prague Castle

St Vitus Cathedral

③

Prague Jewish Museum

Old Town Square

Municipal House

KARLÍN

Florenc, Bus Station

Masarykovo nádraží

Charles Bridge

St Nicholas Church

MALÁ ② STRANA

STARÉ MĚSTO

①

Astronomical Clock

National Memoria on Vítkov Hil

Prague Main Station (Praha- hlavní nádraží)

ŽIŽKOV

STRAHOV

Wenceslas Square

④

NOVÉ MĚSTO

VINOHRADY

SMÍCHOV

Vltava River

M 20min

VYŠEHRAD

④

Praha- Vršovice

Praha Smichov

Vyšehrad Citadel

NUSLE

④ NOVÉ MĚSTO & VYŠEHRAD ⏱ 1 DAY

Walk **Nové Město's** (p72) sweeping Wenceslas Square, bookended at the upper end by the National Museum. Take the metro out to **Vyšehrad** (p100) to see the remains of Prague's 'other castle': Vyšehrad citadel.

Detour: Have dinner and drinks in one of the city's outlying up-and-coming neighbourhoods, like Karlín.

⑤ KARLŠTEJN ⏱ 1 DAY

Hop the train for a 45-minute ride to **Karlštejn** (p104) to tour the impressive castle, which once protected the Bohemian crown jewels. Be sure to book the tour in advance via the castle website.

Detour: Hike to nearby Svatý Jan pod Skalou and Beroun. From Beroun, catch the train back to Prague.

⑥ TEREZÍN ⏱ 1 DAY

An hour-long bus ride brings you to the former fortress of **Terezín** (p107) and back to a grimmer time during World War II. The Nazis transformed the town into a bizarre, horrific showcase camp to trick the world into believing their policies were 'humane'. Sadly, it worked.

🚌 1 hour from Prague

ITINERARIES

Highlights of Bohemia

PRAGUE

Allow: 8 days
Distance: 400km

From the sublime to the macabre, discover the best of Bohemia's cultural and historical attractions. Take in the prettiest towns and most vibrant cities as well as a historic beer tour and a mind-bending 'bone church'.

❶ PRAGUE ⏱ 2 DAYS

Start in **Prague** (p43) and spend a couple days exploring the Old Town and Malá Strana. Walk across Charles Bridge and climb up steep Nerudova street to pay your respects at Prague Castle.

🚗 *Rent a car or catch a bus from Florenc bus station for the two-hour journey to Karlovy Vary.*

❷ KARLOVY VARY ⏱ 1 DAY

The gorgeous spa of **Karlovy Vary** (p120) drew celebrities from all around Europe back in the day for its unique, health-giving spring waters and elegant, 19th-century colonnades. Walk through the town's magnificent spa area.

🚂 *Detour: Plan a day trip to picture-postcard **Loket** (p123) or explore the smaller and quieter nearby spa town of **Mariánské Lázně** (p127).*

❸ PLZEŇ ⏱ 1 DAY

Beer-lovers will make a bee-line to **Plzeň** (p132) to tour the brewery where Pilsner Urquell is made and where modern lager was invented in the 19th century. Parents with kids in tow will want to pay a visit to Techmania, which is like a science fair on steroids.

🚗 *2-hour drive to České Budějovice*

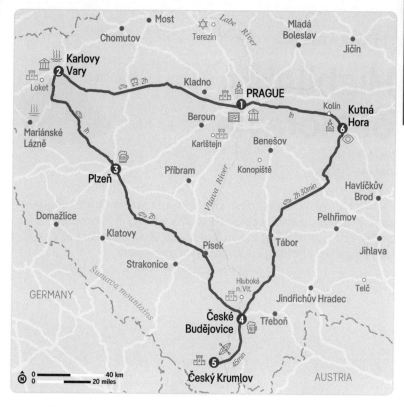

4 ČESKÉ BUDĚJOVICE
⏱ 1 DAY

Continue the beer theme at České Budějovice (p140), home of the Budvar brewery and one of Central Europe's largest and prettiest town squares. From here, it's an easy 45-minute drive or train ride to Unesco-protected Český Krumlov.

🚗 3/4-hour drive to Český Krumlov

5 ČESKÝ KRUMLOV
⏱ 2 DAYS

It's true, **Český Krumlov** (p136) rivals Prague in sheer beauty. Amble around the town's impossibly picturesque alleyways and climb up to the spectacular Renaissance pile of Krumlov Castle. Spend the second day out in nature. One option is to hire kayaks for a jaunt out on the Vltava River.

🚗 2 & 1/2 hour drive to Kutná Horat

6 KUTNÁ HORA ⏱ 1 DAY

On the return to Prague, make a slight detour to Kutná Hora (p163) to take in the town's medieval opulence and to visit Czechia's oddest attraction: the 'Bone Church' in the suburb of Sedlec. The interior is sculpted from the bones of 40,000 people.

🚗 1-hour return drive to Prague

ITINERARIES

Highlights of Moravia

✪ PRAGUE

Allow: 8 days
Distance: 300km

Slow down, relax, enjoy some wine and get to know Czechia's quieter eastern province and its colourful towns. The south is covered in vineyards and cycling trails. Like Prague, Brno offers big-city amenities, but attracts just a fraction of the visitors.

① BRNO ⏱2 DAYS

Start in the Moravian capital, **Brno** (p178), and take advantage of the city's excellent pubs and restaurants. Book a tour (well in advance) to see the interiors of the Vila Tugendhat. Spend a second day visiting Brno's spookier attractions, including a climb up to Špilberk Castle.

🚗 *1-hour drive to Olomouc*

② OLOMOUC ⏱1 DAY

A former Moravian capital, **Olomouc** (p192) was known for centuries as a Catholic bastion and has the magnificent baroque Holy Trinity Column and big churches to prove it. Be sure not to miss the string of parks and walks that surround the walls of the old town.

🚗 *1-hour drive to Kroměříž.*

③ KROMĚŘÍŽ ⏱1 DAY

Sleepy **Kroměříž** (p196) can be visited as a day trip from Olomouc. It's worth a stopover to see the sumptuous baroque Archbishop's Chateau and its certifiable artistic masterpiece: Titian's Flaying of Marsyas.

🚗 *2-hour drive to Mikulov*

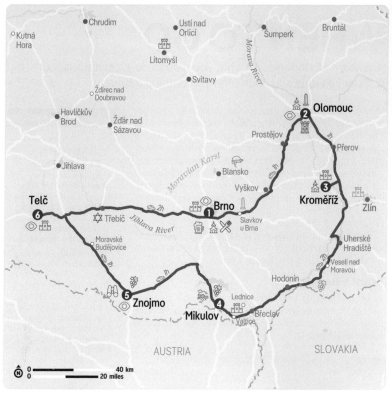

❹ MIKULOV ⏱ 2 DAYS

Stunning **Mikulov** (p185), in the heart of wine country, looks like a piece of Italy plunked down in South Moravia. Walk the cobbled main square and admire the mix of stately Renaissance and baroque buildings. On the second day, visit the Liechtenstein family chateau at nearby Lednice or head to Valtice to taste some Czech wines.

 1-hour drive to Znojmo

❺ ZNOJMO ⏱ 1 DAY

The wine theme carries over to pretty **Znojmo** (p187). In addition to tasting local wines, explore the extensive tunnels that run below the town and catch some breathtaking vistas out over the Thaya River valley.

🚗 1-hour drive to Telč

❻ TELČ ⏱ 1 DAY

Unfortunately, the Renaissance jewel and Unesco-protected town of Telč (p194), with Czechia's most beautiful town square, is relatively remote. Try to squeeze it in as a day trip from Brno or as a stopover on the return to Brno or Prague.

🚗 2-hour return drive to Prague

WHEN **TO GO**

Answer: it all depends on what you plan to do. Czechia has four distinct seasons and each offers something different.

Most visitors travel to Prague and Czechia in summer (from June through August), and it's not hard to see why. The days are long (in late June, it stays light until 10pm), the weather is sunny, and just about everything a visitor might want to do is open. Prague, though, can get uncomfortably crowded during this time. Add in the potential for a midsummer heat wave, and you have the ingredients for a less-than-optimal stay. Consider travelling in spring or autumn, when the crowds are lighter and the temperatures are cooler.

Bear in mind that some attractions, like castles and museums – particularly in smaller towns – shut down for the season from October to April.

Want a Bargain?

Prices for lodging in Prague drop considerably during the colder months from November through March – the exceptions being around the Christmas, New Year and Easter holidays.

Brno (p178)

> ⊛ I LIVE HERE
>
> ### AUTUMN REFLECTION
>
> **Prague-based Markéta Hradecká is a private tour guide (www.caputregni. cz). She spends lots of time wandering the streets of the capital city.**
>
> "Autumn always brings a touch of melancholy and introspection to Prague. The late afternoon casts a long shadow over the city, and I can feel the first cold wisps of winter. On these days, I like to walk along the Vltava riverbank. Watching the water during these last golden hours can feel like an existential experience."

> ### EARLY SNOWFALL
>
> Winter can come relatively early to higher-elevation areas. While September and October can still be warm and sunny in places like Prague and Brno, early autumn often brings the season's first snowfall to mountainous parts of the country.

Weather through the year

JANUARY	FEBRUARY	MARCH	APRIL	MAY	JUNE
Ave. daytime max: **2°C**	Ave. daytime max: **4°C**	Ave. daytime max: **9°C**	Ave. daytime max: **19°C**	Ave. daytime max: **22°C**	Ave. daytime max: **24°C**
Days of snow/ rain: 6 (Prague)	Days of snow/ rain: 5 (Prague)	Days of snow/ rain: 6 (Prague)	Days of rainfall: 9 (prague)	Days of rainfall: 10 (Prague)	Days of rainfall: 10 (Prague)

PRAGUE SPRING

Spring truly is a glorious season in Prague and around the country. April, in particular, is an eye-catching month. That's when the first trees start to bud, and Czechia's parks and gardens explode in riotous pinks and yellows.

Major Festivals

The **Prague Spring International Music Festival** is the undisputed high point of the cultural calendar. The festival starts on 12 May, the anniversary of the death of Czech composer Bedřich Smetana, with a rousing rendition of his symphony *Má vlast* (My Country). ⚙ **May**

Olomouc's **Festival of Songs** (p192) is a five-day celebration of choral music. ⚙ **May/June**

In a nation of cinephiles, Czechia's most prestigious film festival is the **Karlovy Vary International Film Festival** (p120). The event attracts both international and local film stars and plays against a backdrop of steep hills and gorgeous, 19th-century spa architecture. ⚙ **July**

The biggest cultural event in South Bohemia, the **Český Krumlov International Music Festival** is a month-long festival of classical music, with a nod to folk, pop and jazz. ⚙ **August**

⊙ I LIVE HERE

MULLED WINE IN WINTER

Czech Martina Sulková manages social media accounts for a large data company in Prague.

"Winter here can be magical. I love the Christmas markets, and the mulled wine you find everywhere (even hipster cafes serve it). The mood quiets down after New Year. That's when I head to the cinema or outdoors on a ski adventure. This time of year is perfect for a visit to the fairy tale town of Český Krumlov."

Local & Quirkier Events

On 6 January, **Three Kings' Day** marks the formal end of the Christmas season. Czechs celebrate with carol-singing, bell-ringing and gifts to the poor. ⚙ **January**

Once banned by the communists, the annual carnival, **Masopust**, involves street parties, fireworks and concerts. Celebrations start on the Friday before Shrove Tuesday (aka Mardi Gras). ⚙ **February**

Each spring, people around Czechia gather to light bonfires in an annual ritual called **Burning of the Witches** (Pálení čarodějnic). In German it's known as Walpurgisnacht. ⚙ **April**

On the night of 5 December, the eve of **St Nicholas Day**, people around the country dress up as St Nicholas, or as an angel or (scary-looking) devil to hand out treats to children who have been good. (Bad kids get a piece of coal). ⚙ **December**

HOT, HOT, HOT

Climate change is having a noticeable effect on Czechia's summer temperatures. Not that long ago, temperatures rarely exceeded 30°C. Now, 30°C days are relatively common and temps occasionally even reach as high as 35°C.

JULY	**AUGUST**	**SEPTEMBER**	**OCTOBER**	**NOVEMBER**	**DECEMBER**
Ave. daytime max: **24°C**	Ave. daytime max: **24°C**	Ave. daytime max: **19°C**	Ave. daytime max: **13°C**	Ave. daytime max: **7°C**	Ave. daytime max: **3°C**
Days of rainfall: 10 (Prague)	Days of rainfall: 10 (Prague)	Days of rainfall: 7 (Prague)	Days of rainfall: 6 (Prague)	Days of snow/ rain: 6 (Prague)	Days of snow/ rain: 6 (Prague)

LEFT: VITALI MATOKHA/SHUTTERSTOCK © RIGHT: ALBUM/ALAMY STOCK PHOTO ©

GET PREPARED FOR CZECHIA

Useful things to load in your bag, your ears and your brain.

Clothes

Layers: Czechia's weather can be impossible to predict. Wherever you go, summers can be stiflingly hot or unseasonably cool. Even on hot days, evening temps can drop to the point where you'll need a pullover or jacket outdoors. Winters can be cold or extremely cold, especially in higher-elevation areas.

Shoes: A trip to Czechia invariably means lots of walking. Many historic areas, including much of central Prague, are covered in cobblestones. Flat, comfortable shoes are much better than heels. Pack hiking boots if you plan on hitting the trails.

Dressing up: Casual clothes are fine for most occasions, but men should bring along a nice jacket and women a dress or skirt if there are plans to attend a concert, opera or theatre performance.

Manners

Czechs can be formal with strangers. Shake hands on first meeting. Use the more formal dobrý den instead of the casual ahoj to say hello.

Take your shoes off when entering someone's home. Always check your socks for holes before heading out.

Bring a small gift if you're invited to a party. A bottle of wine or a small bouquet of flowers make a nice gesture.

📖 READ

The Glass Room
(Simon Mawer; 2009)
Entertaining look at
Brno life in the interwar
years of the 20th
century.

**The Book of Laughter
and Forgetting**
(Milan Kundera; 1979)
Tragic-comic aspects
of life in communist
Czechoslovakia.

The Trial
(Franz Kafka; 1925)
Classic Kafka tale about
bureaucracy seemed to
foretell the communist-
era horrors.

**I Served the
King of England**
(Bohumil Hrabal; 1983)
Tales from Nazi-occupied
Prague from Czechia's
favourite author.

Words

Ahoj (h·hoyge) It's true.
Landlocked Czechs use
this common aquatic (or
pirate) greeting as the most
common way to say hello.
It's informal, though, and
only used between friends.
When addressing a stranger
or to show respect, say
dobrý den (doh-bree den),
literally good day.

Na shledanou (nuh-skhle-
duh-noh) is the way Czechs
say goodbye.

Děkuji (dye-ku-yi) means
thank you.

Prosím (pro-seem) is Czech
for please.

Ano/ne (uh-no/ne) is
straightforward and means
yes/no. In conversation,
Czechs often shorten ano to
simply no.

Promiňte (pro-min-te) is
how to say excuse me. It's
handy if you accidentally
bump into someone or need
someone's attention.

Pivo (pee-voh) means beer.
To order a beer in a bar, say
jedno pivo, prosím (jed-no
pee-voh pro-seem), literally
one beer, please.

Na zdraví! (nah zdrah-vee)
means cheers! Don't forget
to look the person in the eye
as you raise your glass.

Jídelní lístek (jee-del-nee
lee-steck) or simply **lístek**
is how to ask for a menu in a
restaurant.

Nerozumím (ne-ro-zu-meem)
means I don't understand –
probably another word that
will come in very handy.

🖥 WATCH

Loves of a Blonde (Miloš Forman;
1965; pictured) Bittersweet love
story between a factory girl and
her beau.

Closely Watched Trains (Jiří
Menzel; 1966) Brilliant adaptation
of WWII classic put the Czech
New Wave on the radar.

Kolya (Jan Svěrák; 1996) Heart-
warming, Oscar-winning tale of an
aging bachelor and a Russian kid.

Cosy Dens (Jan Hřebejk; 1999)
Czech directors have yet to
make the definitive film about
communism, but this comedy
comes close.

🎧 LISTEN

Prayer for Marta
(Marta Kubišová; 1969)
This moving ballad
became an informal
anthem of the 1989
Velvet Revolution.

**O' Brother, Shut
the Door** (Karel Kryl;
1969) Echoes the
hopelessness that many
Czechoslovaks felt after
the 1968 Warsaw Pact
invasion.

Safe (Karel Gott; 1964)
One of an endless
number of hits by
the Czech crooner
extraordinaire, who
passed away in 2019.

Traktor (Visací Zámek;
1990) Punk's (still)
not dead, as they say.
Popular, catchy rocker
with an excellent video
to boot.

STEPANEK PHOTOGRAPHY/SHUTTERSTOCK ©

THE FOOD SCENE

Czech food is classic meat-and-dumpling fare, which can be immensely satisfying when prepared well.

Czech food, even when served in restaurants, always has a distinctive homemade quality. The classic pairings – braised beef with gravy and dumplings, or roast pork and sauerkraut – feel like they came straight from the family kitchen. While the dishes appear simple on the surface, the sauces, soups and stews can hide complexity.

Sunday afternoon dinners often involve hours of preparation. Czech food is part of the Central European family and resembles German and Austrian cooking. The mains revolve around meat, with pork being the most common. Beef, chicken and duck are popular too. Czechs are avid hunters and enjoy game, so scan menus for more exotic options featuring rabbit, venison or boar.

Let your waiter choose the proper side. The correct pairings appear to be etched in stone and rarely vary. If a main is served with gravy, then knedlíky (bread dumplings) are the usual go-to. For 'dry' dishes (without gravy), choose a potato or vegetable. Wash it down with a local beer (or two).

Czech home staples

The typical Czech spice rack will have all the usual suspects, plus local faves like paprika, dill, marjoram and caraway seeds (a must for making goulash). Home-cooked meals invariably begin with soup. These are usually made with pork or beef and feature whatever root vegetable looks good at the market, like fennel, leek, onion, celery root, carrot or beet .

| Best Czech dishes | VEPŘO KNEDLO ZELO Roast pork with bread dumplings and sauerkraut. | SVÍČKOVÁ NA SMETANĚ Marinated roast beef, served in cream sauce. | GULÁŠ A stew of beef or pork in a tomato, onion and paprika gravy. | VEPŘOVÝ ŘÍZEK Czech schnitzel; fillet of pork coated in breadcrumbs. |

32

Eggs, flour and bread crumbs are essentials for making řízek – schnitzels of chicken or veal pounded out flat and crumbed and fried. Flour is frequently used to thicken soups and sauces (gluten-free diners take note). It's also an essential ingredient for making knedlíky, big bread dumplings.

Most Czechs buy their bread at the shop, though traditional home-bakers favour darker flours and season their loaves with caraway or rye.

Eating Out

Under communism, the restaurant scene was stifled for decades. Restaurant menus were standardised and quality suffered. In the past two decades, dining options have exploded. Standing alongside family-owned restaurants that use fresh, locally sourced ingredients, you'll find a dazzling array of international choices. Pizza is ubiquitous. A sizable local Vietnamese community means you'll always find places serving classic dishes like pho (a hearty noodle soup).

Vegetarians & Vegans

The last decade or so has witnessed a revolution in healthy dining, with a growing number of vegetarian and vegan

restaurants sprouting up around Prague and other large cities. Alas, vegetarian options at traditional Czech restaurants seem to be as limited as ever, with your best bet being the ubiquitous (yet often excellent) fried cheese (smažený sýr), served with a dollop of cranberry and/or tartar sauce.

Larger cities have promising non-Czech options, such as Indian or Vietnamese food.

PECOLD/SHUTTERSTOCK ©

FOOD & WINE FESTIVALS

Gastronomic Festival of MD Rettigovát (*gastroslavnosti.cz; May*) A tribute to the author of one of the country's first cookbooks and a celebration of traditional Czech cooking.

Prague Festival of Micro-Brewers (*minipivo.cz; Jun*) Small-scale brewers and craft-beer makers from around the country – and their fans – descend on Prague Castle.

Prague Burgerfest (Sep) This annual celebration of burgers and beer at the city's Výstaviště exhibition grounds is arguably Prague's most popular food festival.

Znojmo Wine Festival (*www.znojem skevinobrani.cz; Sep*) Czechia's premier wine festival is much more than wine, with music, parades and street theatre (pictured).

St Martin's Day On 11 November each year, restaurants around the country put out the white linens to serve sumptuous meals built around roast goose.

CCAT82/SHUTTERSTOCK ©

SMAŽENÝ SÝR	KULAJDA	BRAMBORÁK	KAPR	ŠPANĚLSKÝ PTÁČEK
A wedge of cheese that's breaded and fried to perfection.	Hearty soup made of sour cream, potatoes, dill, mushrooms and egg.	Filling, savoury pancake made from shredded potatoes, flour and garlic.	Pond-raised carp, often served breaded and fried.	Beef roulade with pickles, boiled egg and pork.

Specialities

A land of delicious desserts and unusual pub treats.

Dare to Try

Dršťková polévka: tripe soup, favoured in pubs and school canteens.
Olomoucké tvarůžky: pungent Czech cheese that tastes better than it smells.
Koprová omáčka: dill sauce served splodged over dumplings.
Utopence: fat, pickled sausages served in pubs and known as 'drowned men'.

Beer Snacks & Street Food

Klobásy: spicy pork or beef sausages that are a great accompaniment to beer.
Párky: frankfurters served with mustard on rye bread or stuffed in a roll.
Chlebíčky: open sandwiches, often with ham, cheese, egg and mayo.
Nakládaný hermelín: pickled and marinated soft cheese.
Trdelník: ubiquitous chimney cakes made from soft rolled

Koláč

dough and served with sugar or ice cream. Despite claims, these cakes have little to do with Czech traditions.

Desserts & Sweets

Ovocné knedlíky: flour dumplings, stuffed with berries, plums or apricots.
Palačinky/lívance: pancakes topped with jam.
Jablkový závin: apple strudel, usually served with a dollop of whipped cream.
Koláč: sweet pastries, filled with fruit or poppy seed.
Zmrzlina: ice cream; available in a variety of flavours.

MEALS OF A LIFETIME

Field (p70) Michelin-starred Prague destination spot that features traditional recipes and home-grown ingredients.

U Modré Kachničky (p59) Beautiful restaurant in Prague's Malá Strana is ideal for a splurge.

La Villa (p183) At this Zlín restaurant, the Michelin-standard tasting menus offer arguably Moravia's best cooking.

Entree Restaurant (p192) Well-known chef Přemek Forejt plates up top-notch fare in Olomouc that regularly features in national Top 10 lists.

Pension Kladská (p131) Country-style dining amid the splendours of the Slavkovský Forest, and near Mariánské Lázně's spa area.

THE YEAR IN FOOD

SPRING

Easter brings painted eggs, baked meats, cakes and breads. Sweet mazanec bread is made with raisins and almonds, while beránek cake is baked in the shape of a lamb.

SUMMER

The first fruits of the season – strawberries and wild cherries – are soon followed by plums, apricots, pears and watermelon. Czechs are expert grillers, so look out for barbecues.

AUTUMN

Mushroom pickers head to the woods in early autumn. Wine festivals take place throughout September and October. St Martin's Day, on 11 November, is celebrated with young wine and roast goose.

WINTER

Czechs are keen picklers, so there's no shortage of preserves in winter. Carnival season in February occasionally involves a pig slaughter, with buckets of pork fat and garlicky blood sausage.

LUMAXX/SHUTTERSTOCK ©

THE OUTDOORS

Czechia, with its undulating landscapes and seasonal, Central European climate, is perfect for outdoor activities year-round.

Czechs love to be active and spend time outdoors. As soon as the snow melts, you'll find people are ploughing along mountain trails, traversing steep gorges, zipping along cycle paths, rolling over river rapids, climbing foreboding rock faces and floating peacefully on lakes and reservoirs. And just as the last of the autumn rays dip below the horizon, the skiers and snowboarders are out once again carving up the slopes.

Walking & Hiking

With a network of some 40,000km of well-marked hiking trails, Czechia is superbly equipped for walking or hiking. There are hikes to suit every taste, from one or two hours to one or two months. The way-marked, colour-coded trails are clearly indicated on KČT (Klub českých turistů – Czech Hiking Club) hiking maps.

The gentle hills of Šumava (p135) offer the best and longest hikes. The thinly forested Krkonoše Mountains (p153) contain the highest peaks; a way-marked trail follows a ridge on both sides of the border. Czech Switzerland (p156) is laced with trails along hilly terrain and amazing sandstone rock formations.

Several long-distance European footpaths pass through Czechia. Route E8 runs near the southern border. The E10 traverses the country from north to south. The Czech Trail (Cesta Českem; stezkaceskem. cz) is a 10-stage, 1000km path that begins

Popular Sports

SWIMMING
Swimming season runs from June through August. Find a clean and popular swimming lake at the **Brno Reservoir**. (p178)

CAVING
Czechia is honeycombed with dramatic caves; the best are in the **Moravian Karst**, just north of Brno. (p183)

RAFTING & CANOEING
Head south along the Vltava to **Český Krumlov**, where outfitters run relaxing floats and more ambitious trips. (p136)

FAMILY ADVENTURES

Splash around on waterfalls, slides, heated outdoor pools and hot tubs at **Aquaforum** (p126) in Františkovy Lázně.

Climb Prague's Petřín Hill (or ride the funicular) to find a whole range of hilltop diversions, including a lookout tower, a rose garden and a great mirror maze. (p59)

Treat the little ones to a gentle, guided horse ride at the Boheminium miniature park in **Mariánské Lázně** (p127).

Take in a football (soccer) match at Sparta's **Letná stadium** (p95).

Ride a boat through the Punkva Cave of the Moravian Karst; a weird-and-wonderful experience for all ages (p183).

in the western mountains and follows the rugged north to Slovakia.

Cycling

One of the best ways to see the country is by bike. Mountain- and gravel-biking have taken off in a big way, and Czechia is crisscrossed by dozens of marked cycling paths, known as cyklotrasy. Big cities like Prague and Brno are building out their local networks. The trails sometimes follow roads (suitable for road cyclists), though many deviate along forest paths or open fields and are better tackled with wider tires. Cycling maps are widely available. Moravian wine country, particularly around Mikulov, Valtice and Lednice, is laced by scenic marked trails that make it easy to pair a day on the bike with stops at local wineries. Other good regions for riding include the foothills of Šumava (p135) and Czech Switzerland (p156). The 456km Greenway Prague–Vienna Trail (pragueviennagreenways.org) links the two capital cities and follows a mix of roads and trails. A 240km-long trail links Prague to Dresden (in Germany), along the Vltava and Elbe rivers. The path is still under construction in spots. Cycle paths also link up with the Europe-wide network of trails, Euro Velo (eurovelo.org). Three routes pass through Czechia: EV4 runs west–east via Prague and Brno, EV7 north–south through Prague and onto Berlin, and EV9 north–south via Olomouc to Vienna or Poland.

GRAB YOUR SKIS

It's not the Alps, but skiing and snowboarding in Czechia is very popular

Skiing & Snowboarding

It's not the Alps, but skiing and snowboarding in Czechia is popular and relatively inexpensive. The downhill ski areas tend to be small, however, and during school holidays you'll be jostling with other snow lovers for a place in the queues. The season lasts from late December to early April. The best ski area is the Krkonoše Mountains (p153) in north Bohemia, at the resorts of Špindlerův Mlýn, Pec pod Sněžkou and Harrachov. Ranges with lower peaks and gentler terrain are better suited to cross-country skiing and ski touring.

These include Šumava in Bohemia and the Beskydy and Jeseníky mountains in Moravia.

MARTIN VOREL/SHUTTERSTOCK ©

MOUNTAINEERING & ROCK CLIMBING	RUNNING	FISHING	GOLF
Czechs are inveterate climbers. A good place to try is at the **Svatošské skály** on the Ohře River. (p123)	Running has taken off in a big way; virtually any trail that can be hiked can be run (with care). The **Prague marathon** is held in May.	The rivers of South Bohemia and Moravia are popular with local fishermen, but you'll need a permit. Try your luck on the lakes around **Telč.** (p194)	Golf has become increasingly popular the past decade; find a beautiful, historic course in **Mariánské Lázně.** (p127)

ACTION AREAS

Where to find Czechia's best outdoor activities.

GERMANY

Jizerské hory

Hřensko **4** **5**

Děčín

Teplice

Ústí nad Labem

Liber

5

Most

Terezín

Český ráj

Krušné hory

Chomutov

Kokořín

Jič

1 **3**

Jáchymov

Labe River

Mladá Boleslav

Karlovy Vary **1**

Loket **1**

Cheb

Kladno

Lidice

⚙PRAGUE

Kolín

Křivoklát

5

Mariánské Lázně

Beroun

Kutná Hora

Karlštejn

Benešov

Plzeň

Konopiště

Příbram

BOHEMIA

Domažlice

Pelhřimov

GERMANY

Klatovy

Písek

Vltava River

Tábor

Šumava

Jindřichův Hradec

Strakonice

4

České Budějovice

2

Třeboň

Český Krumlov

National Parks

1 The Czech Switzerland National Park (p156)
2 Krkonoše National Park (p153)
3 Podyjí National Park (p190)
4 Šumava National Park (p135)

N 0 / 0

100 km

50 miles

Skiing/Snowboarding
1 Klínovec (p124)
2 Pec pod Sněžkou (p212)
3 Špindlerův Mlýn (p153)
4 Harrachov (p153)
5 Ještěd (p149)

Walking/Hiking
1 Svatošské skály (p123)
2 Mount Kleť (p139)
3 Sněžka mountain (p152)
4 Pravčická Gate (p156)
5 Around Jetřichovice (p157)

Cycling
1 Ohře cycle path (p123)
2 Mikulov Wine Trail (p188)
3 Klínovec Bike Park (p124)
4 Lednice-Valtice (p190)
5 Vltava river ride (p79)

POLAND

Trutnov

Krkonoše

Hradec Králové

Rychnov

Orlické hory

Jeseníky

Pardubice

Chrudim

Ustí nad Orlicí

Šumperk

Bruntál

Opava

Ostrava

SILESIA

Karviná

Litomyšl

Vysočina

Frýdek-Místek

Havlíčkův Brod

Žďár nad Sázavou

Boskovice

Prostějov

Olomouc

Nový Jičín

Přerov

Rožnov pod Radhoštěm

Jihlava

Velké Meziříčí

Blansko

Vyškov

Kroměříž

Zlín

Třebíč

Brno

Slavkov u Brna

Jihlava River

Telč

Morava River

Uherské Hradiště

Beskydy

SLOVAKIA

MORAVIA

Hodonín

Znojmo

Mikulov

Lednice

Valtice

Břeclav

AUSTRIA

VIENNA

BRATISLAVA

THE GUIDE

North & East Bohemia
p143

PRAGUE
p42

South & West Bohemia
p115

Moravia
p173

Chapters in this section are organised by hubs and their surrounding areas. We see the hub as your base in the destination, where you'll find unique experiences, local insights, insider tips and expert recommendations. It's also your gateway to the surrounding area, where you'll see what and how much you can do from there.

Old Town (p62), Prague

ARTONO/SHUTTERSTOCK ©

PRAGUE

MEDIEVAL YET MODERN

Czechia's capital city is a living textbook of European
history – and so much more.

The ups and downs of centuries past, of empires, wars, plagues and prosperity, are etched into the city's soul like lines carved onto the facades of its Gothic towers and Renaissance palaces. A little more than three decades ago, Prague re-emerged on the European stage after languishing for years under communism, and the world was agog.

Those years trapped behind the Iron Curtain left Prague looking neglected and rundown, but it was obvious the city's rich history and intrinsic beauty – the hypnotic, visual tension between Charles Bridge and Prague Castle – had survived intact.

In the years since the fall of communism, as the scaffolding was pulled down from the faces of rehabilitated buildings, the number of visitors to the city has exploded. Indeed, Prague became so popular that in the years immediately preceding the COVID-19 pandemic, the city sadly found itself – along with places like Venice and Amsterdam – as one of Europe's leading poster children for over-tourism.

The pandemic froze the city's tourist economy in its tracks and allowed authorities to hit the reset button. The mayor's office has promised big changes in tourism going forward, including positioning Prague less as a destination for raucous pubs and cheap beer, and more for the city's appealing cultural amenities, museums and parks.

The authorities have their work cut out for them. Prague remains immensely popular. Part of the city's enduring appeal owes something to the whimsical nature of the 1989 Velvet Revolution itself that installed a playwright, Václav Havel, as the first president of the newly liberated country. An even bigger part of the city's attraction might be its own storybook mystique: the dramatic way the floodlit twin towers of the Týn Church rise behind Old Town Square like something from Grimms' Fairy Tales, or the play of shadows on the back streets of the Old Town after dark. A little over a century ago, these same streets inspired the darker sensibilities of writers such as Franz Kafka.

ADISA/SHUTTERSTOCK ©

THE MAIN AREAS

PRAGUE CASTLE & HRADČANY	MALÁ STRANA	STARÉ MĚSTO	NOVÉ MĚSTO	ŽIŽKOV & KARLÍN
Regal and refined.	Less is always more.	The heart of Prague.	Prague's commercial area.	Hillside pubs, riverside revival.
p48	p54	p62	p72	p80

DENIS POLTORADNEV/SHUTTERSTOCK ©

VINOHRADY & VRŠOVICE	**HOLEŠOVICE**	**BUBENEČ & DEJVICE**	**SMÍCHOV**	**VYŠEHRAD**
Regal and rowdy.	Art and street vibe.	Villas, parks and gardens.	Prague's beer quarter.	Prague's 'other' castle.
p84	p88	p92	p96	p100

Find Your Way

Prague has an excellent integrated public transport system of metro lines, trams, buses and night trams, but when it comes to moving around the relatively compact historic neighbourhoods of Staré Město (Old Town), Malá Strana and Prague Castle, it's more convenient – and more scenic – to travel by foot.

THE GUIDE

FROM THE AIRPORT

Bus 119 runs regularly from the airport to metro stop Nádraží Veleslavín (Line A, green line) to catch the metro to the centre. The Airport Express (AE) bus ferries passengers between the airport and main train station at 30-minute intervals. Bus services run daily from around 5am to 11pm.

WALK

The historic core is compact and flat (though the trek to Prague Castle involves a climb) and walking is the best way to get around. Much of Staré Město and Malá Strana is paved with cobblestones, so sneakers or comfortable walking shoes work best.

METRO

Prague's metro is handy for covering long distances in a short amount of time. Several stops on Line A (green line) are useful for reaching sights around Staré Město, Malá Strana and central Wenceslas Square. Line C serves the main train station, Hlavní nádraží.

TRAM & TRAIN

Use trams to cover shorter distances or to reach Prague Castle (and spare the climb). Tram 22 is known as the 'tourist' line as it runs through many historic areas, including Prague Castle and Malá Strana, before heading out to pretty and lively Vinohrady.

Bubeneč & Dejvice

Prague Airport (2 km)

Prague Castle & Hradčany

Prague Castle

St Vitus Cathedral

St Nicholas Church

Malá Strana Charles Bridge

STRAHOV

Smíchov

Praha-Smíchov

RADLICE

TROJA

LIBEŇ

Praha-Holešovice

Stromovka

Holešovice

PALMOVKA

LETNÁ

🏛 Veletržní Palác

Letná Gardens
(Letenské sady)

Prague Jewish
Museum

🏛 Old Town
Square

Staré
Město

🏛

Žlžkov & Karlín

🏛 National Memorial
on Vítkov Hill

Astronomical
Clock

Municipal House

Wenceslas
Square

Praha-hlavní nádraží
(Main Train Station)

Nové Město

Vinohrady & Vršovice

🏰 Vyšehrad

Vyšehrad
Citadel

NUSLE

NA BOHDALCE

Veslařský
ostrov

N   0
    0   1 mile   2 km

45

Plan Your Days

Three days is ideal for taking in Prague's historical sweep at a leisurely pace. Put on comfortable shoes, get ready to walk over 10,000 steps a day, and prepare to be dazzled.

Charles Bridge (p54)

ALEXANTON/SH-JTTERSTOCK ©

DAY 1

Morning
● Start the exploration in **Staré Město** (Old Town), with the hourly chiming of the **Astronomical Clock** (p63), then wander through the **Old Town Square** (p63), taking in the array of architectural styles and the spires of the **Church of Our Lady Before Týn** (p64). Freshen up at **Bakeshop Praha** (p70).

Afternoon
● Spend the afternoon exploring the buildings of the **Prague Jewish Museum** (p65). For art lovers, the nearby **Convent of St Agnes** (p66) holds a valuable collection of medieval art.

Evening
● Return to Old Town Square and follow the twisting alleyways for a first glimpse at stunning **Charles Bridge** (p54) and **Prague Castle** (p48) in the backdrop.

YOU'LL ALSO WANT TO...

Get out of the centre and see the rest of the city without the tourists, stop in at a pub and check out some ice hockey.

DRINK BEER AT A TRADITIONAL PUB

The quintessential Prague experience. One classic pub, Hostinec U Černého vola, is temptingly close to Prague Castle.

SEE AN ICE HOCKEY MATCH

The Czech Extraliga is one of the most competitive hockey leagues in the world and features Prague's HC Sparta Praha.

SAMPLE CZECH FOOD

Hearty and delicious like a home-cooked meal. Go the whole nine yards, with roast duck and dumplings at U Modré Kachničky.

DIETMAR RAUSCHER/GETTY IMAGES ©, CTK/ALAMY STOCK PHOTO©, KAPRIK/SHUTTERSTOCK ©, MARKETA1982/SHUTTERSTOCK ©

DAY 2

Morning
● Get an early start and return to the Staré Město side of **Charles Bridge** for the crossing over to pretty Malá Strana. Spend the morning exploring the quaint backstreets and **Kampa park** (p57). Stop for lunch at **Cafe Savoy** before hiking up to Prague Castle.

Afternoon
● Visiting the Castle complex and **St Vitus Cathedral** (p50) will easily take the rest of the day. Don't miss the **Royal Gardens** (p53) on the castle's northern side.

Evening
● Spend the evening strolling the pretty lanes of **Hradčany** (p48) and reward yourself with traditional Czech food (and home-brewed beer) at the **Klášterní Pivovar Strahov** (p53).

DAY 3

Morning
● Start with coffee at **Cafe Slavia** (p78), with a view of Prague Castle. Check in at the **National Theatre** (p76) to see if any last-minute tickets are available to the opera or ballet. From here, walk up Národní třída to historic **Wenceslas Square** (p72).

Afternoon
● Pop into the **National Museum** (p73) to admire the interiors. Lunch at **Styl & Interier** (p78) before taking the metro to **Vyšehrad** (p100) to admire the former fortress and visit the graves of Dvořak and Mucha.

Evening
● Spend the evening outside the centre. Book a table at **Eska** (p82) in Karlín for a modern take on Czech cooking.

VISIT A FARMERS' MARKET

On Saturdays in warm weather, the entire city turns out to stock up and hobnob. Find a good market at Náplavka.

HEAR A CLASSICAL CONCERT

Dvořák and Smetana are national heroes, and opulent concert halls like the Rudolfinum often feature them.

RELAX IN A PRETTY PARK

Prague is surprisingly green, and the city's most beautiful park is the former royal hunting grounds Stromovka.

GET OUT ON THE RIVER

Several outfitters organise boating tours on the Vltava but renting a pedal boat on Slovanský ostrov can be fun too.

PRAGUE CASTLE & HRADČANY

REGAL AND REFINED

The hilltop neighbourhood of Hradčany, home to Prague Castle, retains a whiff of exclusivity, centuries after the emperors and kings who once lived here have gone. Years ago, noble families competed for access to the rulers and built grand chateaux around the castle. Those opulent piles are still here, many converted to museums and government offices. Most visitors come for attractions like Prague Castle and St Vitus Cathedral, but there are several other places to see. Loreta Church is a baroque, 17th-century pilgrimage site. Strahov Monastery has been here since at least 1140. The monks' adjoining library is one of the most beautiful in Europe. Scattered among the incredible palaces are pubs, restaurants and breath-taking vistas out over Malá Strana and the Old Town.

GETTING ORIENTED

Most visitors come to Hradčany by walking up steep Nerudova street from Malá Strana. To spare the climb, tram 22 stops just outside the castle gates. A more adventurous approach involves taking the Petřín Funicular to the top and walking across the upper end of a wide meadow. The views are spectacular.

Prague Castle (Pražský hrad)

SEAT OF EMPERORS AND KINGS

Looming high above the Vltava River, Prague Castle, with its ranks of spires and palaces, dominates the city centre like a fairy tale fortress. Within its walls lie a fascinating collection of historic buildings, museums and galleries that are home to some of Czechia's greatest artistic and cultural treasures.

The grounds of the Castle complex are free to enter, though to see the interiors (including **St Vitus Cathedral**) requires an admission ticket. The highlights of a visit inside the castle include the Old Royal Palace, dating from 1135, and Vladislav Hall (built between 1493–1502), famed for its beautiful, late-Gothic vaulted ceiling. The former offices of the Bohemian Chancellery gained notoriety in May 1618, when Protestant noblemen rebelled against the Habsburg emperor and threw two Catholic councillors and their secretary out of the window.

They survived, but this 'Second Defenestration' of Prague sparked the Thirty Years' War. Housed in the Gothic vaults beneath the Old Royal Palace, the Story of Prague Castle traces 1000 years of the castle's history, from building the first wooden palisade to the present day. Exhibits include the grave of a 9th-century warrior discovered in the castle grounds, the helmet and chain mail worn by St Wenceslas, and a replica of the gold crown of St Wenceslas, which was made for Charles IV in 1346.

TICKETS

The main Prague Castle ticket includes entry to the Old Royal Palace as well as the Basilica of St George, Golden Lane and St Vitus Cathedral. An extra ticket is required to see the Story of Prague Castle exhibition. Buy tickets at information centres in the second and third courtyards. Time your visit for the top of the hour to see an impressive changing-of-the-guard at the main gate.

PRAGUE CASTLE & HRADČANY

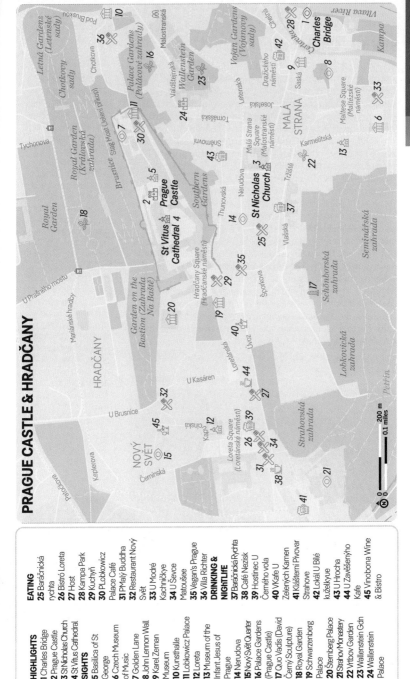

HIGHLIGHTS
1 Charles Bridge
2 Prague Castle
3 St Nicholas Church
4 St Vitus Cathedral

SIGHTS
5 Basilica of St George
6 Czech Museum of Music
7 Golden Lane
8 John Lennon Wall
9 Karel Zeman Museum
10 Kunsthalle
11 Lobkowicz Palace
12 Loreta
13 Museum of the Infant Jesus of Prague
14 Nerudova
15 Nový Svět Quarter
16 Palace Gardens (Prague Castle)
17 Quo Vadis (David Černý Sculpture)
18 Royal Garden
19 Schwarzenberg Palace
20 Šternberg Palace
21 Strahov Monastery
22 Vrtbov Garden
23 Wallenstein Gdn
24 Wallenstein Palace

EATING
25 Baráčnická rychta
26 Bistró Loreta
27 Host
28 Kampa Park
29 Kuchyň
30 P Lobkowicz Palace Café
31 P Malý Buddha
32 Restaurant Nový Svět
33 U Modré Kachničky
34 U Ševce Matoušee
35 Vegan's Prague
36 Villa Richter

DRINKING & NIGHTLIFE
37 Baráčnická Rychta
38 Café Nezisk
39 Hostinec U Černého vola
40 V Kafe U Zelených Kamen
41 Klášterní Pivovar Strahove
42 Lokál U Bílé kuželkyue
43 U Hrocha
44 U Zavěšenýho Kafe
45 Vinobona Wine & Bistro

St Vitus Cathedral

THE NATION'S HOUSE OF WORSHIP

Czechia's most important church was begun in 1344 by Emperor Charles IV, on the site of a 10th-century Romanesque rotunda. Although the structure appears Gothic, much of St Vitus Cathedral was only completed in time for its belated consecration in 1929. The coronations of Bohemia's kings were held here until the mid-19th century. Today it's the seat of Prague's Archbishop and the final resting place of some of the nation's most illustrious figures. On entering the cathedral, visitors are wowed by the massive nave. The original architect, Matthias of Arras, began work in French Gothic style. His German successor, Peter Parler – a veteran from styling Cologne's cathedral – built most of the eastern part. The room is flooded with colour from stained-glass windows created by renowned Czech artists of the early 20th century – note the one by Alfons Mucha in the third chapel on the northern side. The huge and colourful south window, depicting the Last Judgement, is from Czech master Max Švabinský. The eastern end of the cathedral is ringed by side chapels. In the centre lies the ornate Royal Mausoleum. Round the far end of the ambulatory to pass the tomb of St Vitus. Further around is the spectacular, baroque silver tomb of St John of Nepomuk.

CHAPEL OF ST WENCESLAS

The biggest and most beautiful of the cathedral's numerous side chapels is Peter Parler's Chapel of St Wenceslas. Its walls are adorned with gilded panels containing polished slabs of semiprecious stones. Wall paintings from the early 16th century depict scenes from the life of the Czechs' patron saint, while older frescoes show scenes from the life of Christ. After admiring the interior, climb 297 steps up the cathedral's bell tower for some excellent views. Admission to the tower requires a separate ticket.

St Vitus Cathedral

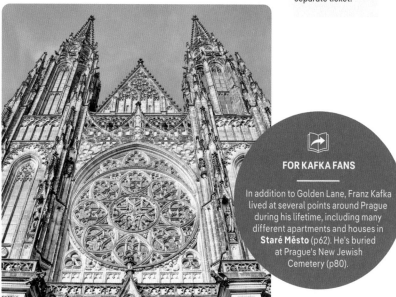

ARTONO/SHUTTERSTOCK ©

FOR KAFKA FANS

In addition to Golden Lane, Franz Kafka lived at several points around Prague during his lifetime, including many different apartments and houses in **Staré Město** (p62). He's buried at Prague's New Jewish Cemetery (p80).

Golden Lane

While strolling the castle grounds, be sure to nip down this colourful picturesque alleyway (entrance included in the main Prague Castle admission) that runs along the castle's northern wall. The impossibly tiny cottages here were built in the 16th century for the sharpshooters of the castle guard but were later used by goldsmiths. In the 19th and early 20th centuries, they were occupied by artists, including the writer Franz Kafka, who frequently stayed at his sister's house at number 22 from 1916 to 1917.

Golden Lane

Basilica of St George

BEST-PRESERVED ROMANESQUE

Just beyond St Vitus Cathedral stands Czechia's best-preserved Romanesque basilica (pictured), hiding behind a brick-red, early-baroque facade. The church was established in the 10th century by Vratislav I (the father of St Wenceslas). What you see today is mostly the result of more-recent restorations. The austerity of the Romanesque nave is relieved by a baroque double staircase leading to the apse, where fragments of 12th-century frescoes survive. In front of the stairs lie the tombs of Prince Boleslav II (d 997) and Prince Vratislav I (d 921). The arch beneath the stairs allows a glimpse of the 12th-century crypt; Přemysl kings are buried here.

Lobkowicz Palace

PRICELESS PAINTINGS AND MUSICAL SCORES

This 16th-century palace houses a private museum known as the Lobkowicz Collections, which include priceless paintings, furniture and musical memorabilia. The tour includes an audio guide narrated by the owner William Lobkowicz and his family. The palace has been home to the aristocratic Lobkowicz family for around 400 years. Confiscated by the Nazis in WWII, and again by the communists in 1948, the palace was finally returned in 2002 to William Lobkowicz, an American property developer and grandson of Maximilian, the 10th Prince Lobkowicz, who fled to the US in 1939. Highlights include paintings by Cranach, Breughel the Elder, Canaletto and Piranesi, original musical scores annotated by Mozart, Beethoven and Haydn, and an impressive collection of musical instruments.

Šternberg Palace

BAROQUE GALLERY

Stately baroque Šternberg Palace dates from the 18th century and originally served as a base for one of Bohemia's most powerful noble families. In addition to housing part of the National Gallery's collection of European masters, the palace has a beautiful, hidden baroque garden (open from May to September). The museum's treasures include a rare collection of Russian Christian icons and of early Italian paintings from the 14th and 15th centuries that formerly belonged to Austrian Archduke Franz Ferdinand.

Šternberg Palace

Schwarzenberg Palace

MASTERS IN A RENAISSANCE SETTING

One of two museums housing the National Gallery's impressive collection of paintings by European masters (the second is across the street at Šternberg Palace). Schwarzenberg Palace (pictured left) was built in north Italian Renaissance style by the noble Lobkowicz family in 1567 (though it didn't get its signature Renaissance sgraffito exterior until the 19th century).

The permanent exhibition focuses on works from the 16th to the 18th centuries, including from notable artists such as Lucas Cranach, Albrecht Dürer, El Greco, Hans Holbein, Rembrandt and Rubens.

Loreta

PLACE OF PILGRIMAGE

This baroque place of pilgrimage was founded in 1626 and features a rare replica of the 'Santa Casa' (Holy House) of the Holy Lands at the centre of the complex. Above the entrance to the courtyard, 27 bells – made in Amsterdam in the 17th century – play 'We Greet Thee a Thousand Times' on the hour. Behind the Santa Casa is the Church of the Nativity of Our Lord, built in 1737 to a design by Kristof Dientzenhofer. At the corner of the courtyard is the unusual Chapel of Our Lady of Sorrows, featuring a crucified bearded lady, St Starosta. The treasury is a bastion of over-the-top religious bling, centred on the 90cm-tall 'Prague Sun', made of silver and gold, and studded with 6222 diamonds.

Explore the Royal Gardens

PARK OF RENAISSANCE SPLENDOUR

Prague Castle is not only a collection of buildings, but also a scenic spread of greenery. To reach the Royal Garden, follow the gate on the northern side of the castle that leads to the Powder Bridge, which spans an even wilder piece of green called Stag Moat. The Royal Garden started life as a classic Renaissance garden, built by Ferdinand I in 1534. It's graced by several gorgeous Renaissance follies that feel almost forgotten amid the trees. The most beautiful of the buildings is the 1569 Ball-Game House, a masterpiece of Renaissance sgraffito where the Habsburgs once played a primitive version of badminton. To the east is the Summer Palace, or Belvedere (1538–60), the most authentic Italian Renaissance building outside Italy, while to the west is the former Riding School (1695). All three are used as venues for temporary exhibitions.

Wander quiet Nový Svět

HAVE PRAGUE TO YOURSELF

Head to the lovely, lonely quarter of Nový Svět (New World) to escape the crowds and find some headspace. The diminutive cottages that line this curving cobbled street, north of the Loreta, date from the 16th century and once housed members of the castle staff. Today, many have been restored and painted in pastel shades – a perfect alternative to the castle's crowded Golden Lane. Danish astronomer Tycho Brahe once lived at Nový Svět.

Discover Strahov Monastery

AN ANCIENT ORDER

Tucked away in a quiet corner of Hradčany, the Strahov Monastery for the Premonstratensian order has stood here since 1140, when it was founded by Vladislav II. The present monastery buildings, completed in the 17th and 18th centuries, were used until the communist government closed them down and imprisoned most of the monks; they returned in 1990.

Inside the main gate is the 1612 Church of St Roch, now a picture gallery, and the Church of the Assumption of Our Lady, built in 1143 and heavily decorated in the 18th century in the baroque style. Mozart is said to have played the organ here.

I LIVE HERE: HRADČANY

Johana Grohova, magazine editor, is a life-long Prague resident and worked at Hradčany's Černín Palace for years. She shares her favourite spots for lunch or drinks.

"I totally adore Cafe Novy Svět for coffee. Bistro Loreta and Kavárna Fejeton on Uvoz are also great choices. For lunch, I would go to Malý Buddha, U Zavěšenýho Kafe or U Ševce Matouše. On Pohořelec street, there's a new charity-run place called Café Nezisk, which supports a different non-profit organisation every week. The tiny quarter of Novy Svět has a new wine place called Vinobona Wine & Bistro. And, of course, there's always Kuchyň – for excellent Czech cooking – right next to the castle."

WHERE TO DRINK

Klášterní Pivovar Strahov
Convivial pub near Strahov Monastery serves its own St Norbert beers – and very good Czech food.

Hostinec U Černého Vola
Rough-and-tumble, authentically Czech pub stands a stone's throw from the gates of Prague Castle.

Lobkowicz Palace Café
This café is the best pitstop in the castle complex. The back balcony has superb views of the city.

MALÁ STRANA

LESSER IS MORE

Visitors are often shocked to discover that Malá Strana – 'Lesser Quarter' – in some ways is grander and more beautiful than the Old Town. In the 17th and 18th centuries, many noble families built their sumptuous palaces and spacious gardens here.

Malá Strana feels quieter and more relaxed than Staré Město. The neighbourhood is home to some of the city's top sights, including the beautiful baroque Church of St Nicholas, the elegant Wallenstein and Vrtbov gardens, and pretty aristocratic gardens. The best way to explore the quarter is simply to amble along the cobblestoned backstreets, or through Kampa park along the river, and admire the many handsome buildings and tiny squares.

Malá Strana's western boundary is formed by the steep ridge of the Petřín Gardens. Climb (or ride a funicular) to the top to a lookout tower that bears an uncanny resemblance to the Eiffel Tower, and a host of diverting, kid-friendly amusements.

TOP TIP

The grandest way of accessing Malá Strana, like kings of yore, is to walk across Charles Bridge (which we've included here within the Malá Strana neighbourhood). Several trams, including 9, 12, 20, 22 and 23, stop at the quarter's main square, Malostranské náměstí. The area is serviced by metro Line A (green line), stop 'Malostranská'.

Charles Bridge

BRIDGE WITH A VIEW

Who knew that a bridge could be this beautiful – or that mounting 30 baroque statues along its edges might elevate what in any case would have been a handsome Gothic structure into a public work of art?

Charles Bridge is a world-class attraction; and one of the signature Prague enjoyments is emerging from the crowded streets of the Old Town out onto a sunny bridge and into the open air. Prague Castle standing in the backdrop adds to the spectacle, as do the dozens of spires and cupolas that punctuate both sides of the river. The bridge began life in 1357 when Emperor Charles IV commissioned Peter Parler (architect of St Vitus Cathedral) to replace the older, 12th-century Judith Bridge, which had been washed away by floods in 1342. The new bridge was completed in 1390 and took Charles' name only in the 19th century – before that it was known simply as Kamenný most (Stone Bridge).

The statues came three centuries later, when the bridge's first monument, the crucifix near the eastern end, was mounted in 1657. The first statue – the Jesuits' 1683 tribute to St John of Nepomuk – inspired other Catholic orders, and over the next 30 years a score more went up. Not everyone loved the new statues at the time, which some viewed as Catholic over-reach to mark new territory.

Rub the Plaque

MOST FAMOUS STATUE

Tradition says if you rub the bronze plaque on the statue of St John of Nepomuk, you will one day return to Prague. According to legend, Wenceslas IV had John thrown off the bridge in 1393 for refusing to divulge the queen's confessions (he was her priest).

NOT ALL THE STATUES ARE ORIGINALS

Over the years, several weathered originals of the Charles Bridge statue have been replaced with copies. Some of the originals are housed in the casements at **Vyšehrad** (p100) and in the **Lapidárium** in Bubeneč (p92).

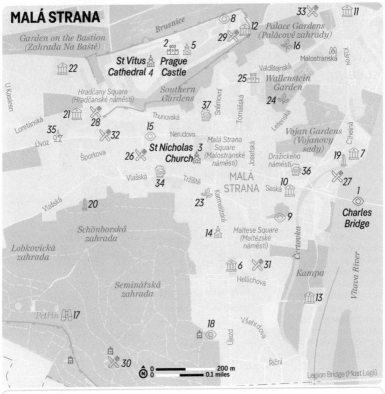

MALÁ STRANA

HIGHLIGHTS
1 Charles Bridge
2 Prague Castle
3 St Nicholas Church
4 St Vitus Cathedral

SIGHTS
5 Basilica of St George
6 Czech Museum of Music
7 Franz Kafka Museum
8 Golden Lane
9 John Lennon Wall
10 Karel Zeman Museum
11 Kunsthalle
12 Lobkowicz Palace
13 Museum Kampa
14 Museum of the Infant Jesus of Prague
15 Nerudova
16 Palace Gardens (Prague Castle)
17 Petřín
18 Funicular Railway
19 Proudy
20 Quo Vadis (David Černý Sculptures)
21 Schwarzenberg Palace
22 Šternberg Palace
23 Vrtbov Garden
24 Wallenstein Garden
25 Wallenstein Palace

EATING
26 Baráčnická rychta
27 Kampa Park
28 Kuchyň
29 Lobkowicz Palace Café
30 Restaurant Nebozízek
31 U Modré

Kachničky
32 Vegan's Prague
33 Villa Richter

DRINKING & NIGHTLIFE
34 Baráčnická Rychta
35 Kafe U Zelených Kamen
36 Lokál U Bílé kuželky
37 U Hrocha

St Nicholas Church

BAROQUE MASTERPIECE

Praguers generally have a love-hate affair with baroque architecture. Many residents find it too 'over the top'. Everyone, though, loves St Nicholas Church, one of Central Europe's finest baroque buildings. It's easy to find – just look for the church's oversized green cupola. Mozart himself tickled the ivories on the 2500-pipe organ in 1787. Take the stairs up to the gallery to see Karel Škréta's gloomy 17th-century Passion Cycle paintings and the scratchings of bored 1820s tourists and wannabe Franz Kafkas on the balustrade. (stnicholas.cz)

Franz Kafka Museum

CONNECTING AUTHOR AND CITY

Franz Kafka is perhaps Prague's most famous son. The German-Jewish author was born here in 1883, and the city played an important role as the setting for much of his work (though Prague is rarely – if ever – mentioned in the stories). This museum is directed more at true Kafka fans and explores the complex relationship between the author and his birth city through exhibits featuring letters, photographs, period newspapers and publications, as well as video and sound installations.

Proudy by David Černý

Czech Museum of Music

IMPRESSIVE COLLECTION OF INSTRUMENTS

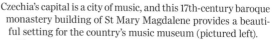

Czechia's capital is a city of music, and this 17th-century baroque monastery building of St Mary Magdalene provides a beautiful setting for the country's music museum (pictured left).

The permanent exhibition, entitled 'Man–Instrument–Music', explores the relationship between people and their musical instruments through the ages, and showcases an incredible collection of violins, guitars, lutes, trumpets, flutes and harmonicas. The highlights here include a grand piano that was played by Mozart in 1787, and the woodwind instruments of the16th-century Rožmberk Court Ensemble.

The exhibits are brought to life by recordings played using the actual instruments on display.

Museum of the Infant Jesus of Prague

WAX OBJECT OF ADORATION

Prague is under-rated as a place of religious pilgrimage. There's the Loreta (p52) near Prague Castle, and this even more-popular holy pursuit: the Church of Our Lady Victorious and its world-famous wax figurine, the Infant Jesus of Prague. The 47cm-tall waxwork figure of baby Jesus was brought here from Spain in 1628. The Infant is said to have protected Prague from the plague and the Thirty Years' War. An 18th-century German prior, ES Stephano, wrote about the miracles, kicking off what became a worldwide cult. It was traditional to dress the figure in beautiful robes, and over the years various benefactors donated richly embroidered dresses. A tiny museum at the back of the church shows off the Infant's impressive wardrobe.

Museum Kampa

MILL WITH MODERN ART

This often-overlooked museum in a renovated old mill in Kampa Park will appeal mainly to lovers of modern art from the first half of the 20th century. The highlights of the permanent exhibition are extensive collections of bronzes by cubist sculptor Otto Gutfreund and paintings by the celebrated Czech master František Kupka. The most impressive canvas is Kupka's Cathedral, a pleated mass of blue and red diagonals. The museum also hosts high-quality temporary exhibitions.

RADOMIR REZNY/SHUTTERSTOCK ©

Museum Kampa

MORE DAVID ČERNÝ

David Černý's street art, statues and installations can be found all over Prague. Other statues worth seeking out include **Kůň** (Horse; p74) at the Lucerna Palace, and **K** (p76), Černý's giant, mesmerising rotating bust of Franz Kafka. Both are located in Nové Město.

Proudy & Quo Vadis

STREAMS AND CONSCIENCE

Malá Strana is home to two David Černý sculptures – one ridiculous and one of historical importance. The first (*Proudy*) is open to the public; the second (*Quo Vadis*) sadly locked in the garden of the German embassy (Vlašská 19). Sounds of laughter greet *Proudy* (Streams; 2004), a saucy animatronic sculpture of two guys peeing in a puddle shaped like Czechia. *Quo Vadis* depicts a bronze Trabant (an East German car) on four legs. It's a tribute to the thousands of East Germans who fled to Prague in late-1989, before being granted asylum (and leaving their cars behind).

John Lennon Wall

COLOURFUL GRAFFITI WALL

Long before street art was cool, Prague had its 'Lennon Peace Wall' – a place where people could express themselves through imagery and spray paint. The wall began life under the former communist regime, following the death of John Lennon on 8 December 1980. The Beatles' frontman became a pacifist hero for many young Czechs and someone painted an image of Lennon on a wall in this secluded square opposite the French embassy. Despite repeated coats of whitewash, the secret police never managed to keep it clean, and the wall evolved into a symbol of resistance. These days, the Lennon Wall has long lost its potency, though tourists still scrawl messages and buskers come to sing and soak up the lingering counter-culture vibe.

Kunsthalle

BRAND NEW ART SPACE

In 2022, this long-underutilised electricity substation opposite the Malostranská metro station was re-opened as a multifunctional art space. The curators here are promising a demanding, eclectic program of exhibitions going forward. The first shows have been world class – and even played a bit on the building's roots as a power station. The Kunsthalle (pictured left) also has a bistro and gift shop. Check the website (kunsthallepraha.org) to see what's on.

Karel Zeman Museum

ANIMATION AND FILM EFFECTS

Karel who? Bohemia-born film director Karel Zeman (1910–89) was a pioneer of special effects in his day, though his work remains little known outside his home country. Movie buffs will want to pop in here to see some of the tricks and techniques he perfected. Zeman's inventive use of animation and matt paintings combined with live action – seen in films like Czech cult classics Journey to the Beginning of Time (Cesta do pravěku; 1955) and The Fabulous Baron Munchausen (Baron Prášil; 1962) – influenced more-famous directors, including George Lucas, Tim Burton and Terry Gilliam. Some exhibits allow for hands-on interaction.

Wallenstein Palace

Wallenstein Palace

A WANNABE EMPEROR

In his day in the early 17th century, the Habsburg general Albrecht of Wallenstein (1583–1634) was a larger-than-life figure and widely viewed as a rival to the emperors and kings who financed his war-making. This enormous town palace – now home to the Czech Senate (the parliament's upper chamber) – was intended to rival Prague Castle itself and stands as a testament to his wealth and ego. Access for the general public is limited, though a self-guided tour takes in the more spectacularly decorated parts of the palace. The ceiling fresco in the Baroque Hall shows Wallenstein as a warrior at the reins of a chariot, while the unusual oval Audience Hall has a fresco of Vulcan at work in his forge.

Climb Petřín Hill

FUNICULAR AND MIRROR MAZE

Climbing (or riding the funicular) up the 318m-high **Petřín Hill**, which marks the steep western boundary of Malá Strana, is one of the city's favourite activities. It's particularly lovely in April or early May to catch the buds on the trees.

The climb takes 20 minutes of moderate exertion. There's no direct path to the summit; the best plan is to keep moving uphill. To avoid the climb, the handy **Petřín funicular railway** runs to the summit every 10 to 20 minutes from near the Újezd tram stop (lines 9, 12, 20, 22). You will need a full-price transport ticket or day pass to ride.

The funicular's been in operation since the Prague Exposition of 1891; in some years, incredibly, it numbers among the city's most popular tourist attractions.

Petřín is ideal for families; the two main sights atop the hill are the kid-friendly, 62m-tall **Petřín Observation Tower** and an old-fashioned **Mirror Maze** that's stuffed with circus-style mirrors that make you look wide, tall or comically short.

Climb the tower's 299 steps (or take the lift) for dramatic views of the city below or – out in the distance – the forests of Central Bohemia. The tower, which resembles the Eiffel Tower, was built in 1891 by the Czech Hikers Club after members visited Paris and became overly inspired.

Petřín Hill itself is lovely. Once upon a time the hill was draped with vineyards. Look for the huge stone fortification, the **Hunger Wall**, that cuts across Petřín's peak. It was constructed in 1362 under Emperor Charles IV to protect the city from invasion; the name comes from the fact that it was built by the city's poor in return for food.

Return to the centre via the funicular or downhill path. The funicular's midway stop, **Nebozízek**, has a good Czech restaurant for lunch or dinner. Paths lead north to **Prague Castle** and **Hradčany** (p48).

Petrin Hill Funicular

BEST TRADITIONAL CZECH PUBS

Kolkovna Olympia
Big, tourist-friendly beerhall, with lots of Pilsner Urquell on tap and a menu of decent, reasonably priced Czech dishes.

Baráčnická rychta
The hard wooden benches, parquet floors and hunting trophies take you back to the Prague of yesteryear.

Hostinec U Kocoura
Old-school Czech boozer with excellent beer on tap and a – usually – rowdy local crowd.

U Hrocha
Very popular Malá Strana watering hole that hasn't changed much since the days of the people's republic. Beloved by staff from the nearby British embassy.

 WHERE TO EAT

U Modré Kachničky
This feels like an old-fashioned hunting lodge, with quiet, candlelit nooks. The traditional roast duck is very good. €€€

Terasa U Zlaté Studně
Perched atop a Renaissance mansion close to the castle, 'At the Golden Well' combines great dining with a fine setting. €€€

Ichnusa Botega Bistro
Superb Italian food and wines ferried to Prague directly from the owner's homeland of Sardinia. €€

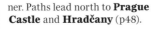

**I LIVE HERE:
MALÁ STRANA**

Bonita Rhoads,
an American who
has lived in Prague
for 19 years, is co-
founder of Insight
Cities (insightcities.
com), which offers
tours of Prague
and neighbouring
capitals. These are
some of her favourite
places.

Vrtbov Garden
Often overlooked by
visitors, the walled-in
baroque landscaping
here gives a luminous
glimpse into the life of
the nobility. Climb to
the top courtyard for
panoramic views.

Wallenstein Garden
This hidden garden
offers albino
peacocks, mannerist
statues, mythical
fountains and tragic
family histories
spanning 400 years.
Note the garden is
closed in winter.

**Palace Gardens
Beneath Prague
Castle**
Travellers, alas, also
often frequently miss
these meticulously
maintained terraced
gardens on the hills
below the castle. Also
closed for winter.

Find the Hidden Gardens

PEEK BEHIND HIGH WALLS

Malá Strana is home to Prague's greatest concentration
of manicured parks and gardens; the problem is many
are hidden behind high walls. Visitors and residents alike
typically walk right past and miss the little piece of paradise
that lies within. The Palace Gardens Beneath Prague Castle
are a unique composition of baroque terraced gardens dating
from the 17th and 18th centuries, notched into the southern
hillside below the castle. Not far away, the eye-popping
Wallenstein Garden is an immense, unexpected oasis. It was
created for the mighty Duke Albrecht of Wallenstein in the
17th century. Its finest feature is the huge loggia decorated
with scenes from the Trojan Wars, flanked on one side by an
enormous fake stalactite grotto. Toward the southern end
of Malá Strana, beyond and below Charles Bridge, find the
leafy riverside park known as Kampa. This park, bordered
on its western end by the Čertovka stream, is a popular spot
for picnics and throwing Frisbees. On Malá Strana's western
end, rising up a steep slope, find the Vrtbov Garden, one of
the quarter's least visited but most beautiful places. It's a
formal baroque space that crawls up a hillside to a terrace
graced with statues of Roman mythological figures by the
baroque master Matthias Braun. Take in the views up here in
all directions.

Wallenstein Gardens

CATARINA BELOVA/SHUTTERSTOCK ©

BEST PLACES TO STAY

Dům U Velké Boty
The quaint 'House at the Big Boot' is set on a quiet square, just five minutes' walk from the castle and Charles Bridge. €€

Golden Well Hotel
A secluded and elegant Renaissance house that is often a popular choice for honeymooners in Prague. €€€

Aria Hotel
Five-star luxury residence. Each room sports a musical theme and the roof-top views are phenomenal. €€€

Nerudova Street

Spot the House Signs on Nerudova

FIDDLES, HORSESHOES AND SUNS

Steep Nerudova leads from Malá Strana to Prague Castle. It's named after Czech poet Jan Neruda and has a long, rich history – much of it written on the symbols that adorn the fronts of the houses.

The House at Three Fiddles (Nerudova 12; pictured right) once belonged, fittingly, to a family of violin-makers. St John of Nepomuk House (No 18) is adorned with an image of the patron saint. Bretfeld Palace (No 33) was a social hotspot, entertaining the likes of Mozart and Casanova.

The House of the Golden Horseshoe (No 34) is named after St Wenceslas' horse, which was said to be shod with gold. Neruda himself lived at the House of the Two Suns (No 47) from 1845 to 1857.

STARÉ MĚSTO

THE HEART OF PRAGUE

Staré Město, Prague's Old Town, has been the city's beating heart for at least 1000 years. The grand buildings, churches and squares, the Old Town Hall, Astronomical Clock and Church of Our Lady Before Týn stand as testimony to the growing wealth and influence over the centuries of Prague's merchants and craftsmen. This splendour rivalled that of the emperors, kings and noble families on the other side of the river. Centuries ago, the Old Town was protected by high walls, moats and grand gates. The path of the former moat still defines Staré Město's borders and can be traced along Na příkopě and Národní streets. Of the former gates, only the Powder Tower survives. The best way to take in Staré Město's sights is simply to wander. Most visitors stick to popular routes like Karlova and Celetna street, but be sure to break away into intriguing lanes or courtyards. The street plan appears to have little logic; perfect for wandering.

TOP TIP

Much of Staré Město is closed to cars, so walking is often the best way of getting around. The closest metro station to Old Town Square is Staroměstská (Line A, green line). Metro stations Můstek (on lines A and B) and Náměstí Republiky (Line B, yellow line) are located just a short walk away.

Old Town Square

MARKET FROM THE MIDDLE AGES

For first-time visitors to the city, nothing quite beats the thrill of stepping back several centuries in time and onto the medieval marketplace of Old Town Square. The square appears particularly majestic at night, when the Gothic and baroque buildings are bathed in floodlight. The old merchants are long gone, replaced these days by a motley collection of tourists, touts, buskers and seasonal Christmas and Easter markets.

The square is surrounded by the quarter's most important buildings, including the 14th-century Old Town Hall, presided over by a tall Gothic tower and splendid Astronomical Clock. The most dramatic structure is the twin-spired Church of Our Lady Before Týn (p64), which stands incongruously behind a row of baroque facades. Next door (to the left), the 14th-century House at the Stone Bell (p64) is considered the square's oldest building.

This solemn Gothic structure shares the same block with the attention-grabbing, late-baroque Kinský Palace from 1765 with its riotous, pinkish facade. The balcony of the Kinský Palace played an infamous role in modern Czechoslovak history. It was from here in February 1948 that communist leader Klement Gottwald proclaimed the 'February Revolution' (or communist coup, depending on your point of view). Find another important church, the baroque Church of St Nicholas (p64), wedged into the square's northwestern corner.

Jan Hus & Mary

RELIGIOUS REFORMER

Two pieces of statuary stand at the centre of Old Town Square. Ladislav Šaloun's brooding art nouveau statue of religious reformer Jan Hus was unveiled on 6 July 1915, the 500th anniversary of Hus' death at the stake. The newer Marian Column, nearby, was installed in 2020 to replace the baroque original pulled down by anti-Habsburg nationalists in 1918. The jury is still out on whether restoring the Marian Column was a good idea, but both statues provide places to sit and relax.

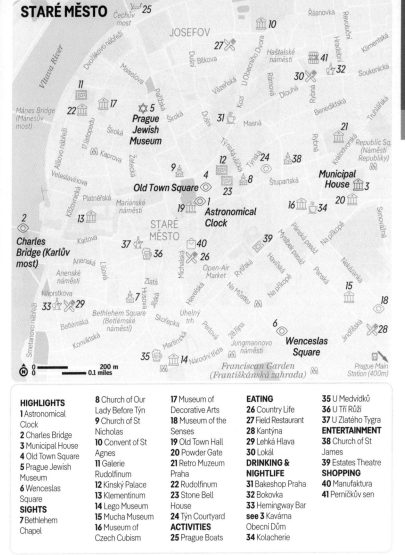

STARÉ MĚSTO

JOSEFOV

STARÉ MĚSTO

Vltava River

Mánes Bridge (Mánesův most)

Prague Jewish Museum

Old Town Square

Astronomical Clock

Charles Bridge (Karlův most)

Municipal House

Open-Air Market

Bethlehem Square (Betlémské náměstí)

Wenceslas Square

Franciscan Garden (Františkánská zahrada)

Prague Main Station (400m)

200 m
0.1 miles

HIGHLIGHTS
1 Astronomical Clock
2 Charles Bridge
3 Municipal House
4 Old Town Square
5 Prague Jewish Museum
6 Wenceslas Square
SIGHTS
7 Bethlehem Chapel

8 Church of Our Lady Before Týn
9 Church of St Nicholas
10 Convent of St Agnes
11 Galerie Rudolfinum
12 Kinský Palace
13 Klementinum
14 Lego Museum
15 Mucha Museum
16 Museum of Czech Cubism

17 Museum of Decorative Arts
18 Museum of the Senses
19 Old Town Hall
20 Powder Gate
21 Retro Muzeum Praha
22 Rudolfinum
23 Stone Bell House
24 Týn Courtyard
ACTIVITIES
25 Prague Boats

EATING
26 Country Life
27 Field Restaurant
28 Kantýna
29 Lehká Hlava
30 Lokál
DRINKING & NIGHTLIFE
31 Bakeshop Praha
32 Bokovka
33 Hemingway Bar
see 3 Kavárna Obecní Dům
34 Kolacherie

35 U Medvídků
36 U Tří Růží
37 U Zlatého Tygra
ENTERTAINMENT
38 Church of St James
39 Estates Theatre
SHOPPING
40 Manufaktura
41 Perníčkův sen

Old Town Hall & Astronomical Clock

MUST-SEE MEDIEVAL SPECTACLE

Prague's Old Town Hall, founded in 1338, was once the most important building in the Old Town. The eastern edge of the building was destroyed by Nazi gunfire at the end of World War II. The Astronomical Clock is one of Prague's most famous sights. On the hour, from 9am to 9pm, spectators are treated to a 45-second mechanised marionette display. The figures beside the clock represent the deepest anxieties of 15th-century Praguers: 'Vanity' (with a mirror), 'Greed' (with a money bag), 'Death' (the skeleton) and 'Pagan Invasion' (represented by a Turk). On the hour, 'Death' rings a bell and the 12 Apostles parade past. **63**

📷

Stone Bell House

SIMPLE GOTHIC DIGNITY

During restoration in the 1980s, a baroque stucco facade was stripped away from this elegant medieval building next to the Church of Our Lady Before Týn to reveal the original 14th-century Gothic stonework. The stone bell that gives the building its name is on the corner. Inside the building, two restored Gothic chapels now serve as branches of the Prague City Gallery (ghmp.cz), with changing exhibits of modern and contemporary art, including a very good retrospective of Mexican painter Frida Kahlo in 2021.

Stone Bell House

St Nicholas Church

BAROQUE CONCERT VENUE

This baroque wedding cake of a church in the far northwestern corner of Old Town Square was built in the 1730s by Kilian Dientzenhofer (not to be confused with the Dientzenhofers' masterpiece of the same name in Malá Strana). The church was built on top of a much older house of worship dedicated to St Nicholas from the 13th century. Considerable grandeur has been worked into a very tight space. Originally the church was wedged behind the Old Town Hall's north-running eastern wing (destroyed by the retreating Nazi soldiers in May 1945). The church is frequently used as a venue for chamber concerts.

St Nicholas Church

Church of Our Lady Before Týn

TWIN SPIRES AND TYCHO BRAHE

Its twin Gothic spires make Týn Church an unmistakable landmark. Like something out of a 15th-century – and probably slightly cruel – fairy tale, they loom over the square, decorated with a golden image of the Virgin Mary made in the 1620s using the melted-down Hussite chalice that previously adorned the church. Though impressively Gothic on the outside, the church's interior is smothered in heavy baroque. Two of the most interesting features are the main altar with its Virgin and the Holy Trinity by Baroque painter Karel Škréta, and the tomb of Tycho Brahe, the Danish astronomer who was one of Rudolf II's most illustrious court scientists. (He died in 1601 of a burst bladder following a royal piss-up.)

Prague Jewish Museum

HISTORIC SYNAGOGUES AND CEMETERY

Prague's historic Jewish quarter, Josefov, is a few blocks north of Old Town Square. For centuries, the Jewish community was forced to live in this relatively small area. The remarkable Prague Jewish Museum consists of six important structures that document the long history of Prague's Jews and aspects of Jewish life and faith. These include the Maisel Synagogue, Pinkas Synagogue, Spanish Synagogue, Klausen Synagogue, Ceremonial Hall and Old Jewish Cemetery. There is also the Old-New Synagogue, which is still used for religious services, and requires a separate ticket or additional fee.

Josefov has an interesting history. The neighbourhood was razed around the turn of the 20th century in an effort to clear what had become a slum. During the German occupation in World War II, most Jewish residents were tragically sent to the Terezín concentration camp (p107) and eventually to Nazi-run death camps in Poland.

The most interesting sights here include the Pinkas Synagogue, built in 1535. The walls are inscribed with the names of the 77,297 Czech victims of the Nazis. The synagogue holds a moving collection of drawings by children held at Terezín. The adjoining Old Jewish Cemetery is Europe's oldest surviving Jewish graveyard, founded in the early 15th century. It has a palpable atmosphere of mourning even after centuries of disuse (it was closed in 1787).

VISITING THE MUSEUM

One basic admission ticket allows entry to all six main monuments. The ticket, however, doesn't include admission to the evocative Old-New Synagogue, which dates from 1270 and is Europe's oldest working synagogue. Buy tickets on the museum website (jewishmuseum.cz) or at the Reservation Centre on Maiselova 15. Some individual synagogues also have ticket windows. Several local agencies offer tours of the museum and to other historical sites, including Terezín. One of the best of these is Wittmann Tours (wittmann-tours.com). Choose and book tours online.

Prague Jewish Museum

MAZARZ/SHUTTERSTOCK ©

KAFKA'S TOMBSTONE

Kafka is buried in Prague's **New Jewish Cemetery** (p80), just beyond the limits of Žižkov.

Rudolfinum

GRAND CONCERT HALL

The grand 1884 Rudolfinum, designed by architects Josef Schulz and Josef Zítek, is considered one of Prague's finest neo-Renaissance buildings. It served as the seat of the Czechoslovak Parliament between the two world wars, and as administrative offices of the occupying Nazis during WWII. These days, it's home to the Czech Philharmonic Orchestra, and the impressive 'Dvořák Hall' is one of Prague's great venues for listening to classical music. Check out the program or book guided tours on rudolfinum.cz.

TOP RIGHT: POPOVA VALERIYA/SHUTTERSTOCK © BOTTOM LEFT: BELIKART/SHUTTERSTOCK ©

Rudolfinum

Convent of St Agnes

MEDIEVAL AND EARLY-RENAISSANCE ARTS

In the northeastern corner of Staré Město, in a maze of hidden alleyways, the former Convent of St Agnes holds the National Gallery's priceless collection of medieval and early Renaissance art (1200–1550). It's a veritable treasure trove of glowing Gothic altar paintings and polychrome religious sculptures. The building itself is considered Prague's oldest surviving example of Gothic architecture and has a fascinating history. In 1234 the Franciscan Order of the Poor Clares was founded by Přemysl king Wenceslas I, who made his sister Anežka (Agnes) the first abbess of the convent. Agnes was beatified in the 19th century and, with hardly accidental timing, she was canonised as St Agnes of Bohemia just weeks before the revolutionary events of November 1989.

Convent of St Agnes

Museum of Decorative Arts

VINTAGE GLASS AND TAPESTRIES

This graceful old museum is packed with vintage Czech glassware, furniture, tapestries and period clothing, though at the time of writing the full collection is not yet open to the public. The museum began in 1900 as part of a Europe-wide arts and crafts movement to encourage a return to the aesthetic values sacrificed to the Industrial Revolution. The space was renovated several years ago, and since then it has only hosted temporary shows (to be fair, some of these have been very good). Check upm.cz for a list of what's on.

Retro Muzeum Praha

COMMUNIST-ERA KITSCH

Three decades since the fall of communism and Prague still lacks a comprehensive museum that would help visitors better understand that period. This exhibition on the fourth floor of the Kotva department store isn't quite it, but it comes close. It includes several rooms of communist-era household goods, clothing, toys and furnishings that will impress both budding historians and interior designers alike.

Retro Muzeum Praha

Church of St James

IS THAT A SHRIVELLED HUMAN ARM?

From outside, the Gothic Church of St James looks deceptively small. It's only on the inside where its girth takes shape. St James started in the 14th century as a Minorite monastery and, like many Prague churches, got a baroque facelift in the early 18th century. In the midst of the gilt and stucco, the interior holds a grisly memento: on the western wall (look right as you enter) hangs a shrivelled human arm. Legend claims that when a thief tried to steal the jewels from the statue of the Virgin, the Virgin grabbed his wrist in an iron grip and his arm had to be lopped off.

LEARN MORE ABOUT COMMUNISM

In addition to the **Retro Muzeum Praha**, contemporary history buffs can find more communist memorabilia at the **Museum of Communism** (p74) and at the **National Memorial** on Vítkov Hill (p80).

Estates Theatre

MOZART AND DON GIOVANNI

This colourful neo-Classical theatre from 1783, incredibly, hosted Mozart himself for the premiere of his opera Don Giovanni on 29 October 1787.

The theatre was originally patronised by upper-class German citizens and thus came to be known as the Estates Theatre – the Estates being the traditional nobility at this time.

These days it serves as part of the National Theatre's family of dramatic venues and makes an unforgettable setting for a piece of theatre or the occasional, highly popular concert of baroque music. Check the National Theatre website (narodni-divadlo.cz) to arrange a guided tour of the entire building and to see what's on.

Municipal House

ART NOUVEAU ELEGANCE

Just near the Powder Tower, Prague's most exuberantly art nouveau building was a labour of love, with every detail of its design and decoration carefully considered, and every painting and sculpture loaded with symbolism. The Municipal House stands on the site of the former Royal Court, seat of Bohemia's kings from 1383 to 1483 (when Vladislav II moved to Prague Castle), which was demolished at the end of the 19th century. Between 1906 and 1912 this magnificent art-nouveau edifice was built in its place – a lavish joint effort by around 30 leading Czech artists of the day, including Alfons Mucha.

While it looks almost too pretty to enter, don't be afraid to walk in. The building's purpose was always to serve as a place of recreation for city residents. To that end, the ground floor holds both a grand cafe and an unspeakably opulent restaurant. The interior is home to Smetana Hall, Prague's biggest classical concert hall, with seating for 1200 beneath an art nouveau dome.

This is the customary venue for the start of the annual Prague Spring on 12 May, and an excellent place to catch a concert. Walk downstairs to find an ornately decorated Czech pub and an early-20th-century American-style cocktail bar.

PRACTICAL INFO

Guided tours in English can be booked on obecnidum.cz or at the venue box office. The highlight of the tour is the octagonal Lord Mayor's Hall, the windows of which overlook the main entrance. Every aspect of its decoration was designed by Alfons Mucha, who also painted the superbly moody murals that adorn the walls and ceiling. The website also carries a handy program for what's on at Smetana Hall.

Municipal House

SVETLANASF/SHUTTERSTOCK ©

A PLACE OF RECREATION

The ground floor of the **Municipal House** holds both a grand cafe and an unspeakably opulent restaurant. The interior is home to **Smetana Hall**, Prague's biggest classical concert hall, with seating for 1200 beneath an art nouveau dome.

Museum of Czech Cubism

UNIQUE CUBIST DESIGN

Among Prague's early-modern designers, cubism was regarded as not just a painting technique, but rather a thorough-going approach that could be applied equally to architecture and industrial design. This museum, with its collection of cubist furniture, ceramics and glassware, is housed in Josef Gočár's eye-catching House of the Black Madonna (Dům U černé Matky Boží). This is arguably Prague's finest example of cubist architecture. Don't miss the arresting interiors of the adjoining cubist cafe, the Grand Cafe Orient.

House of the Black Madonna

Týn Courtyard

KEEPER OF THE CUSTOMS

The small lane that begins just to the left of the Church of Our Lady Before Týn leads back to a sort of medieval caravanserai – a fortified hotel, trading centre and customs office for visiting foreign merchants. Now attractively renovated, the space houses shops, restaurants and hotels. The courtyard is still often referred to by its German name, Ungelt (meaning 'customs duty'). The courtyard may be from as far back as the 11th century and was busiest and most prosperous in the 14th century during the reign of Charles IV. In the northwest corner is the 16th-century Granovsky Palace, with an elegant Renaissance loggia, and sgraffito and painted decorations depicting biblical and mythological scenes.

Týn Courtyard

Powder Tower

SURVIVING OLD TOWN ENTRY

Back in the day, Prague's Old Town was surrounded by walls and moats, and could only be accessed through one of thirteen town gates. The splendour of the 65m-tall Powder Tower, which dates from 1475 and marks the start of the royal route, gives us an idea of the grand scope of those old town entryways.

The Powder Tower remained unfinished until the 19th century; neo-Gothic architect Josef Mocker put the final touches to the building in 1886. The name comes from the tower's function in the 18th century as a gunpowder store. The top affords pretty views of the Old Town.

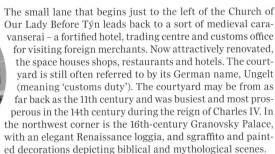

WHERE TO STAY

Ahoy! Hostel
Pleasant, welcoming and peaceful hostel (definitely not for the pub-crawl crowd), with eager-to-please staff. €

Design Hotel Josef
The work of London-based Czech architect Eva Jiřičná, the minimalist theme is evident in the stark white lobby with glass spiral staircase. €€

Dominican Hotel
Housed in the former monastery of St Giles, this luxury hotel is bursting with character. €€€

WHERE TO DRINK

U Zlatého Tygra
The 'Golden Tiger' is a classic Czech pub and Prague legend, but it's carefully protected by locals (don't come in large groups).

Bokovka
A crumbling, atmospheric cellar bar and a great place to sample the best Czech wines.

U Tří Růží
The 'Three Roses' offers six of its own beers on tap and is at the forefront of the movement to revive local brew-pubs.

Listen to a Classical Concert

SMETANA, DVOŘÁK AND MORE

Staré Město lords over Prague's best venues for listening to classical concerts. Pride of place goes to both the **Rudolfinum** (p66) and Smetana Hall at the **Municipal House** (p68) for having the best acoustics and skilled musicians. But churches all around the Old Town open up their pulpits to chamber concerts and the results aren't bad. Two churches to look for include **St Nicholas Church** (p55) on Old Town Square and **Church of St James** (p67), with its enormous pipe organ. The **Estates Theatre** (p67) occasionally hosts highly worthwhile baroque music concerts.

Cruise the Vltava

DAY (OR NIGHT) ON THE WATER

Several tour-boat operators run daytime and evening cruises up and down the Vltava. Some cruises are paired with live jazz or dance music, others with dinner and drinks, and some are just sightseeing excursions. **Prague Boats** (prague-boats.cz) runs a variety of popular cruises. Check the website to see if something appeals. Most cruise boats tie up at the embankment just below Čech Bridge (Čechův most) at the northern end of Pařížská street. **Prague Venice** (prazskebenatky.shop) runs entertaining 45-minute cruises in small boats under the hidden arches of Charles Bridge and along the Čertovka stream near **Kampa** (p57).

Taste the Green Fairy

IMBIBING ABSINTHE

Prague isn't only about beer. In the past three decades, the city has become a mecca for absinthe – the allegedly hallu-

cinatory 'green fairy' cocktail of 1920s' Paris fame. It's legal to buy and imbibe in Czechia, but not every place pours the same quality of drink.

Hemingway Bar (hemingwaybar. cz) is arguably one of Prague's best cocktail bars and has a wide selection of absinthe brands and knowledgeable staff. Book a table in advance.

ROMAN YANUSHEVSKY/SHUTTERSTOCK ©

 WHERE TO EAT

Field
Michelin-starred destination spot features farm-fresh ingredients, minimalist design and an unfussy attitude. €€€

Lehká Hlava
The emphasis is on healthy, fresh vegetarian and vegan dishes, often with an international theme. €

Bakeshop Praha
Lifesaver bakery sells pastries, cakes and takeaway sandwiches and salads. Gets busy at lunch. €

Walk in Kafka's Footsteps

WHERE HE LIVED AND WORKED

Prague's fingerprints are all over Franz Kafka's books and stories, and Kafka's footprints can still be traced throughout Prague's Old Town. Kafka was born in a house on today's **náměstí Franze Kafky**, just west of the Church of St Nicholas (p55). The house is no longer there, but is marked with a bust.

Kafka spent his early years (1889–96) living at the **House of the Minute**, a Renaissance building attached to the Old Town Hall. Not far from here, at Celetná 3 is the **House of the Three Kings**, where the Kafka family lived from 1896 to 1907.

Also nearby, Kafka and a young Albert Einstein attended literary salons hosted by socialite Berta Fanta in a building called **At the Unicorn** (Staroměstské náměstí 17).

Kafka's fiction was informed by his mundane day job as an insurance clerk – he worked for 14 years at the Worker's Accident Insurance Company at Na poříčí 7, not far from Náměstí Republiky.

Franz Kafka bust, sculptor Karel Hladík

FRED DE NOYELLE/GETTY IMAGES ©

I LIVE HERE: STARÉ MĚSTO

Eva Brejlová was born and raised in Prague and leads tours for Eating Prague (www. eatingeurope.com/ prague). These are some of her favourite places to eat.

Loď Pivovar (Brewery Boat)
Find this ship-based microbrewery in the Vltava River below Štefánik bridge. They serve unique craft beers hopped with Czech 'green gold': the country's fabled Saaz hops. Sample the nakladaný hermelín (marinated cheese).

Perníčkův sen (Gingerbread Dream)
This family-owned, Old Town bakery is the only place in Prague to taste a traditional Bohemian sakrajda roll. It's gingerbread strudel, stuffed with plum jam and walnuts.

Kolacherie
Forget those phony trdelník (chimney cakes). These koláče (soft, round pastries) are as Czech as it gets.

Lokál	U Medvídků
Excellent beer and Czech comfort food served in a modern take on a communist-era canteen. €	Bustling pub serves Czech Budvar beer, plus some of its own home-brew, and very good Czech food. €€

NOVÉ MĚSTO

PRAGUE'S COMMERCIAL CENTRE

The busy streets in Prague's main commercial area is where Prague actually starts to feel like a real city (and less like a living museum). Nové Město translates as 'New Town', but there's little 'new' about it. It was laid out by Emperor Charles IV in the mid-14th century to alleviate overcrowding in Staré Město. Nové Město hugs the borders of Staré Město in a wide arc that traces the former walls and moats of the Old Town from Revoluční (east of Old Town Square) along pedestrianised Na Příkopě street and out along the main avenue of Národní třída, south of Staré Město. It's a sprawling quarter that lacks a true neighbourhood feel. That said, Nové Město is home to some of Prague's most interesting sights as well as excellent restaurants, pubs, clubs and shops. It's also the location of the city's most important public gathering area and former horse market, Wenceslas Square.

GETTING ORIENTED

Wenceslas Square is the quarter's main hub and is well-served by metro. On the square's northern (lower) end, lines A (green) and B (yellow) intersect at station Můstek station, once the site of a small bridge that connected Nové Město and Staré Město. At the top of the square, lines A and C (red) cross at Muzeum station.

Wenceslas Square

HISTORY-MAKING HORSE MARKET

The centre of Nové Město is dominated by this massive square that for centuries was known simply as the horse market. In more modern times, it has evolved into the heart of Prague's commercial life (pictured). It's dominated at the top by the massive National Museum and along the sides by hotels, fast-food outlets, shops and hidden shopping passages that parallel the square. This gathering spot has witnessed a great deal of Czech history – a giant mass was held here during the revolutionary upheavals of 1848; in 1918 the creation of the new Czechoslovak Republic was celebrated here; and it was here in 1989 that many anti-communist protests took place. The square is currently undergoing a massive multi-year renovation that will eventually limit car traffic and return tram service to the square.

At the southern end of the square is Josef Myslbek's muscular equestrian statue of St Wenceslas, the 10th-century pacifist Duke of Bohemia and the 'Good King Wenceslas' of Christmas carol fame. Flanked by other patron saints of Bohemia – Prokop, Adalbert, Agnes and Ludmila – he has been plastered with posters at every one of the square's historical moments. Today it is the most frequented meeting place for locals as the statue stands at one of the entrances to Muzeum metro station. Near the statue, a small memorial to the victims of communism bears photographs and epitaphs to anticommunist rebels Jan Palach and Jan Zajíc.

VELVET REVOLUTION

Wenceslas Square will be forever embedded in Czech history for the role the space played during the anti-communist uprising of November 1989. Following a police attack on a student demonstration on 17 November 1989 (find a memorial at Národní 16), angry citizens gathered on the square by the thousands night after night. A week later, Václav Havel, flanked by popular reform politician Alexander Dubček, stepped onto a balcony over the square to a thunderous ovation and proclaimed the end of communism.

TATIANA DIUVBANOVA/SHUTTERSTOCK ©

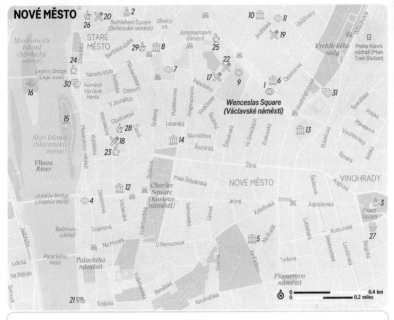

NOVÉ MĚSTO

HIGHLIGHTS	Nuclear Bunker	Heroes of the	store & Café	25 Dobrá Čajovna
1 Wenceslas Sq	7 K (David Černý	Heydrich Terror	19 Kantýna	26 Hemingway Bar
	Sculpture)	13 National	20 Lehká Hlava	27 Prague Beer
SIGHTS	8 Lego Museum	Museum	21 Náplavka	Museum
2 Bethlehem	9 Lucerna Palace	14 New Town Hall	22 Styl & Interier	28 U Fleků
Chapel	10 Mucha Museum	15 Slav Island		
3 Church of	11 Museum of	16 Střelecký ostrov	DRINKING &	ENTERTAINMENT
St Ludmilla	the Senses		NIGHTLIFE	29 National
4 Dancing House	12 National	EATING	23 Artic Bake-	Theatre
5 Dvořák Museum	Memorial to the	17 Cukrárna Myšák	house	30 State Opera
6 Hotel Jalta		18 Globe Book-	24 Café Slavia	

National Museum

PRIDE OF CZECHIA

Looming high above Wenceslas Square is the neo-Renaissance bulk of the National Museum, designed in the 1880s by Josef Schulz as an architectural symbol of the Czech National Revival. The building is so outwardly impressive that in 1968 invading Russian soldiers mistook it for the country's parliament and shot at it.

The museum's magnificent interior is a shrine to the cultural, intellectual and scientific history of Czechia. The new permanent exhibitions, added in 2022, highlight the 'miracles of evolution' and the history of the Czech lands from the 8th to 20th centuries. The restored interiors are worth the price of admission alone.

Museum of the Senses

OPTICAL ILLUSIONS

Keep this family-friendly museum (muzeumsmyslu. cz) in mind as an option for a rainy-day.

A sure-fire winner with kids and young teens, this interactive centre bamboozles visitors with its optical illusions. Have your head served on a platter of fruit, enter the infinity disco or the upside-down bathroom, lie down on a bed of nails, or get lost in a world of virtual reality.

Budget around an hour for this and try to go in the morning to avoid the crowds.

TOP RIGHT: MUZEUMSMYSLU.CZ ©; BOTTOM LEFT: ANIBAL TREJO/SHUTTERSTOCK ©

Museum of the Senses

Lucerna Palace

ART NOUVEAU SHOPPING PASSAGE

Easily the most elegant of the shopping arcades that run alongside Wenceslas Square is the art nouveau Lucerna Palace from 1920. The complex was designed by former president Václav Havel's grandfather and is still partially owned by the family. The attractions include a glamorous cinema, the evocative Kavárna Lucerna café, and the ever-popular Lucerna Music Bar, an excellent venue to catch live music. In the marbled atrium hangs artist David Černý's sculpture Kůň (Horse), a wryly amusing counterpart to the more-imposing equestrian statue of St Wenceslas in Wenceslas Square. Here, St Wenceslas sits astride a horse that is decidedly dead. The neighbouring Novák Arcade, connected to Lucerna, has one of Prague's finest art nouveau facades, complete with mosaics of country life.

Museum of Communism

BEHIND THE IRON CURTAIN

Put together by an American expat, this private museum tells the story of Czechoslovakia's years behind the Iron Curtain in photos, words and a fascinating and varied collection of ... well, stuff.

The empty shops, corruption, fear and doublespeak of life in socialist Czechoslovakia are well conveyed, and there are rare photos of the Stalin monument that once stood on Letná terrace (where the

metronome now stands) – and its spectacular destruction. Be sure to watch the moving video loops about protests leading up to the Velvet Revolution: you'll never think of it as a pushover again.

Mucha Museum

ART NOUVEAU MASTER

The fascinating, busy Mucha Museum (mucha.cz) features the sensuous art nouveau posters, paintings and decorative panels of internationally renowned Czech illustrator Alfons Mucha (1860–1939), as well as sketches, photographs and other memorabilia. The exhibits include countless artworks showing Mucha's trademark Slavic maidens with flowing hair and piercing blue eyes, bearing symbolic garlands and linden boughs.

There are also photos of the artist's Paris studio, one of which shows a trouser-less Gaugin playing the harmonium; a powerful canvas entitled *Old Woman in Winter*; and the original of the 1894 poster of actress Sarah Bernhardt as Giselda, which shot him to international fame.

A video documentary about Mucha's life is well worth watching and helps put his achievements in perspective.

MORE FROM MUCHA

To see more examples of Mucha's art, book a tour to explore the interiors of the art nouveau **Municipal House** (p68). Mucha was the main designer of one of the highlights of the tour, the Lord Mayor's Hall.

DANCING HOUSE

One of Prague's best-known modern buildings is the so-called **Dancing House**, just back from the Vltava River along the Rašínovo embankment. The building was designed in 1996 by architects Vlado Milunić and Frank Gehry. The curved lines of the narrow-waisted glass tower clutched against its more upright and formal partner led to it being christened the 'Fred & Ginger' building, after the legendary dancing duo.

Spy Museum at Hotel Jalta

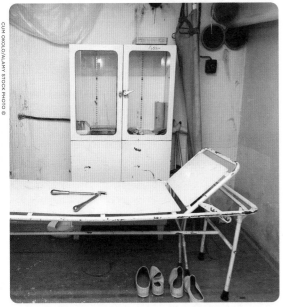

CUM OKOLO/ALAMY STOCK PHOTO ©

Hotel Jalta Nuclear Bunker

WIRETAPS

Hidden far beneath the 1950s Hotel Jalta on Wenceslas Square lies a communist-era nuclear shelter that is open to the public. The tour, led by a guide in period security-police uniform, takes in a series of secret chambers. The highlight is the chilling communications room which was used to spy on important hotel guests. Reserve tour spots on the hotel's website (hoteljalta. com).

Dvořák Museum

CZECHIA'S MOST FAMOUS COMPOSER

This museum, dedicated to the life and work of Czech composer Antonín Dvořák, is probably only really for die-hard fans. The museum is set in the Vila Amerika, a French-style summer house designed in the 1720s by the baroque master Kilian Dientzenhofer. Special concerts of Dvořák's music are staged here between May and October. The museum is operated as a branch of the National Museum. See nm.cz for details.

K (David Černý Sculpture)

KAFKA ON A SWIVEL

This relatively recent David Černý sculpture (from 2014) – a giant, rotating bust of Franz Kafka – may just be the artist's most popular work of all.

Find it in the courtyard of the upmarket Quadrio shopping centre, just above and behind the Národní třída metro station (line B).

The bust is formed from 39 tonnes of mirrored stainless steel. It's a mesmerising show as Kafka's face rhythmically dissolves and re-emerges, possibly playing on notions of the author's ever-changing personality and sense of self-doubt.

TOP LEFT: VERONIKA PRIMM/LONELY PLANET ©; BOTTOM RIGHT: STLJB/SHUTTERSTOCK ©

The National Theatre

National Theatre

CZECHIA'S LEADING STAGE

The National Theatre is the neo-Renaissance architectural flagship of the Czech National Revival, and one of Prague's most impressive buildings. Architect Josef Zítek's masterpiece was funded entirely by private donations from across the land and decorated inside and out by a roll call of prominent Czech artists. It burned down within weeks of its 1881 opening but, incredibly, was funded again and restored in less than two years. Today, it's the city's most prestigious venue for dramatic works as well as opera and dance. Be sure to walk past in the evening, when the theatre is decked out in dazzling light. Check the website (narodni-divadlo.cz) for the current program.

National Memorial to the Heroes of the Heydrich Terror

New Town Hall

THE 'FIRST' DEFENESTRATION

The New Town Hall has been around for several centuries (built in the late 14th century), but is not nearly as picturesque as the Old Town Hall. The building's historical high point came in 1419, when two of Wenceslas IV's Catholic councillors were flung to their deaths by followers of the Hussite preacher Jan Želivský. The event sparked the bloody Hussite Wars, and gave 'defenestration' a lasting political meaning. A similar scenario was repeated at Prague Castle in 1618. Visit the Gothic Hall of Justice – the site of the defenestration – and climb the 221 steps to the top of the tower.

National Memorial to the Heroes of the Heydrich Terror

GRIPPING WORLD WAR II HISTORY

The Church of Sts Cyril & Methodius houses a moving memorial to the seven Czechoslovak paratroopers who were involved in the assassination of German Reichsprotektor Reinhard Heydrich in 1942, with an exhibit and video about Nazi persecution of the Czechs. The church appeared in the 2016 movie based on the assassination, Anthropoid. The paratroopers hid in the church's crypt for three weeks after the killing, until their hiding place was betrayed. Three paratroopers were killed in the ensuing fight; the other four took their own lives. In the crypt itself, note the bullet marks and shrapnel scars on the walls, and signs of the paratroopers' last desperate efforts to dig an escape tunnel to the sewer under the street.

ANOTHER TRAGIC DEFENESTRATION

Prague's other defenestration, sometimes called the 'Second Defenestration', took place in 1618 at Prague Castle (p48). Like the first window-pushing, this one also ignited a catastrophic European war.

BEST PLACES TO EAT

Kantýna
Wildly popular local butcher. Choose your own piece of meat for the chefs to prepare, and enjoy it in the opulent former bank. €€

Styl & Interier
A passage opposite the Vodičkova entrance to the Lucerna Palace leads to this secret garden. Perfect for lunch or just coffee and sweets. €€

Cukrárna Myšák
Historic confectionery from 1911, redesigned by artist Josef Čapek in 1922, with top-notch cakes and coffee. €

Globe Bookstore & Cafe
Beloved by foreign residents for its good American-style bar food and many English books for sale. €

Sansho
Groundbreaking restaurant that uses locally sourced ingredients reformulated into sumptuous Asian-fusion concoctions. €€€

Pedal the Vltava
SELF-POWERED ADVENTURE

A favourite summertime activity among locals is to head to Slovanský ostrov, an island at the base of the National Theatre, and rent a pedal boat for some self-propelled fun on the Vltava. Be sure to pack a lunch and perhaps a bottle of wine to celebrate once you're out on the water.

Hang out at Náplavka
LIVELY RIVERBANK

Praguers have rediscovered the Nové Město waterfront in recent years. The most popular spot is called Náplavka, which starts just below the Dancing House (p75) and runs for about 2km south to the Výtoň tram stop. Saturday is the most popular day here when, from around 8am, farmers start setting up stalls along the river, but any nice evening in summer brings out hundreds of people to sit along the banks and relax with a glass of wine or beer.

A Night at the Opera (or Ballet)
HIGH-BROW CULTURE

Nové Město is the quarter of culture. Two of the country's pre-eminent cultural institutions, the State Opera (Státní opera) and the National Theatre (p76), are both based here. The stately State Opera, near the National Museum, has just emerged from a fabulous renovation.

The program is heavy on traditional Italian opera and operetta. The National Theater performs virtually anything from Czech opera to avant-garde dance, but everything is top-notch. Check the websites for the full programme and how to buy tickets.

Explore the Islands
NEARBY OASIS

The quickest way to escape the crowds in this busy part of the city is to walk out to one of the islands floating just offshore in the Vltava.

Beautiful Slovanský ostrov, home to elegant Žofín Palace, has been magnificently manicured and has an ex-

JAKAPONG PAOPRAPAT/SHUTTERSTOCK ©

WHERE TO DRINK

Vinograf	**U Fleků**	**Cafe Slavia**
Appealingly modern wine bar great for discovering the best Moravian wines.	Don't mind the tourists, come to this ancient beer-house for its signature home-brewed dark beer.	This old favourite of late president Václav Havel offers good coffee and food, and views of Prague Castle.

tensive playground at the southern end. Střelecký ostrov (pictured facing page) is bigger and more peaceful. Bring a drink, find a bench and stare out into the water.

Cycle along the River

STRETCH THE LEGS

One of the city's most scenic (and flattest) cycling routes begins in Nové Město and follows the Vltava River south for at least 20km.

Find the trail, signposted as the A2, along the embankment just below the Dancing House (p75). The trail doesn't require any special cycling skill. Plan on around four hours out-and-back. Rent bikes at Praha Bike (prahabike.cz) or from local bike-share operator Rekola (rekola.cz; look for stands with pink bikes).

FILIP KOSKA/SHUTTERSTOCK ©

I LIVE HERE: NOVÉ MĚSTO

Nina Rail, a pottery designer (ninarail.com), makes her own hand-thrown pottery, bottles and jewellery in a studio near her home in Nové Město. Here are some of her favourite spots:

100 Class Concept Store
Everything in Vendula Stoklásková's cosy boutique is selected from independent designers in Czechia and nearby countries.

Restart Shop
This second-hand clothing resource always has something lovely in the window, and the proceeds fund meaningful social programs.

Výtvarné Potřeby v Soukenicke
The art-supply shop in Soukenická street stocks oil paints, notebooks, pencils, canvases and other design essentials.

Artic Bakehouse
My husband loves the rustic loaves of bread, but they also have great cinnamon rolls, croissants and pastries.

 WHERE TO STAY

Alcron Hotel
Glamorous hotel from the 1930s with many original art deco marble-and-glass fittings €€€

Icon Hotel
Pretty much everything in this gorgeous boutique hotel has a designer stamp on it. €€

Sophie's Hostel
Big step up from a typical hostel; contemporary style, with oak-veneer floors and stark, minimalist decor. €

ŽIŽKOV & KARLÍN

HILLSIDE PUBS, RIVERSIDE REVIVAL

Many a night has been spent – and lost – at a Žižkov pub. This hilly, traditionally working-class quarter, east of the centre, is easily Prague's rowdiest neighbourhood, with only a few tourist sights. It is a place to unwind after a long day of sightseeing. Bořivojova street is famous for its workers' watering holes, but many of the steep streets are filled with pubs and clubs that haven't changed much since the quarter's heyday 100 years ago. To Žižkov's south and east are two important cemeteries, including the New Jewish Cemetery, Franz Kafka's final resting place. The adjacent riverfront district of Karlín, north of the National Memorial, is connected to Žižkov via a long pedestrian tunnel. Like other neighbourhoods along the Vltava, Karlín was flooded in 2002 and has since been rebuilding. The transformation has been nothing short of miraculous. It's now one of Prague's most desirable residential neighbourhoods, with lovely art nouveau buildings housing dozens of good restaurants, cafes, pubs and wine bars.

GETTING ORIENTED

There are no metro stations in Žižkov, though several stations on metro Line A (green line), including Jiřího z Poděbrad, Flora and Želivského, pass within walking distance. Trams 5, 9, 15 and 26 bisect Žižkov. Karlín lies on metro line B (yellow line), stations Florenc and Křižíkova. The quarter is accessible by trams 3, 8 and 24.

National Memorial on Vítkov Hill

NATIONAL EXCESS AND MACABRE

Žižkov's prominent Vítkov Hill is punctuated by an enormous equestrian statue of 15th-century Hussite general (and Czech hero) Jan Žižka. The national monument on top of the hill is a spectacular tribute to nation-building, with a structure and location so distinctive that the directors of Netflix's 2022 blockbuster *The Gray Man* even used it as a stand-in for a dictator's palace in Azerbaijan. The monument was originally conceived as a tribute to the heroes of newly independent Czechoslovakia, but was used first by the occupying Nazis in the 1940s and later by Czechoslovakia's own communist leaders to serve their propaganda ends.

The interior is a jaw-dropping extravaganza of polished art deco marble, gilt and mosaics, and is home to a small museum of 20th-century Czechoslovak history. The most grimly fascinating part of the building, though, is the Frankenstein-like laboratory that lies beneath the structure's 'Liberation Hall'. It was here, following the death of Czechoslovak communist leader Klement Gottwald in 1953, where scientists battled in vain to prevent Gottwald's corpse from decomposing.

The original plan was to preserve his body in state – not unlike Lenin at Moscow's Lenin Mausoleum. Gottwald's body was initially placed on display in a glass-walled sarcophagus by day and lowered into the white-tiled crypt here each night for a frantic round of maintenance and repair. He was eventually removed and buried in Prague's Olšany Cemetery (p000).

PRACTICAL INFO

The Vítkov memorial is maintained by the National Museum (nm.cz). The main entry ticket allows access to the entire building, including the museum, the former Gottwald laboratory, and an adjoining Memorial to the Unknown Soldier. There's a small cafe on the top floor for refreshments. The upper-level space offers panoramic views out over neighbouring Žižkov and the Žižkov TV tower. Paths surround the memorial and make for a scenic walk down. The memorial is closed for the season from November to March.

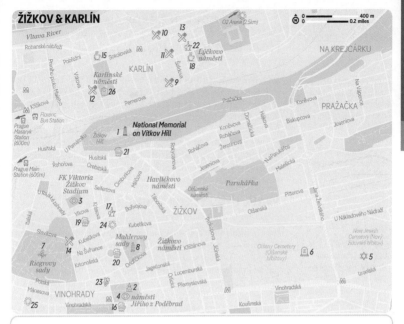

ŽIŽKOV & KARLÍN

HIGHLIGHTS
1 National Monument

SIGHTS
2 Church of the Most Sacred Heart of Our Lord
3 FK Viktoria Žižkov Stadium

4 Náměstí Jiřího z Poděbrad
5 New Jewish Cemetery
6 Olšany Cemetery
7 Riegrovy sady
8 TV Tower

EATING
9 Eska

10 Krystal Bistro
11 Můj Šálek Kávy
12 Nejen Bistro
13 Proti Proudu
14 The Tavern

DRINKING & NIGHTLIFE
15 Antonínovo Pekárna

16 Beer Geek
17 Bukowski's
18 Loft Cafe Karlín
19 U Houdků
20 U Sadu
21 U Vystřeleného Oka
22 Veltlin
23 Vinotéka Noelka

ENTERTAINMENT
24 Palác Akropolis
25 Radiopalác

SHOPPING
26 Karlín Farmers Market

Olšany cemetery

PRAGUE'S BIGGEST BURIAL GROUND

Prague's main burial ground lacks the stark beauty of the **Vyšehrad Cemetery** (p101), but it is peaceful and pretty. It was founded in 1680 to handle increased deaths during a plague epidemic.

The most prominent grave belongs to Jan Palach, the student who set himself on fire in January 1969 to protest the 1968 Soviet-led invasion. To find Palach's grave, enter the main gate on Vinohradská and turn right – it's 50m along on the left.

Czechoslovakia's first communist president, Klement Gottwald, is also buried here. The oldest gravestones can be found in the northwestern corner of the cemetery, near the 17th-century Chapel of St Roch.

THE TRAGEDY OF JAN PALACH

The site where student Jan Palach set himself ablaze to protest the 1968 Warsaw Pact invasion is located at the top of Wenceslas Square, in front of the **National Museum** (p73). The location is designated by a marker in the pavement.

BEST WATERING HOLES IN ŽIŽKOV

Bukowski's
More cocktail 'dive' than cocktail bar, but beloved for its debauched rep and generous 3am closing times.

U Vystřelenýho oka
A Žižkov classic; a wild bohemian hostelry with a raucous Friday-night atmosphere where just about anything goes.

U Sadu
Popular, slightly upscale (compared to the other places on this list) pub, with its very own 'Sádek' beer, brewed specially for customers here.

U Houdků
A classic Žižkov boozer, on pub-strewn Bořivojova street, that entices with decent Czech food and a secluded summertime beer garden.

Hear Some Live Music
LEGENDARY CLUBS

Žižkov and Karlín both have excellent venues for catching a live show. Palác Akropolis (palacakropolis.cz) is a former theatre that's been transformed into a labyrinthine, sticky-floored shrine to alternative music and drama. Its various performance spaces host a smorgasbord of musical and cultural events, from DJs and string quartets to local rock gods and visiting talent. Forum Karlín (forumkarlin.cz) is a spacious, thoroughly modern concert hall that regularly attracts the best international bands on tour in Central Europe.

Walk the Žižkov 'Highline'
ŽIŽKOV FROM THE BACK SIDE

It's not quite New York City's more famous highline, but this former elevated railway line has been transformed into a popular recreation trail for walkers, cyclists and rollerbladers. The trail passes just below the National Memorial on Vítkov Hill (p80) and it's easy to pair a visit. Pick up the trail at an overpass on the western end of Seifertova street and follow it eastward as it runs behind some colourful Žižkov townhouses all the way to a pedestrian tunnel that leads to Karlín. Stay on the trail to find a spooky, abandoned railway tunnel. The trail also passes just behind popular Žižkov pub U Vystřelenýho oka.

Chill out at Kasárna Karlín
CULTURE IN A FORMER BARRACKS

For a taste of Karlín's growing cultural aspirations, drop by this popular hang-out spot set in a former barracks facilities. Depending on the day, catch an outdoor film screening, a concert, an art exhibition or maybe a sports competition, such as volleyball. There's also a big children's playground on the premises and a unique, very cool cafe located in a former swimming-pool hall.

Drink & admire the river
KARLÍN BY THE WATER

Karlín has rediscovered its riverfront in the past couple of years, and the district's shady embankment is a pretty spot to relax over a beer. From April through September, shaggy Přístav 18600 serves as an

ARAZU/ALAMY STOCK PHOTO ©

WHERE TO DRINK

Eska	**Krystal Bistro**	**Lokál Hamburk**
Artisanal bakery and industrial-chic restaurant that does interesting things with basic Czech ingredients. Book ahead. €€	Unpretentious Austro-Bohemian food with a touch of Gallic sophistication, using quality local produce. €€	Popular, upscale pub serving good-value Czech comfort-food classics and well-cared-for Pilsner beer. €

impromptu open-air beer garden, with a couple of beer kiosks and a few scattered tables and oversized pieces of concrete to sit on. It's a popular after-work venue for the district's many office workers. There's a big sandy playground too, which makes it convenient for families, and plenty of hiking and cycling paths to follow the river. From here, it's a short walk to a new pedestrian bridge that leads across the river over to Holešovice (p88).

Cheer on Viktoria Žižkov

LOCAL HEROES

Žižkov's local football (soccer) club, Viktoria Žižkov, plays in a lower division, and watching a match here feels far more low-key and local than cheering on Sparta Praha across the river in Bubeneč. The home stadium on Seifertova street holds just over 3000 spectators. Buy tickets on the team website (fkvz. cz) or at the stadium box office 90 minutes before the match.

Viktoria Žižkov football stadium

I LIVE HERE: KARLÍN

Caroline Holoubek grew up in Sweden and has lived in Prague since 2000. She now calls Karlín home. She shares her favourite places for coffee or wine:

Muj Šálek Kávy
This is the oldest coffee kid on the block but still one of the best. The menu is creative and the food and pastries excellent.

Antonínovo pekárna
Mainstream bakery, but with excellent coffee. The south-facing location overlooking the park and church gets plenty of sun.

Veltlin
A niche selection of natural wines from Central Europe (the countries of the former Habsburg Empire) and great outdoor seating.

 WHERE TO STAY

Nejen Bistro
Super steaks, ribs and burgers. Best in the evening when the ambiently illuminated dining room feels even cosier. €€

Proti Proudu
Clean, casual Karlín bistro serves all-day breakfasts, soups and sandwiches. Book ahead. €

U Kurelů
Classic Žižkov pub re-imagined as an American-style pizza parlour, with great cocktails and drinks. €

VINOHRADY & VRŠOVICE

REGAL AND ROWDY

Centuries before Czechia was famous for beer, Prague was known for its wine, and much of it was grown and produced here in Vinohrady ('vineyards'). Some vineyards can still be seen at the back of the pretty hillside park, Havlíčkovy sady. The rows of elegant 19th- and early-20th-century apartment buildings, along handsome tree-lined streets like Mánesova and Americká, are home to some of Prague's most-prosperous residents. This concentration of wealth helps to support the city's best restaurants, pubs and cafes. Vinohrady is the heart of Prague's LGBTIQ+ community and home to the best gay-friendly clubs and bars. The adjacent quarter of Vršovice, to the south and east, is a mixed industrial and residential neighbourhood that's gained new life in recent years as a party 'hood, particularly along narrow Krymská street.

GETTING ORIENTED

Vinohrady is easy to reach from the centre by metro. Line A (green line) stops at both of the quarter's main hubs: Náměstí Míru and Jiřího z Poděbrad. Tram 22, sometimes called the 'tourist' tram, stops at Náměstí Míru before continuing on to Vršovice. Tram lines 4, 10 and 16 also service Vršovice.

PTTY/SHUTTERSTOCK ©

Rieger Gardens

CHURCH OF THE MOST SACRED HEART OF OUR LORD

This Catholic church from 1932, on one of Vinohrady's liveliest squares, Jiřího z Poděbrad, is arguably one of Prague's most original pieces of 20th-century architecture. It's the work of Jože Plečnik, a Slovene designer who's best known for installing decorative pillars and obelisks in his home capital of Ljubljana. He also worked on revitalising Prague Castle in the 1920s.
   The church is said to recall the shape of Noah's Ark and, through squinted eyes, it does resemble a boat. The interior is strikingly minimalist. The church is normally only open during Mass.

Rieger Gardens

SUNSET PHOTO OPPORTUNITY

This spacious park, modelled on a classic 19th-century English garden, is a favourite among residents for strolling, jogging or simply walking the family dog. The park encloses a cosy beer garden that's popular from May to September. The high-altitude bluff towards the back of the park affords photo-ops of the Old Town and Prague Castle in the distance. It's one of the city's most picturesque venues for throwing down a blanket and watching the sun set in the western sky.

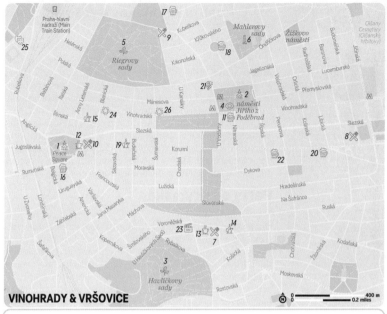

VINOHRADY & VRŠOVICE

SIGHTS		DRINKING &	17 U Houdků	ENTERTAINMENT
1 Church of St Ludmilla	5 Riegrovy sady	NIGHTLIFE	18 U Sadu	23 Kino Pilotů
2 Church of the Most Sacred Heart of Our Lord	6 TV Tower	11 Beer Geek	19 Vinograf Korunní	24 Radiopalác
	EATING	12 Café Nový Svět	20 Vinohradský Pivovar	25 State Opera
	7 Cafe Sladkovský	13 Cafe V Lese		26 TerMIX
3 Havlíčkovy Sady	8 La Farma	14 Krymská street	21 Vinotéka Noelka	
4 Náměstí Jiřího z Poděbrad	9 The Tavern	15 Ossegg	22 Výčep	
	10 Vinohradský Parlament	16 Prague Beer Museum		

Church of Saint Ludmila

SPIRITUAL HEART OF VINOHRADY

For Praguers, this beautiful neo-Gothic Catholic church on central Náměstí Míru symbolises the heart of Vinohrady. The church was built between 1888 and 1892, based on plans by the Czech Gothic enthusiast, Josef Mocker. In addition to designing churches, Mocker was responsible for adding neo-Gothic spires to many of Prague's older buildings in the late-19th century (and thus inspiring Prague's nickname of 'City of 100 Spires').

The small square in front of the main entrance is home to the city's most-festive Christmas market outside of the Old Town Square.

THE FIRST CZECH SAINT

The Church of Saint Ludmila is named after the first Czech saint. She's the grandmother of Bohemian patron saint St Wenceslas, and plays an important role in the legend of Prague's founding at **Vyšehrad** (p100).

THE GUIDE

PRAGUE

I LIVE HERE: VINOHRADY

Lori Wyant, an American who has lived in Vinohrady for almost three decades, owns and operates The Tavern (thetavern.cz) restaurant with her husband, Dean Selby. Here are some of her favourite Vinohrady venues:

BoHo Café
This beautifully lit, charming cafe and bar serves excellent cocktails amid racks of stylish vintage garb. Get drunk and walk out with a cool retro jacket.

Lokál U Benyho
Old dessert shop revamped as a retro Czech pub. Super-friendly vibes and unbeatable goulash, matched with perfectly poured Pilsner.

Kro Kitchen Bistro
Their signature rotisserie chicken, with a side of demi-glace sauce and roast potatoes, is addictive. Save room for an almond croissant from their bakery next door.

Hang out on JZP
FARMERS' MARKET AND FUN

Always-active Jiřího z Poděbrad square – Jiřák to Czechs and often shortened by non-Czech speakers to 'JZP' – is surrounded by cafes, bars and trendy restaurants. The inviting benches in front of the Church of the Most Sacred Heart of Our Lord (p84) are perfect perches for people-watching. From February to December, the square hosts a popular farmers' market that runs through the day from Wednesday to Saturday. On Saturdays, many locals make a day of it – they come early for the shopping and then relax on the square, picnic-style, with drinks and food.

Party on Krymská
VRŠOVICE NIGHTLIFE

On weekend nights, residents decamp to Vršovice's hilly Krymská street for a night of drinking and carousing. The bars can get crowded, and many places thankfully allow customers to take their drinks outside (as long as they don't make too much noise). Popular venues include Café V lese, which hosts live music, the arthouse cinema Kino Pilotů, with its cosy, adjoining cocktail bar, and nearby Café Sladkovský, for food and drinks. The best thing is to walk around and see which place fits the mood.

Don't Forget the Pubs
MICROBREWS AND CRAFT BEERS

Vinohrady has some excellent Czech pubs and microbrewers. Both the popular Vinohradský Pivovar and Ossegg Praha brew their own and serve excellent Czech food to go with it. Náměstí Míru's Prague Beer Museum has a big cellar space for drinking and keeps some 30 beers on tap. Across the street, Vinohradský Parlament toes a fine line between pub and restaurant. JZP's BeerGeek has 32 taps and specialises in local craft beers, like Matuška, Clock and Klášterní Strahov.

Hike & 'Wine' at Grébovka
ENJOY THE VINEYARDS

Vinohrady's 'other' pretty park, Havlíček Gardens (Havlíčkovy sady), known as Grébovka by residents, occupies a steep hillside at the southern end of Americká street. The park was inspired by Italian

PAJKA87/SHUTTERSTOCK ©

🍷 WHERE TO DRINK

Le Caveau	Kavárna Šlágr	Café Kaaba
JZP staple and a popular spot to relax with coffee or French wine. Also serves French-style pastries, sandwiches and cheese.	Old-fashioned bakery-cafe with a big pastry counter; feels like stepping back into the last century.	Stylish cafe-bar with retro furniture and pastel-coloured decor straight out of the 1959 Ideal Homes Exhibition.

neo-Renaissance design and it's a small piece of paradise, with hidden grottoes, big rocks and finely manicured ponds. There's no prescribed walk for exploring the park – simply choose the most inviting path downhill. The Gröbe Villa, toward the bottom, offers more stunning vistas and two venues for sampling wine: Pavilon Grébovka and an informal, open-air gazebo.

Go Dancing at TerMIX

GAY-FRIENDLY VINOHRADY

Over the past decade, Vinohrady has evolved into the informal epicentre of Prague's LGBTIQ+ community and the ever-lively TerMIX dance club is a good place to experience the community's energy and vitality. Weekend nights draw a mixed crowd of gay and straight partiers, who compete for space on a tiny dance floor. Arrive soon after the 10pm opening or be prepared to wait in line. When it's time to move on, TerMIX is within easy walking distance of a mix of gay-friendly venues at the enormous Radiopalác building in the heart of Vinohrady.

Andrea Kotašková, Vinohrady native and recognised wine expert, is co-owner of a wine-themed travel agency, Wine Travel in Czech (winetravelinczech. com). She shares her Vinohrady wine tips:

I LIVE HERE: VINOHRADY

Grébovka
This beautiful park (also known as Havlíčkovy sady) has dramatic vineyards. Sample wines in the Pavilon Grébovka or at a wooden gazebo overlooking the vineyard.

Vinograf Korunní
A modern wine bar with a beautiful brick cellar. Come for a glass or pair your wine with a good meal.

Vinotéka Noelka
Do like the locals and stop over at this busy vinothèque for a glass or two. They have a great selection of Czech wines.

Vinograf wine bar

SATURNO DONÀ/ALAMY STOCK PHOTO ©

 WHERE TO EAT

Výčep
High-end gastropub offers updated takes on classic Czech dishes. €€

The Tavern
Great for burgers, pulled pork and other comfort food; vegetarian-friendly as well. €

La Farma
Perfect lunch or dinner choice offers a mix of well-done Czech favourites and international dishes. €€

87

HOLEŠOVICE

ART AND STREET VIBE

Historically working-class Holešovice, with abandoned factories
and lofts, has recast itself as the city's contemporary-arts hub.
Building on the National Gallery's superb collection at the Trade
Fair Palace, a smattering of edgy galleries have opened up. Holešovice has also emerged as the epicentre of hip design in Prague,
with many boutiques around central Milady Horákové street.
Holešovice is essentially two distinct districts, separated by an
old railway line. The more prosperous western half is a rapidly
gentrifying residential neighbourhood of late 19th-century townhouses, anchored by the Trade Fair Palace and National Technical Museum. This is also home to Letná gardens on a high ridge
over the Vltava. The scruffier eastern half is filled with old factories, many now converted to design studios and loft residences. The mood here is edgier, with late-night clubs like Cross Club
and the always interesting DOX Centre for Contemporary Art.

GETTING ORIENTED

Holešovice is situated
across the river from Staré
Město (Old Town) and
Nové Město (New Town).
To access Letná Park
from Staré Město, cross
Čechův bridge and climb
the stairs. Holešovice is
served by metro line C (red
line), Vltavská and Nádraží
Holešovice stations.
Strossmayerovo náměstí is
an important tram junction
(lines 1, 6, 8, 12, 17, 25, 26).

Trade Fair Palace
MASTERS OF MODERN ART

The National Gallery's collection of 19th- and 20th-century
art is spread out over several floors and is a strong contender for Prague's best museum. It has an unexpectedly rich
collection of world masters, including Van Gogh, Picasso,
Schiele, Klimt and so on, but the holdings of Czech interwar
abstract, surrealist and cubist art are worth the trip alone.
Take a moment to admire the building's exterior. When construction was completed in 1928, the Trade Fair Palace was
Prague's first functionalist building and the largest building
of its kind in the world.

The star-studded third floor holds an impressive collection
of late-19th- and early-20th-century art, including works by
Monet, Gauguin, Cézanne, Picasso, Delacroix and Rodin. Look
for Gauguin's Flight and Van Gogh's Green Wheat. It's also
home to a stunning assembly of interwar (1918–38) Czech
art. Standouts include the geometric works by Czech master
František Kupka, and Cubist paintings, ceramics and design
by several artists – these paintings show an interesting parallel with the concurrent art scene in Paris.

The fourth floor shows off the breathtaking landscapes and
portraiture of the 19th century (which the curators define as
running from 1796 to 1918). This floor also boasts works by
some major names: Klimt, Schiele and Munch, to list a few.
Two highlights take on feminine themes: Klimt's luscious, vi-
brantly hued The Virgins and Schiele's much darker, foreboding Pregnant Woman and Death.

SAVING MONEY

The Trade Fair Palace
is part of the National
Gallery's (ngprague.
cz) collection of
museums. For 500Kč,
you can buy a ticket for
combined admission
to all of the member
buildings that host
permanent exhibitions.
These include
**Schwarzenberg
Palace** (p52),
Šternberg Palace
(p52) and the **Convent
of St Agnes** (p66), as
well as the Trade Fair
Palace. The ticket is
good for 10 days from
first entry. Children
under 18 years (and
students under 26)
enter for free.

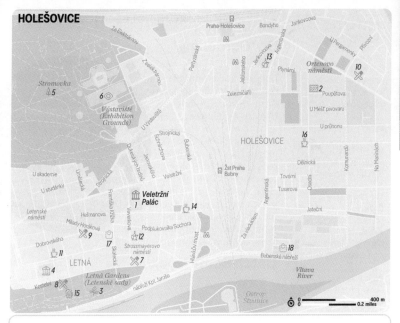

HOLEŠOVICE

HIGHLIGHTS
1 Veletržní Palác

SIGHTS
2 DOX Centre for Contemporary Art
3 Letná Gardens

4 National Technical Museum
5 Stromovka Park
6 Výstaviště Exhibition Grounds

EATING
7 Bistro 8
8 Letenský Zámeček
9 Mr Hot Dog
10 The Eatery

DRINKING & NIGHTLIFE
11 Café Letka
12 Cobra
13 Cross Club
14 Kavárna Liberál

15 Letná Beer Gdn
16 Osada

SHOPPING
17 Milady Horákové Street
18 Pražská Tržnice

National Technical Museum

PLANES, TRAINS AND AUTOMOBILES

Prague's interactive National Technical Museum has a kind of industrial-age, steampunk feel. The main hall is filled to the rafters with historic planes, trains, automobiles and motorcycles that are close enough to touch.

Separate halls scattered throughout the rest of the building are devoted to displays on Czech industrial prowess in photography, printing, household design, architecture and astronomy, among others.

A high-tech renovation carried out a few years back brought the exhibitions up to date and added some hands-on experiences. The museum is especially popular with kids and families.

THOMAS PILLER/GETTY IMAGES ©

BEST PLACES TO SHOP

Charaktery
Designer collective turns out exquisitely formed jewellery and accessories.

Kurâz
Clothing, accessories and gift ideas from producers in both Czechia and Slovakia.

The Chemistry Gallery
Eclectic, occasionally affordable photos and paintings from leading local artists.

Page Five
Colourful collection of books, maps and prints on Veverkova.

Guilt
Carefully selected second-hand clothing and coats with an emphasis on sustainability.

Go 'Gardening'
CITY'S BEST BEER GARDEN

Hang out at the Letná beer garden, one of Prague's signature warm-weather experiences (May to September). Line up with everyone else at a small beer-dispensing kiosk to buy a glass of Gambrinus, served in half-litre plastic cups (there's a 50Kč deposit for the cup). Find a nearby picnic table, relax and enjoy the view and convivial mood. On warm nights, in high summer, the kiosk stays open until around midnight.

RIVAL BEER GARDENS

After you've chugged a few at Letná's beer garden, check out its cross-town rival in Vinohrady. That quarter's Rieger Gardens (**Riegrovy sady**; p84) has a quieter open-air garden that locals say might be even better.

Catch Some Hockey
ACTION ON THE ICE

From September through April, sleek O2 Arena (o2arena.cz), 5km east of Holešovice in the district of Libeň, is home ice for local hockey club, Sparta Praha. Quality of play is high and the Czech Extraliga is arguably the most competitive national league outside of North America's NHL. Even non-fans will enjoy the spectacle and intensity of the players and fans alike. Find a schedule and buy tickets online at Ticketportal (ticketportal.cz). The arena is located on metro line B (yellow line), Českomoravská stop.

Head to the Market
RENOVATION PROJECT

Prague Market (Pražská tržnice; prazska-trznice.cz), in the eastern part of Holešovice, functioned for years as the city's main market for food and household goods. In the 1990s and early 2000s, the area fell on hard times. Now the complex is in the throes of a major renovation. Saturdays are the liveliest, when food trucks move in and crafters set up shop. The market is home to alternative theatre Jatka 78 (jatka78.cz) and the funky Trafo gallery (trafogallery.cz). It's also home to a very good Vietnamese restaurant, Tràng An, in Building 5.

WHERE TO EAT

Bistro 8
Welcoming, vegan-friendly space with all-day breakfasts, lunch specials and good coffee. €

Letenský zámeček
Upscale dining on a terrace adjacent to the Letná beer garden. Book in advance. €€

Cobra
Combination popular restaurant and cocktail bar stands at the heart of hipster Holešovice. €€

Do Some Window Shopping
TRENDY BOUTIQUES

In the past few years, dozens of small shops, designer paper sellers, booksellers and boutiques have popped up in the western end of Holešovice. The best hunting grounds run along the area's main street, Milady Horákové, and side streets like Veverkova, Františka Křížka and Kamenická.

See DOX Centre for Contemporary Art
ZEPPELIN ON THE ROOF

This alternative art gallery, occupying a former factory, stands at the heart of Holešovice's artistic ambitions. Exhibitions here highlight a wide range of media, including video, sculpture, photography, sound and painting. There's a decent cafe and bookstore that's heavy on art and architecture. Don't miss the Gulliver Airship, a giant wooden zeppelin that's been perched atop the building since 2016.

DOX Centre for Contemporary Art

JONATHAN STOKES/LONELY PLANET ©

**I LIVE HERE:
HOLEŠOVICE**

Jan Valenta, Prague native, is co-owner, along with his wife Zuzi, of the popular Taste of Prague (tasteofprague.com) food tours. He shares some of his Holešovice food scene's favourites:

Hall 22
This cavernous hall within the Prague Market complex is a good place to pick up local organic fruit and veg.

**Mr Hot Dog/
Big Smokers**
Mr Hot Dog serves sliders, hot dogs and chili, while its sister restaurant, Big Smokers, does pulled pork and barbecued meats.

Osada
Search out Osada in a hidden courtyard in the eastern part of Holešovice for specialty coffees and light meals.

The Eatery
Offers upscale, modern Czech cuisine in a tastefully designed, minimalist main dining room.

 **WHERE TO DRINK**

Cafe Letka
Beautifully ornate neighbourhood coffeehouse stands just a few steps away from Letná gardens.

Kavárna Liberál
Viennese-style coffeehouse with echoes of the 1920s and very good food.

Cross Club
Holešovice's best-known bar and nightclub is a celebration of steampunk and must be seen to be believed.

BUBENEČ & DEJVICE

VILLAS, PARKS AND GARDENS

The adjoining districts of Bubeneč and Dejvice stretch out to the northwest of the city centre, north of Prague Castle and west of Holešovice. Both are handsome, prosperous residential areas laid out in the late 19th and early 20th centuries. Bubeneč, in particular, is home to stunning villas that have now been converted to embassies and official residences. Bubeneč is also home to Stromovka Park, the city's largest and prettiest piece of green, hugging the Vltava's southern bank.

Adjoining Stromovka, the Výstaviště exhibition grounds – built for the 1891 Prague Jubilee – look neglected, though they hold an interesting branch of the National Museum and the city's largest aquarium. Across the river, north of Stromovka, find the Prague Zoo, Troja Chateau and the Prague Botanical Gardens. Further west, in Dejvice, hiking trails follow Šárka creek all the way out to Divoká Šárka, a striking piece of urban wilderness.

GETTING ORIENTED

Both Bubeneč and Dejvice are easily reachable by metro line A (green line), to stations Hradčanská and Dejvická. Both neighbourhoods are well-served by tram. Lines 1, 8, 25 and 26 run to Letenské náměstí – from where it's an easy walk to Stromovka Park. Výstaviště can be reached via trams 12 and 17.

MILONK/SHUTTERSTOCK ©

Troja Château

Villa Müller

MASTERPIECE OF DESIGN

Fans of modern architecture will enjoy this masterpiece, located just west of Dejvice in the district of Střešovice. Built in 1930 for construction entrepreneur František Müller, it was designed by the Brno-born architect Adolf Loos. The clean-cut, ultramodern exterior contrasts with the polished wood, leather and oriental rugs of the interior. Book in advance (muzeumprahy.cz).

Troja Château

BAROQUE BLING

Across the Vltava from Stromovka (accessible via footbridge), the delightful Troja Château was originally conceived as a kind of grand, Roman-style suburban villa. It was designed in baroque style in the 17th century by French architect Jean Baptiste Mathey for the noble Šternberk family. The permanent exhibit is devoted to the interior furnishings of the chateau and shows off the villa's lavish chambers and frescoes. The grounds are free to enter, and the baroque stone giants and winding French gardens make for beautiful photographs.

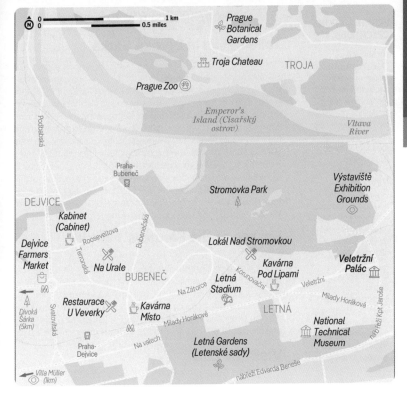

Prague Botanical Gardens

BUTTERFLIES AND BONSAI TREES

The gently rolling hills across the Vltava river, north of Stromovka, create an idyllic setting for these sprawling botanical gardens, one of Prague's most under-appreciated attractions. There's something for every budding botanist, including the S-shaped 'Fata Morgana' greenhouse, which features free-range butterflies, a small aquarium and many exotic plants from Latin America, Australia and Africa. A smallish Japanese garden holds an impressive display of Japanese bonsai and other plants. Trails run here and there, with breathtaking views out over the Vltava river valley. A visit could easily take up the better part of a day. Vineyards climb up the south-facing hillside and tastings can sometimes be organised via botanicka.cz. Buy bottles of local wine at the garden gift shop.

ANOTHER ADOLF LOOS

The modern master architect Adolf Loos had a hand in designing several villas in and around Prague over the years. One of his most impressive works, and the last to be completed during his lifetime, is the 1932 **Villa Winternitz** (p98) in Smíchov.

93

BEST TRADITIONAL
CZECH PUBS

Na Slamníku
More like a welcoming
roadside inn, with
two handsome dining
rooms and a roaring
fire. Pilsner-Urquell and
local Únětice beer are
served, plus very good
food. Live music on
Friday nights.

Na Urale
Popular
neighbourhood pub,
with plenty of sidewalk
tables, on Bubeneč's
quiet Puškinovo
náměstí.

U Veverky
People come here
not so much for the
beer – though it is very
good – but rather for
the excellent Czech
home cooking. Book in
advance for dinner.

Take a Hike in Divoká Šárka'

STUNNING ROCKS AND NATURE

Divoká Šárka, west of Dejvice, is one of the city's prettiest and most
remote nature parks. The area is best known for its unique landscape of barren rocks and hills at its western end, but it goes on
for kilometres through forests and valleys along the Šárka Creek
(Šárecký potok). The easiest way to access the park is by tram;
lines 20 and 26 from Vítězné náměstí terminate at the park's edge
(Divoká Šárka stop). Return by tram or, for a longer outing, find a
red-marked trail that runs for about 7km all the way to the suburb
of Podbaba, where the creek empties into the Vltava. Once at the
river, look for the tower of the Hotel International (with a star on
top). Head towards the hotel to find tram 8 or 18 for the return to
Vítězné náměstí and Dejvická metro station (Line A).

Forage at the Farmers' Market

SATURDAY MORNING FUN

From March to November, get out of bed early on a Saturday
morning to join the crowds at the Dejvice farmers' market, spread
across a grassy field adjacent to Dejvická metro station. The
mood is more akin to a carnival than a market. Sure there's lots
of fresh fruits and vegetables, but there's usually also live music
and plenty of food truck fare, like tacos and burgers, to munch on.

Visit the Zoo

ELEPHANTS, GORILLAS AND RARE HORSES

Prague's attractive zoo is immensely popular with families, so much
so it's best to avoid going on the weekend. The 2002 Prague flood hit
the zoo hard and many animals were lost in the inundation. Over
the past two decades, officials have invested greatly to improve the
grounds and animal safety. There are sizable collections of giraffes
and gorillas, but pride of place goes to a herd of rare horses.

Attractions include a miniature cable car and a big play
area. The quickest way to reach the zoo is to take bus
112 from metro stop Nádraží Holešovice (Line C).
If time is no issue, there's a pretty 30-minute walk
to the zoo from the Výstaviště exhibition grounds
through Stromovka Park. Follow the trails north
and west and look for signs to 'Troja' and 'Zoo'. The
walk proceeds through a railway underpass, and the
road eventually leads to a footbridge over the Vltava
and the zoo's main entrance.

SERGEYPHOTO7/SHUTTERSTOCK ©

 WHERE TO EAT

Lokál Nad Stromovkou
Excellent, good-value Czech
cooking and Pilsner beer, served
on a ridge overlooking Stromovka
Park. Book in advance. €€

Kavárna Místo
Creative concoctions from
locally sourced ingredients
offered in a stripped down,
minimalist setting. €

The Farm
Informal spot for great
breakfasts and burgers, a short
walk from the entrance to
Stromovka. €€

Check out Some Footie
CHEER ON THE HOME TEAM

Hometown football (soccer) faves AC Sparta Praha play their home matches in Bubeneč at the 20,000-seat Letná Stadium (Generali Aréna). The stadium is often used for international matches and friendlies. Matches are usually played on weekends and the season runs from August to May. Buy tickets on the team website (sparta.cz) or at the stadium's box office before the match on game day.

Stroll through Stromovka Park
ROYAL HUNTING GROUND

Strolling the long oval corso at the centre of Stromovka Park has been a popular pastime for generations. Centuries ago, Stromovka served as a royal hunting preserve. Emperor Rudolf II had rare trees planted and had several lakes created. Enter from the Výstaviště exhibition grounds or from Letenské náměstí (follow Čechova třída north to a ridge overlooking the park).

Stromovka Park

CAPTURE LIGHT/SHUTTERSTOCK ©

THE GUIDE

PRAGUE

WHERE TO HAVE COFFEE (AND CAKE)

Cukrárna Alchymista
The hidden back garden is the real draw here, though the cakes and pastries are some of the city's finest.

Cafe Pod Lipami
Coffee and light bites under the graceful linden trees of pretty Čechova street.

Kavárna Kabinet
Old-school cafe set in a leafy residential patch of Bubeneč. Good for beer too.

95

SMÍCHOV

PRAGUE'S BEER QUARTER

Smíchov has almost no tourist vibe, and not much in the way of historic architecture. Most of the buildings date from the last half of the 19th or early-20th centuries, when the quarter was still largely industrial. What the district does offer, though, is beer. It is home to the Staropramen brewery and beer plays a strong role in the neighbourhood's identity and day-to-day life. Smíchov can't be far behind Žižkov in terms of most pubs per square kilometre, and the pubs here are just as raucous and unvarnished. Smíchov isn't just about drinking. As the district has slowly changed and become more prosperous, better and more-varied restaurants have sprouted. The presence of places like Meet-Factory for alternative music, Jazz Dock for jazz, and Švandovo Divadlo for theatre has put Smíchov firmly on the city's cultural map. Each year the embankment (Smíchovská náplavka) in this riverfront district adds new places to eat, drink and stroll.

GETTING ORIENTED

Smíchov is located on major transport lines. Metro line B (yellow line) serves both Anděl, the main commercial area, and the Smíchov train station (Smíchovské nádraží). The bustling quarter around the Anděl metro station is crisscrossed by tram lines (4, 5, 7, 9, 10, 12, 16, 20 and 21) that run to all parts of the city.

TOP LEFT: PROFIMEDIA.CZ A.S./ALAMY STOCK PHOTO ©

MeetFactory

Staropramen

PRAGUE'S LAST BIG COMMERCIAL BREWER

Smíchov's Staropramen brewery is the city's last-remaining major commercial brewery (though local micro-brewers have stepped up the pace in recent years to fill the void). Unlike similar big brewery tours in Plzeň and České Budějovice, this 50-minute circuit feels more like a museum stop than an actual factory visit, although you do get to sample several beers along the way. The presentation here focuses on the 100-plus years of tradition at the brewery. See centrumstaropramen. cz for tour times or check them on the door. There are several English tours per day.

MeetFactory

ALTERNATIVE VIBE

It's not easy to find (take tram 4, 5, 12 or 20 to the Lihovar stop and walk across some railway tracks) but, depending on what's on the program, David Černý's MeetFactory is worth the effort. The MeetFactory is a remarkable project that unites artists from around the world in an abandoned factory south of Smíchov train station. The space is used for exhibitions, happenings, screenings, theatrical performances and some of Prague's best alternative concerts. Find the program on meetfactory.cz.

SIGHTS
1 Futura Gallery
2 Staropramen Brewery
3 Villa Winternitz

EATING
4 Manifesto Market
5 Na Verandách
6 Taro
7 Zlatý Klas

DRINKING & NIGHTLIFE
8 Andělský pivovar
9 Hospoda U Buldoka
10 Kavárna Co Hledá Jméno

ENTERTAINMENT
11 Jazz Dock
12 Meet Factory
13 Švandovo Divadlo
Na Smíchově

Smíchov embankment

RIVERSIDE DRINKS AND VIEWS

The Smíchov embankment (Smíchovská náplavka), along the Vltava, defined roughly as the riverbank running south of Vltavská street until approximately Pivovarská street, keeps getting better and better. The area got going a few years ago in response to Nové Město's larger and more popular **Náplavka** (p78) on the other side. In many ways, though, Smíchov's version is superior. It feels much quieter and more refined. Several pubs and restaurants, including the Pitchers (Hořejší nábřeží), a good bar and grill restaurant, put out open-air tables in nice weather, and the views out to the Vyšehrad fortress (p100) are impressive. A river ferry (requiring a tram or metro ticket to ride) connects the embankment to the Výtoň tram stop in Nové Město.

BREWERY TOURS

The Staropramen brewery tour is fine for starters (or if you're only visiting Prague), but the best guided tour of this kind is undoubtedly at the **Pilsner Urquell Brewery** (p132) in Plzeň (Pilsen).

Jazz Dock

JAZZ WITH A VIEW

Prague has had a love affair with jazz going back to the 1920s – and especially during the 1950s and '60s. Most of the city's jazz clubs are dark cellar affairs, and this above-ground riverside club is a definite step up. It draws some of the best local talent and international acts in jazz, blues, swing and pop. Shows normally begin at 7pm and 10pm, and you can pair a show with dinner and drinks. Book a table on the venue website (jazzdock.cz).

Švandovo Divadlo

CZECH THEATRE
IN ENGLISH

The Czechs have a storied tradition in theatrical arts. The Švanda experimental theatre gets props for its commitment to performing or super-titling some of its productions in English to allow access to international audiences, but understandably almost everything is in Czech. The program here leans toward contemporary comedy and drama. The theatre also hosts occasional live music and dance, as well as regular 'stage talks' – unscripted discussions with noted personalities. Look for 'English friendly' or 'English supertitles' on the program at svandovodivadlo.cz.

TOP LEFT: EVA PRUCHOVA/SHUTTERSTOCK © BOTTOM RIGHT: RUEDIGER ETTL/SHUTTERSTOCK ©

Villa Winternitz

Villa Winternitz

EARLY-MODERN MANSION

The fully restored 1932 Villa Winternitz, the work of architects Adolf Loos and Karel Lhota, is a must for fans of early-modern and functionalist architecture. Indeed, Brno-born Loos (1870–1933) is often considered one of the fathers of modern architecture. This villa marks the architect's last design to be fully realised during his lifetime, and Loos' concept of raumplan – minimalist design, lighting and interior spacing – is on full display. The Winternitz family was forced to abandon the villa in 1941 during the Nazi occupation, and the house was later returned to the owner's descendants. Guided tours take place on weekends and can be booked on the website (loosovavila.cz).

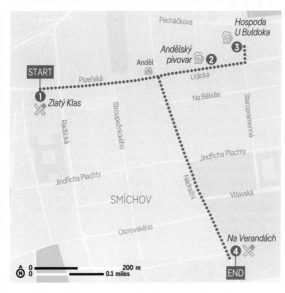

Map labels: Pecháčkova · Hospoda U Buldoka · Andělský pivovar · Anděl · START · Plzeňská · Lidická · Zlatý Klas · Na Bělidle · Staropramenná · Stroupežnického · Radlická · Jindřicha Plachty · Nádražní · Jindřicha Plachty · SMÍCHOV · Vltavská · Ostrovského · Na Verandách · END · 200 m · 0.1 miles

WHERE TO EAT IN SMÍCHOV

Manifesto Market
This open-air eatery, near Anděl metro station (below), is a godsend for something quick and easy. The food stands offer everything from food-truck faves to high-end meals. Card only. €

Taro
One of the district's few destination restaurants, where the chefs turn out meticulously prepared Vietnamese dishes (with some Asian-fusion tossed in). €€€

Kavárna Co Hledá Jméno
Popular hipster-style cafe good for coffee and chilling, but they also feature arguably the city's best eggs Benedict. Book in advance. €

THE GUIDE

PRAGUE

A Pub Tour

SIGHTSEEING BY THE PINT

As the site of the city's last-standing big national brewery, Smíchov is all about beer. This tour only scratches the surface and is in no way meant to be exhaustive. Feel free to branch off to other places as the mood strikes. Start off at one of the neighbourhood's favourite old-school pubs, **(1) Zlatý Klas**. Here, beer is stored in big tanks, called tankové pivo, which is intended to keep it fresher. The traditional pub food, like svíčková (braised beef in cream sauce) and Plzeňský guláš (goulash), is also good.

From here, head east along Plzeňská. This street and a parallel street, Na Bělidle, mark out the area's heartland of pubs. **(2) Andělský pivovar** offers a contrast to older, traditional pubs. It is an airy, renovated space that makes its own very good craft beers. Just around the corner, nip in for a quick one at classic sports bar **(3) Hospoda U Buldoka**. There's a decadent drink-till-you-drop vibe here, but pace yourself. Head south on Nádražní a few blocks to sample beer direct from the Staropramen Brewery at **(4) Na Verandách**. It is housed on the brewery grounds and promises the freshest pour you can find.

 WHERE TO STAY

Red & Blue Design Hotel
Designer boutique set in a smartly renovated 19th-century townhouse. €€

Anděl's By Vienna House
Artful, contemporary hotel with minimalist decor. The location is a short walk from Anděl metro station. €€

Hotel Julian
Small hotel in a quiet location, just south of Malá Strana. The public areas include a clubby drawing room with a library. €€

99

VYŠEHRAD

ONCE PRAGUE'S 'OTHER' CASTLE

Vyšehrad ('Upper Castle') is an enigma. The castle, which once rivalled larger Prague Castle in importance, is long gone, a casualty of war and kingly preference. The early Přemysl rulers made their home here in the 11th century, but soon moved to the other side of the river. A few centuries later, Vyšehrad was just a moody ruin.

In the 17th century, the ruling Habsburg monarchy temporarily revived Vyšehrad by building a baroque fortress here to fend off the Prussians. What's left today is an aura of mystery and legend, and a beautiful park with river views. One Czech folk tale says that a chieftain named Krok built a castle here in the 7th century and his daughter Libuše prophesied a great city would rise in the valley of the Vltava. Maybe it's not so far-fetched. Vyšehrad is home to Prague's oldest surviving building, the 11th-century Rotunda of St Martin, as well as its most prestigious cemetery.

GETTING ORIENTED

The former fortress and scattered ruins of Vyšehrad lie 2km south of the centre. If time is short, grab metro line C (red line) south to Vyšehrad station; from here walk 200m west to the Tábor Gate, the entryway to the complex. For a more leisurely approach, walk uphill along Vratislavova from the Výtoň tram stop near the Vltava river.

TOP LEFT: MARIN GARAJ/SHUTTERSTOCK©

Rotunda of St Martin

Rotunda of St Martin

HERE FOR A THOUSAND YEARS

The dignified, 11th-century Rotunda of St Martin is said to be Prague's oldest-surviving building. The structure's thick walls and high, narrow windows are classic elements of Romanesque architecture. The door and frescoes, though, were added much later, during renovations around 1880. During the bloody 17th century, the rotunda was used to store gunpowder. Alas, the rotunda is normally closed to visitors, but the tiny interior can be viewed during mass times that are usually posted on the door.

Basilica of Sts Peter & Paul

FORMER ST VITUS RIVAL

Vyšehrad's stately Gothic-spired Basilica of Sts Peter & Paul looms over the skyline in the distance and plays an analogous – though lower-key – role to Prague Castle's St Vitus as a royal cathedral. The structure certainly looks as if it may have come from the days of the early Bohemian kings, but it was built and rebuilt several times over the centuries. Like nearly everything here, the basilica suffered greatly from neglect and damage during the wars of the 15th and 17th centuries. Its arresting twin spires date from the 19th century and an architectural craze that gripped Prague at the time known as 'neo-Gothic'.

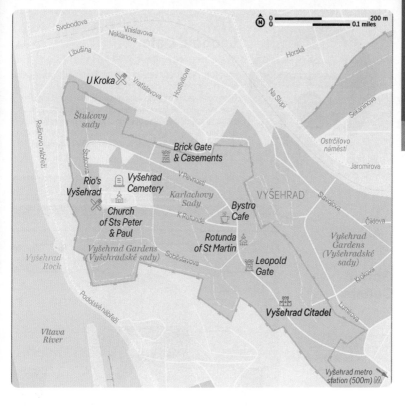

Vyšehrad Cemetery

BEAUTIFUL BURIAL SITE

Much like London's Highgate or Paris's Père Lachaise, Vyšehrad Cemetery is more than a burial ground. It's a pantheon to the leading Czech artists and thinkers of the 19th and early-20th centuries, when the country was first forging its own national identity. Vyšehrad is the final resting place of dozens of Czech luminaries, including Antonín Dvořák, Bedřich Smetana and Alfons Mucha.

Many tombs and headstones are works of art. Dvořák's is a sculpture by Ladislav Šaloun, the art nouveau sculptor who created the Jan Hus monument (p62) in Old Town Square. The cemetery is free to enter and there's a list of famous graves at the door, but the real enjoyment is simply walking the rows and locating the names.

Leopold Gate

OLD ROYAL ENTRYWAYS

Entry to the Vyšehrad complex, when approaching from the metro station, is marked by a series of impressive gates. Beyond the Tábor Gate, continue on to the more impressive 17th-century Leopold Gate. Between these two main gates, note the remnants of an earlier (and what must have been grander) 14th-century Gothic gate, the 'Peak Gate' (in Czech, Špička brána). Today, it's home to the area's main tourist information office (praha-vysehrad.cz).

Gothic Cellars

WHAT'S LEFT
OF THE PALACE

The restored Gothic cellars here were once part of a four-chamber palace complex (other parts of the palace may have held a chapel and dining room) that was built here by Emperor Charles IV in the 14th century. The palace is long gone, but the cellars are used to house a permanent (rather dry) exhibition dedicated to the history and legend of Vyšehrad. The various display panels describe Vyšehrad's transition over the centuries from royal residence to fortress to today's tourist attraction. The high points are the impressive interiors and the relics on display from early pre-Slavic civilisations.

Brick Gate

Brick Gate & Casemates

LESSON IN FORTRESS-MAKING

In the collective imagination, Vyšehrad is often associated with the city's earliest origins, though most of the surviving buildings here, including this gate and casemate complex, date from the 17th and 18th centuries, when the ruling Habsburg dynasty used the fortress to protect against Prussian and French encroachment. The casemates serve as a primer for how baroque fortresses were constructed at the time. A guided, 20-minute tour takes visitors through an elaborate system of vaulted brick tunnels within the ramparts. The highlight is the large, barrel-vaulted Gorlice Hall, where large numbers of troops could muster without being seen by the enemy. Now, the space is home to several statues from Charles Bridge.

TOP LEFT: XLUP/SHUTTERSTOCK ©; BOTTOM RIGHT: SILOTO/SHUTTERSTOCK ©

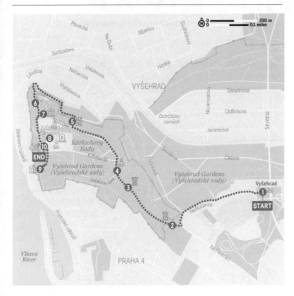

Stroll the Grounds

THE BIRTHPLACE OF PRAGUE

Vyšehrad spreads out over gracious parkland and is best explored on foot. This walk hits the major sights and shows off some pretty vistas. From (1) **Vyšehrad metro station**, walk west 200m to (2) **Tábor Gate**. From here, continue through (3) **Leopold Gate** (p102). Once inside the fortress, bear right to the (4) **Rotunda of St Martin** (p100), a solemn relic that's been standing here 1000 years. Continue along the main path to the fortress' northern ramparts for stunning views over Prague below. Retrace your steps and bear right to see the (5) **Brick Gate and casemates** (p102). From the Brick Gate, walk west and bear right to the fortress' north-western corner, which holds the (6) **Letní scéna**, a summer amphitheatre with dramatic views. Trace the western wall to reach the (7) **Basilica of Sts Peter & Paul** (p100). Just to the left of the church is (8) **Vyšehrad Cemetery** (p101), the final resting place of Czech luminaries from the 19th and 20th centuries. From the cathedral and cemetery, walk south to a large park. A path leads to the (9) **Gothic Cellar** and permanent exhibition on Vyšehrad's history. Reward yourself with lunch or dinner at (10) **Rio's Vyšehrad** (p103) or find nearby Vratislavova street for traditional Czech food at **U Kroka** (p103).

I LIVE HERE: VYŠEHRAD

David Humphreys and **Melissa Joulwan**, Prague-based Americans, host a books-and-travel podcast, *Strong Sense of Place.*

The first time we climbed the steps to Vyšehrad, a string quartet appeared and began to play Mozart. Then we turned a corner and found a cafe selling ice cream. We felt like we'd stumbled into an alternative universe where everything was awesome. Our affection for Prague's 'other castle' has only increased since then. It's our favourite spot to have a picnic, watch people play with their dogs, and admire Prague Castle across the river. It doesn't hurt that myths and eerie legends are attached to every brick, monument and statue.

 WHERE TO EAT

Rio's Vyšehrad
Elegant outdoor dining in nice weather, opposite the beautiful Basilica of Sts Peter & Paul. €€

U Kroka
Traditional pub that delivers not just good beer but excellent food. Book in advance. €€

Bystro Cafe
This pretty terrace makes for an ideal spot to linger over coffee, beer or a light meal. €

BEYOND PRAGUE

BEAUTIFUL CASTLES, CONTEMPORARY HISTORY

Prague is surrounded by rolling hills, river valleys, open fields and scattered woodlands. Thousand-year-old castles and wondrous landscape parks lie just an hour or so in any direction by car, bus or train. Castle lovers will be spoiled for choice. Many visitors take the 40-minute train ride to Karlštejn to see the grand Gothic pile that used to hold the crown jewels. But an equally stunning castle can be found at Křivoklát, and without anywhere near the number of visitors. The 13th-century Konopiště Chateau was the residence of Archduke Franz Ferdinand, whose assassination ignited World War I. During World War II the occupying Germans transformed an Austrian military garrison into the infamous 'Theresienstadt' Jewish ghetto at Terezín. The town still looks largely unchanged, and visitors can walk the grim streets and learn of the awful events.

GETTING ORIENTED

While a car affords more freedom to visit the area around Prague, with some pre-planning most of the attractions here are accessible by bus or train. Many places have decent restaurants but may not offer much in the way of overnight accommodation. We've listed a few places to stay (p113), but some destinations are best explored as a day trip from Prague.

Terezín
Kokořín
Mělník
Lidice
Křivoklát
PRAGUE
Průhonice
Karlštejn
Konopiště

Karlštejn Castle

KEEPER OF THE CROWN JEWELS

A trip out to massive Karlštejn Castle, 35km southwest of Prague, is by far the most popular day-trip from the capital. Part of the appeal is the fact that it's an easy 40-minute train ride out here. The bigger part, of course, is that the medieval fortress is absolutely stunning. It's in such good shape it wouldn't look out of place on Disney World's Main Street. The rustic town that surrounds the castle is perfect for a leisurely stroll, and hiking trails fan out from here through the woods and out over the pretty Berounka River valley.

Karlštejn was built in the 14th century to serve as a hideaway for the Bohemian crown jewels and treasury of the Holy Roman Emperor Charles IV. Run by an appointed burgrave, the castle was surrounded by a network of landowning knight-vassals, who came to the castle's aid whenever enemies moved against it. Karlštejn was again used to shelter the royal valuables during the destructive Hussite Wars of the early 15th century.

Afterward, the castle fell into disrepair as its defences were regarded at the time as being outmoded. Considerable restoration work in the late 19th century returned the castle to its former glory. One of the main architects was Josef Mocker, the king of Prague's neo-Gothic architecture craze.

PRACTICAL INFO

Admission to the castle is by guided-tour only. There are two main tours in English. Tour 1 takes in the historic interiors of the first and second floors of the Imperial Palace. This tour doesn't require advance booking and will suffice for most visitors. Real enthusiasts will want to follow tour 2, which explores the elegant chapels. Book tour 2 in advance on hradkarlstejn.cz.

Karlštejn Castle

The Fate of the Paratroopers

THE ULTIMATE PRICE

Lidice paid the ultimate price for the Czechoslovak action to assassinate Reinhard Heydrich. The **National Memorial to the Heroes of the Heydrich Terror** (p77) in Nové Město is filled with information on the operation.

Lidice Memorial

WWII HORROR STORY

About 20km northwest of Prague, accessible by public transport, the Lidice memorial and museum (lidice-memorial.cz) recalls the tragic events that took place here in 1942 during World War II.

The occupying Nazis senselessly razed the village that stood here in retaliation for the assassination by Czechoslovak paratroopers, a couple of weeks earlier, of Nazi leader Reinhard Heydrich. The Nazis murdered the village's 200 men and sent the women and children to ghettos and concentration camps in Nazi-occupied Poland. The solemn exhibitions tell the story, and the adjoining rose garden is particularly moving and beautiful in springtime. To reach Lidice, take metro Line A (green line) to Nádraží Veleslavín and board bus 300 or 322.

Lidice Memorial

Terezín

HOLOCAUST FORTRESS GHETTO

After the beauty of many Czech towns, the imposing fortress town of Terezín (pamatnik-terezin.cz), 60km north of Prague, comes as a moving reminder of the more tragic aspects of Central Europe's past. The massive bastion of stone and earth was built in 1780 by Austrian Emperor Joseph II to keep the Prussians at bay and could accommodate up to 11,000 soldiers.

The fortress was never used in wartime, instead serving as a prison in the mid-19th century. Gavrilo Princip – the Serb nationalist whose assassination of Archduke Franz Ferdinand in Sarajevo in 1914 ignited WWI – died in the prison in 1918. When the Germans occupied the country during WWII, they transformed the fortress into a grim holding centre for Jews bound for extermination camps. Today, Terezín is the country's most-important Holocaust-remembrance site.

The bleakest phase of Terezín's history began in 1940, when the Gestapo first established a prison in the Lesser Fortress. Evicting the inhabitants from the main fortress the following year, the Germans transformed the town into a transit camp through which some 150,000 people eventually passed, most en route to the death camps. Terezín later became the centrepiece of one of the Nazis' most grotesque public-relations coups. Official visitors to the fortress, including representatives of the Red Cross, saw a town that was billed as a kind of Jewish 'refuge', with a Jewish administration, banks, shops, cafes, schools and a thriving cultural life. That charade, sadly, completely fooled the observers.

PRACTICAL INFO

Terezín is a sprawling, somewhat depressing town. The Terezín Visitor Centre is a good place to start an exploration. The main sights are spread out over several buildings, including the Ghetto Museum, which explores the rise of Nazism and life in the Terezín ghetto, and the former Magdeburg Barracks, which served as the seat of the Jewish 'town council'.
Buses from Prague depart from above the Nádraží Holešovice metro station (Line C, red line). The ride takes a little over an hour.

Terezín

MICHAELA JILKOVA/SHUTTERSTOCK ®

Konopiště Château

HOME TO FRANZ FERDINAND

The 13th-century **Konopiště Château** (zamek-konopiste.cz), about 50km south of Prague, is perhaps less interesting for its architecture or history (though they are impressive) than for its last owner, the **Archduke Franz Ferdinand d'Este**. It was Franz Ferdinand's assassination, along with his Czech wife, in Sarajevo on 14 June 1914 that triggered World War I. A guided tour of the chateau lends insight into the Austrian heir's ill-fated life and habits, and particularly his obsessions with hunting and the cult of St George. Having renovated the massive Gothic and Renaissance building in the 1890s and installing all the latest technology – including electricity, central heating, flush toilets, showers and a lift – Franz Ferdinand decorated his home with hunting trophies.

His game books record that he shot about 300,000 creatures; a whopping 100,000 animal trophies are said to adorn the walls. The crowded Trophy Corridor, with a forest of mounted animal heads, and the antler-clad Chamois Room, with its chandelier fashioned from a stuffed condor, are bizarre sights. The archduke's collection of art and artefacts relating to St George amounts to 3750 items, many of which are in the adjoining St George Museum. You'll need a full day to make the most of a visit here: join one of the tours and then explore the beautiful landscaped grounds and village that surround it.

BOOK A TOUR

Entry to the chateau is by guided tour, with several tours on offer. All take around an hour. Tour 3 is probably the most interesting. This circuit focuses on the private apartments used by the archduke and his family, which have been restored from photographs to appear as they looked when the state took possession of the chateau in 1921. The best way to reach Konopiště is by train from Prague's main station to Benešov u Prahy, and then walk 2km to the chateau.

Konopiště Château

VLADISLAV ZOLOTOV/GETTY IMAGES ©

TROPHY HUNTER

Archduke Franz Ferdinand d'Este's game books record that he shot about 300,000 creatures; a whopping 100,000 animal trophies are said to adorn the walls

Mělník Château

Mělník Château

BOHEMIAN WINE AND VIEWS

Unlike most places in Bohemia, where beer is king, the small city of Mělník, about 30km north of Prague, prides itself on wine, and a visit to Mělník Château (lobkowicz-melnik.cz) includes a chance to sample some of the local vintage. The vines in the small vineyard below the old town are supposedly descendants of the first vines introduced to Bohemia, by Charles IV in the 14th century.

The chateau itself sprawls over a rocky promontory surrounded by the flat Central Bohemian plains. The dramatic setting is amplified by stunning views over the confluence of Czechia's two most-important rivers, the Vltava and Labe (Elbe). The chateau was acquired by the noble Lobkowicz family in 1739 and opened to the public in 1992. You can wander through the former living quarters, which are crowded with a rich collection of baroque furniture and 17th- and 18th-century paintings, on a self-guided tour with English text. A separate tour descends to the 14th-century wine cellars for the tasting sessions.

Next to Mělník Château, 15th-century Church of Sts Peter & Paul sports a Gothic exterior and baroque furnishings. Climb to the top of the tower for superlative views. The church crypt holds an ossuary packed with the bones of around 15,000 people. The space feels even more visceral and claustrophobic than the better-known **Sedlec Ossuary** (p164) in Kutná Hora.

BOOK A TOUR

Mělník makes an easy day trip by bus from Prague. Plan on taking the chateau tour in the morning, followed by lunch and then a stroll around the other sites – they're all close together. Don't miss the terrace on the far side of the chateau, with superb views across the river. Buses run to Mělník from the bus stop outside Prague's Ládví metro station (Line C, red line); buy your ticket from the driver. The ride takes about 45 minutes.

TATIANA POPOVA/SHUTTERSTOCK ©

BOOK A TOUR

Visitors can opt for
an 80-minute 'long'
tour and a shorter
60-minute tour. Both
include the most
important sights:
the second castle
courtyard, royal hall,
prison and dungeon.
The longer tour adds
the library, picture
gallery, museum and
lapidarium (where
stone monuments are
displayed). Křivoklát
is accessible by train
from Prague's main
station; most services
require a change in
Beroun. The castle
is located about a
15-minute walk from
Křivoklát station.

Křivoklát Castle

Křivoklát Castle & Landscape Park

GOTHIC SPLENDOUR, ROYAL DUNGEON

Remote, foreboding Křivoklát Castle (hrad-krivoklat.cz), nestled deep in the woods about 40km southwest of Prague, is one of the area's spookiest castles, yet sees relatively few international visitors. The castle is set amid the sprawling Křivoklátsko Protected Landscape Area, a Unesco-listed biosphere that covers the highlands on both sides of the Berounka River. The surrounding nature once served as a royal hunting ground. The castle's origins date back to the 12th century and the earliest years of the Bohemian kingdom. Visitors are treated to some spectacular Gothic interiors, the Royal Hall (which is second in significance only to Prague Caste's Vladislav Hall), a black kitchen, an immense library, and a prison and dungeon system that over the years held some famous prisoners. One of the towers here was allegedly used to imprison the English occultist and alchemist Edward Kelly, who was arrested in 1591 on the orders of Emperor Rudolf II himself for failing to turn base metals into gold.

Kokořín Castle & Landscape Park

SANDSTONE CASTLE

About 10km northeast of Mělník, the 14th-century Kokořín Castle (Hrad Kokořín; hrad-kokorin.cz) features large sandstone ramparts and a solemn tower that really does feel straight out of a fairy tale.

The castle was badly damaged in the 15th-century Hussite religious wars and stood as a romantic ruin for nearly 500 years, until it was purchased and refurbished in the early 20th century. The castle is open to the public via guided tour. It's surrounded by a stunning landscape park that's marked by steep sandstone rocks and canyons. There are several hiking trails, and a road makes the park accessible to cars and cyclists.

A NEW LEASE OF LIFE

The castle was badly damaged in the 15th-century Hussite religious wars and stood as a romantic ruin for nearly 500 years

Kokořín Castle

DALIU/SHUTTERSTOCK ©

Průhonice Castle & Park

EASY, ELEGANT EXCURSION

The elegant castle and surrounding English-style park (pruhonickypark.cz) in the southern Prague suburb of Průhonice is an easy and popular day trip from the capital. The original castle dates all the way back to the 13th century but has been built and rebuilt several times over the years to today's majestic, 19th-century neo-Renaissance. After visiting the castle, join crowds and stroll the gardens. To get to Průhonice, take metro Line C (red line) to Opatov station and transfer to bus 363, 357 or 385.

111

I LIVE HERE: THE AREAS AROUND PRAGUE

Kateřina H Pavlitová is a communications professional living with her family in a historic villa on the outskirts of Prague.

A short bus ride from the Opatov metro stop brings you to **Průhonice** (p111), with its extensive English park and local chateau. It's especially lovely in spring.

Berounka River, southwest of Prague, has stunning limestone rock formations, a verdant river valley and hills covered by deep woods. There are many hiking and biking options.

I recommend the 15km hike from Karlštejn to the picturesque village of **Svatý Jan pod Skalou** to Beroun along the red trail. In Beroun, reward yourself at the Black Dog Bar & Grill with burgers and regional beers.

MORE IN BEYOND PRAGUE

Hike the Karlštejn Woods

WALK WITH A VIEW

It's easy to combine a visit to **Karlštejn Castle** (p104) with an invigorating three- to four-hour hike in the woods. The hike is moderately difficult, with some climbs, but doesn't demand any specialised hiking skills. Get an early start at Prague's main train station. Instead of buying a ticket to Karlštejn, purchase a ticket for the next town over, Beroun.

Walk out the main entrance at Beroun train station and look for a red-marked hiking trail. This is the path that will eventually bring you to Karlštejn and the castle, about 15km away. The hike itself is surprisingly varied. After passing through the humdrum outskirts of Beroun, descend into the quiet woods.

For part of the walk, the path parallels a long, sloping waterfall. The highlight of the hike to Karlštejn is the small village of Svatý Jan pod Skalou, a picturesque place with a few outbuildings and an evocative chapel and cemetery. After an

 WHERE TO DRINK

Caffé Castello Průhonice
Convenient spot for coffee or snacks at Průhonice Castle.

Kafe Mělník ve Věži
Freshly roasted coffee and snacks within Mělník's distinctive, Gothic Prague Gate (Pražská brána).

Pobuda
Lifesaver cafe and restaurant; one of the few refreshment options near Kokořín Castle.

hour or so from here, you will alight onto a meadow and the towers of Karlštejn Castle round into view. Visit the castle or relax at one of the many restaurants in town and reward your efforts with a beer and hot meal. Take the train back to Prague from Karlštejn station.

Bike to Karlštejn Castle

HIT THE ROAD

Karlštejn (p104) is close enough to Prague to reach by bike for cyclists of at least moderate ability. The path includes a few climbs, but generally passes through secluded woods and along quiet streams as well as the Vltava and Berounka Rivers.

The ride takes three to four hours and is best done as part of a guided excursion. Several outfitters offer a Karlštejn cycling outing. Prague-based **Biko Adventures** (bikoadventures.com) runs an e-bike tour as well as three road-cycling variations: easy, medium and advanced. **Praha Bike** (prahabike.cz) offers a similar tour.

Float a Boat to Mělník

ALL-DAY VLTAVA RIVER TRIP

Most visitors to **Mělník** (p109) from Prague drive or travel by bus, but it's also possible to hop on a boat in Prague and float all the way there along the Vltava River. Several tour boat operators in Prague offer out and back cruises.

The day typically takes around 15 hours, which includes a couple of hours of sightseeing in Mělník. The Prague Steamboats Company offers two cruises to Mělník during the summer season. One is a cheaper, more stripped-down trip; the second includes meals and unlimited drinks. Some of the highlights of the cruise include passing through locks along the river, glancing out at the prominent, 460m-high Říp Mountain, seeing the confluence of the Vltava and Elbe rivers, and of course touring Mělník.

Cruises depart from Nové Město's Rašínovo embankment (Rašínovo nábřeží), located between the Palacký and Jirásek bridges. Check praguesteamboats.com for departure times and pricing, and to book tickets.

BEST PLACES TO EAT

Black Dog Bar & Grill
Enjoy steaks, barbecue, burgers and burritos at Beroun's most popular restaurant. €€

Němý medvěd
Mělník's go-to for burgers, fries and craft beers, served in an informal, family-friendly setting. €€

Restaurace pod Hradem Křivoklát
Decent Czech cooking at the best of a small number of places near Křivoklát Castle. €

Stará Myslivna
At Konopiště, an unashamedly old-fashioned Czech restaurant set in a character-filled, 19th-century gamekeeper's lodge. €€

Restaurace Pod Dračí Skálou
Appealing Karlštejn country inn, with outdoor tables and a barbecue grill. €

 **WHERE TO STAY**

Parkhotel
Decent for a night; one of the few acceptable sleeping options in quiet Terezín. €€

Hotel Mlýn Karlštejn
Clean, bright, romantic choice for anyone planning to stay over in Karlštejn. €€

Pensionl Konopiště
Good-value pension within easy walking distance of Konopiště Château. €

Český Krumlov (p136)

SOUTH & WEST BOHEMIA

◆ PRAGUE

SPAS, BEER AND UNESCO SITES

This area of the country contains some of Czechia's most famous places of interest.

Taking up most of the Czech lands west of Prague, Bohemia's south and west share many things. Unesco listings pepper the landscape, from the medieval brilliance of Český Krumlov to the mines of the Krušné Mountains.

The aroma of hops drift in the air: Plzeň (Pilsen) and České Budějovice's brewing traditions are based on Bohemia's crystal clear water. Saaz hops – grown between Rakovník and Žatec – are said to be the best in the world.

What links the south and west physically are endless forests and mountains, the Krušné Range in the north linked to the Šumava in the far south by an unbroken string of virtually uninhabited, thickly forested peaks and valleys, ideal for backcountry hiking, mountain biking and cross-country skiing.

The spas of the Karlovy Vary (Carlsbad) region form the second-most popular attraction in the country after Prague, with hundreds of thousands arriving each year to take the cure. With its hot thermal water and luxury spa area, Karlovy Vary is essential viewing, while Mariánské Lázně offers a more understated and relaxing experience. The three main spas here (little Františkovy Lázně completing the trio) were Unesco-listed in 2021 as World Cultural Heritage Sites – and not before time.

Other highlights in this incredibly varied wedge of central Europe include the folk traditions of the Chodsko region, spectacular castles at Loket, Český Krumlov and Bečov, and one of the country's best attractions for kids, Plzeň's Techmania.

MICHAEL715/SHUTTERSTOCK

THE MAIN AREAS

KARLOVY VARY	MARIÁNSKÉ LÁZNĚ	PLZEŇ (PILSEN)	ČESKÝ KRUMLOV	ČESKÉ BUDĚJOVICE
The country's biggest spa town. p120	Exquisite spa town at altitude. p127	Bohemia's hop-infused second city. p132	Jaw-droppingly quaint, Unesco-listed town. p136	Capital of the Czech south. p140

Plzeň (Pilsen), p132

Bustling and gritty, Plzeň is all about the world's finest beer, heavy industry and student life. If you are bringing kids to Czechia, do not skip Techmania.

Karlovy Vary, p120

Hot spas and exquisite natural surroundings combine to create the country's finest spa town. Come during the international film festival to rub shoulders with the stars.

Cheb

Karlovy Vary

Mariánské Lázně

Mariánské Lázně, p127

Stylish, relaxing and rejuvenating, little Marienbad is arguably the most attractive of the Czech spas with its countless springs, architecture in myriad 'neo' styles and huge spa park.

Plzeň

Domažlice

Klatovy

CAR

The main motorway west out of Prague is the D5, which will take you to Plzeň and almost to the spas. The permanently-under-construction D6 will one day link the capital to Karlovy Vary. The main route south is the unfinished D3.

BUS

If a train doesn't go there, then a bus will – this is true across Czechia. Coaches link Prague with every major town in the region, local bus companies connect towns to each other. Rare is the bus that runs on Saturday afternoon and Sunday.

TRAIN

The Západní Expres (Western Express) runs between Prague, Plzeň and Mariánské Lázně, with another branch going out to Domažlice. Karlovy Vary is linked to Plzeň, Prague and Mariánské Lázně direct. Train is the way to reach České Budějovice but not Český Krumlov.

Find Your Way

The south and west constitute a large part of Czechia but have no fear - transport links are good here and you'll have no problem reaching even the remotest trailheads.

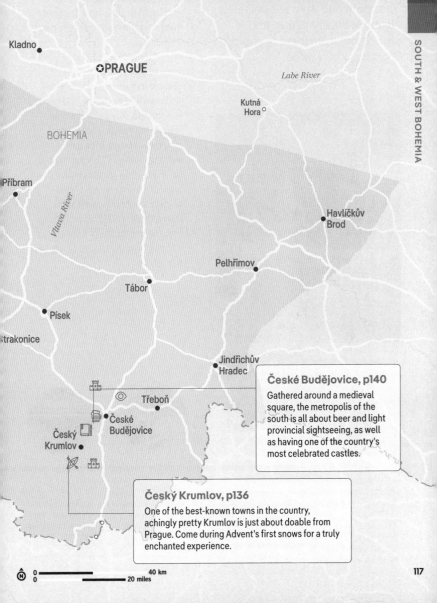

Kladno

⊕PRAGUE

Labe River

Kutná Hora

BOHEMIA

Příbram

Vltava River

Havlíčkův Brod

Pelhřimov

Tábor

Písek

strakonice

Jindřichův Hradec

Třeboň

České Budějovice

Český Krumlov

České Budějovice, p140

Gathered around a medieval square, the metropolis of the south is all about beer and light provincial sightseeing, as well as having one of the country's most celebrated castles.

Český Krumlov, p136

One of the best-known towns in the country, achingly pretty Krumlov is just about doable from Prague. Come during Advent's first snows for a truly enchanted experience.

0   40 km
0   20 miles

Plan Your Time

The south and west are definitely all about finding a base and striking out from there to explore the surrounding area.

Karlovy Vary (p120)

MYROSLAVA BOZHKO/SHUTTERSTOCK ©

A Day Out from Prague

● **Karlovy Vary (p120)** has the most to offer on a day trip from Prague. Start early from Prague's main train station to make the most of your day.

● Head straight to the **Moser glassworks** for a fascinating tour. Then bus it to the centre and head into the **spa**. Buy a spa cup and sample the gurgling hot mineral springs as you go. If it's cold, warm up at the 73°C geyser that splutters into a glass copula.

● Make a lightening visit to the **Diana Tower (p121)** before buying that souvenir bottle of Becherovka and catching the last train back to the capital.

Seasonal highlights

The region enjoys distinct seasons and has food and festivals to fit each one. Don't assume summer is the best time to come – the snowy winters lend a great new dimension.

JANUARY

Snow blankets the mountains and forests, the **skiing season** hits top gear and cosy taverns light their wood burners.

FEBRUARY

Hike or cross-country ski the snowbound trails of the **Krušné Mountains** for an unforgettable, subzero experience.

JULY

July is all about the **Karlovy Vary International Film Festival** (p120), one of the biggest events on the Czech calendar.

A Two-Day Break

● For overnighters from the capital, the first stop should be **Plzeň (p132)**, Bohemia's second city. Here you can combine a visit to the **Urquell Brewery** with some light sightseeing in the historical centre, or you can spend the day experimenting at **Techmania**. (You can't do both in a day).

● On day two it's an hour by train to **Mariánské Lázně (p127)** to explore the spa area with its colonnades, churches, British royal connections and soothing green backdrop of the **Slavkovský Forest**, before making a trip to **Bečov Castle** or **Loket Castle (p125)**, or taking a hike into the surrounding hills.

Take a Week Out

● In a week you can explore the entire region and fit in a hike or two.

● Spend the first day in **Karlovy Vary** enjoying the architecture and thermal springs. Via a stop-off in **Loket**, you'll easily make it for lunch in the tranquil spa town of **Mariánské Lázně** on day two.

● Day three brings you to **Plzeň** for the Urquell Brewery tour and a stroll around the centre. With a car you can detour to **Domažlice** on day four before hitting **Český Krumlov (p136)**.

● Spend day six exploring Krumlov further or hiking the surroundings. Day seven delivers you to the easy-going city of **České Budějovice (p140)**.

AUGUST
The **Chod Festival** in Domažlice and the **Český Krumlov International Music Festival** both take place in August.

SEPTEMBER
The best month to travel when the weather is still good but the crowds have evaporated.

NOVEMBER
Český Krumlov has a lull in November, meaning it's the best month to head there, preferably on a rainy Wednesday.

DECEMBER
The region's best **Christmas markets** take place on Plzeň's main square and on the courtyard of Loket Castle.

KARLOVY VARY

Karlovy Vary ● ☆ PRAGUE

Karlovy Vary (Carlsbad, KV), or simply 'Vary' to Czechs, best captures the lost glamour and elegance of 19th-century spa culture - perhaps more than any other town in Central Europe. The promenades, colonnades and most of all the grand neoclassical buildings dazzle the eye. In the resort's heyday, royals like Russia's Peter the Great and members of the Habsburg monarchy mixed here with the greatest thinkers, writers and composers of their time. Four decades of communism drew a grey curtain across proceedings but, since the 1990s, restoration here was quicker than anywhere else outside Prague.

These days, visitors come mainly to admire the architecture and to stroll the impressive colonnades, sipping on the health-restoring sulphurous waters from spouted ceramic drinking cups. Away from the cure, the town has many other attractions and is a good base for hiking into the surrounding forested hills.

TOP TIP

The vast majority of KV's sights are in the spa area that bulges out from the south of the town. The rest of KV is a rather gritty, workaday affair that goes about its business as regional capital. Buses run between the two parts.

KARLOVY VARY INTERNATIONAL FILM FESTIVAL

The Karlovy Vary International Film Festival in July is the region's biggest annual event. It features around 200 films, tickets are relatively easy to get, and there's a funky array of concurrent events. It always features the year's top films and attracts the odd Hollywood star. Most of the red-carpet action takes place in and around the Hotel Thermal but screenings are spread around the town. The winning filmmakers and actors take home exquisite art deco figurines made by Moser. You can see one at the **Moser Glassworks and Museum** (p123).

Strolling the Colonnades

KARLOVY VARY'S GRAND SPA ARCHITECTURE

As a first-timer, the thing to do straight off the train or bus is walk, admire the architecture and sip the tepid spring waters from a **lázeňský pohárek** (a traditional porcelain drinking cup). So why not give it a go yourself and stroll the spa area? Buy your own cup (they come in myriad designs) from any one of a hundred souvenir shops and kiosks around town.

There are 16 mineral springs housed in or near the four main kolonády (colonnades) along the **Teplá River**. Each spring has its own purported medicinal properties and spurts and splutters out of brass taps at various temperatures, ranging from lukewarm to scalding hot. The tourist information centre has a chart of the springs and temperatures, and can advise on the various health benefits of the waters.

You can fill your cup for free at all public springs along the way, but watch how much you sip, as too much 'health' can cause gastric issues. Spa guests consume the amount strictly prescribed by a spa doctor.

Your stroll begins at the northern end of the spa area, whose entry is marked by the landmark communist-era **Hotel Thermal** (1976) built in the brutalist style. Walk south past the hotel and through a small park to find the first of the colonnades, the white, cast-iron **Park Colonnade** (Sadová kolonáda).

Further on is the biggest and most impressive colonnade, the neo-Renaissance **Mill Colonnade** (Mlýnská kolonáda), with five different springs, a small bandstand and rooftop statues

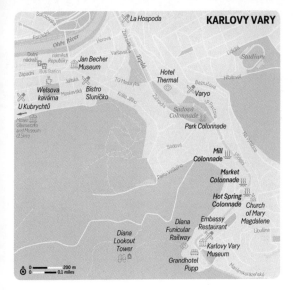

KARLOVY VARY

La Hospoda
Sokolovska
Polzska
Ohře River
Horova
Dolní
nádraží
náměstí
Republiky
Jan Becher
Museum
Varšavská
Stadium
Lidická
Hřbitovní
Západní
Bus Station
Jaltská
TG Masaryka
Hotel
Thermal
Bezručova
Welsova
kavárna
Moskevská
Bistro
Sluníčko
Krále Jiřího
I.P. Pavlova
U Kubrychtů
Varyo
Zámecký
Moser Glassworks
and Museum
(2.5km)
Sadová
Colonnade
Park Colonnade
Sadová
Na Vyhlídce
Mill
Colonnade
Petra Velikého
Vřídelní
Market
Colonnade
Hot Spring
Colonnade
Church
of Mary
Magdalene
Diana
Funicular
Railway
Embassy
Restaurant
Libušina
Diana
Lookout
Tower
Karlovy Vary
Museum
Grandhotel
Pupp
Mariánskolázeňská
0   200 m
0   0.1 miles

BEST SOUVENIRS IN KARLOVY VARY

Becherovka
Often called the 13th spring, this is a strong-tasting herbal liquor made to a secret recipe.

Moser Glass
A piece of Moser glass is an eternal reminder of your trip.

Spa Cup
These curiously-shaped cups are one of the most popular take-home items from Bohemia.

Porcelain
Several porcelain manufacturers are based in the town, producing typically Czech designs.

Petrified Roses
Roses left in the spring water accumulate mineral residue and essentially turn to stone.

depicting the months of the year. It dates from 1881 and is the work of Josef Zítek who built Prague's National Theatre.

Now head up Lázeňská to the impressive **Market Colonnade** (Tržní kolonáda) with its delicately fretted woodwork; one of its two springs, the pramen Karla IV (Charles IV Spring), is the spa's oldest. Just beyond the Market Colonnade stands the granddaddy of them all, the **Vřídelní Colonnade,** now housed in a hulking 1970s brutalist building that was once dedicated to cosmonaut Yuri Gagarin.

The tallest glass copula houses central Europe's only geyser. Here the waters are at their hottest – if it wasn't mineral water spluttering out of the taps you could pop a teabag in for a cuppa (don't try it, it's disgusting). The timepiece Communist-era colonnade has been slated for replacement for decades but there's no sign of the wrecking ball arriving just yet. The street Stará Louka continues south for more splendour. At the end of the stroll stands the magnificent **Grand-Hotel Pupp**, the resort's choicest hotel and still the favoured haunt of well-heeled visitors.

Away from the Colonnades

SAVOURING THE TOWN'S OTHER ATTRACTIONS

The Karlovy Vary experience isn't all about sipping salty mineral water and strolling grandiose colonnades. Spa guests needed other forms of entertainment too and KV has it aplenty. Our walk through the colonnades ended at the Pupp so that's where we will begin on our stroll back, spa cup now stuffed into our bag.

First stop must be the Diana lookout tower high above the town, reached by funicular railway from behind

THE GRANDHOTEL PUPP

Arguably the most illustrious hotel in the entire country, the sumptuous Pupp covers nearly the whole of the spa's southern end and oozes old-world glamour. Though established in the 18th century, the current 1907 building is the work of prolific Viennese architects Fellner and Helmer, the duo behind theatre buildings across the former Habsburg empire. The hotel was featured in the James Bond film *Casino Royale* and inspired Wes Anderson's *Grand Budapest Hotel* which was also mostly filmed there.

These days it's a real budget-blower, but worth the splurge if you can bag one of the period-style rooms inside. Even if you're not staying here, take a peek inside; the restaurants are very good, and the historic atmosphere is perfect.

IGLWCH/SHUTTERSTOCK ©

Karlovy Vary

the Pupp. The tower is free to climb and affords memorable views across the spa and the surrounding forested hills. There's a restaurant and cafe here and other attractions including a worthwhile Butterfly house. Whether you walk or take the funicular down, you'll end up back at the Pupp.

From here, head across the river to the Karlovy Vary Museum with its exhibits on the town's development as a spa resort, Czech glasswork and the region's natural history. A few steps further along Nová Louka is the town's beautiful theatre which has original decorations by the Klimt brothers. Some 300m further is KV's main place of worship, the imposing twin-steepled Church of Mary Magdalene. It dates from the 1730s and is the work of baroque master Kilian Dientzenhofer, the architect of **St Nicholas Church** (p55) in Prague's Malá Strana.

From the church, amble through the spa towards the **Hotel Thermal**. Continue along ulice TG Masaryka to the Jan Becher Museum where you can learn all about the alcoholic phenomenon still made in KV: Becherova. This is a little like Jägermeister or Unicum. The tour ends with a tasting session. Na zdraví!

 WHERE TO SLEEP

Grandhotel Pupp
Book early for this central European gem with five-star service and a guestbook that reads like a Forbes list. €€€

Hotel Romance
Superb spa area location, very comfortable rooms and a cooked breakfast. €€

Pension Villa Rosa
Perched high above the river, the family-run Villa Rosa combines traditional rooms with a spectacular location. €€

The Moser Glass Experience

WATCH THE GLASSBLOWERS AT WORK

The most interesting reason to leave the spa area is to visit the **Moser Glassworks and Museum** around 4km to the west. Take bus 2 from the theatre. The Moser company opened its first workshop in Karlovy Vary in 1857, and by 1873 had established a large glassworks in the town and become the official supplier to the imperial court of Franz Josef I. He obviously put in a good word with his English friend, King Edward VII, as Moser also became the official supplier of glass to British royalty in 1907. Throughout the 20th century, this exquisite glassware was used by governments and heads of state and remains one of the world's most exclusive brands for wealthy clients in the know.

A visit to the glassworks is one of the most memorable things you might do outside Prague. Guided tours begin with a description of the glassmaking process before you are shown into the workshop itself. Here you can watch the glassblowers taking the molten glass out of the furnaces and blowing it into all manner of receptacles using wooden moulds. The high temperatures mean a constant supply of drinks is brought to them. You are allowed pretty close up to feel the heat radiating from the orange-glowing glass.

After the glassworks comes the museum, which traces the history of production in thousands of pieces of priceless glass. After that, head to the shop – prices will come as a shock. Even a single delicate wine glass will set you back around €100, a vase thousands.

If you can't make it out to the glassworks, Moser have a shop at the **Grandhotel Pupp**.

HOT PROPERTY

A visit to the **glassworks** is one of the most memorable things you might do outside Prague

BEST HIKES FROM KARLOVY VARY

Andělská Hora
Around a 10km hike east, the village of Angel's Mount boasts a ruined castle with spectacular views.

Kyselka
A 15km hike east, eerily abandoned Kyselka spa is famous as the erstwhile home of mineral-water magnate Mattoni.

Svatošské Skály
Follow the **Ohře cycle path** from KV's Doubí neighbourhood to some spectacular rock formations where there is climbing.

Šemnická Skála
A wonderful 10km hike through the thick forest ends at this high promontory with camera-impressing panoramas.

Goethova Vyhlídka
The Goethe lookout tower is a 5km round trip along the yellow hiking trail from the Vřídelní Colonnade.

GETTING AROUND

Karlovy Vary has two train stations, Dolní (Lower) and Horní (Upper). Trains from Prague pull in at the Upper station, those from Mariánské Lázně at the Lower station. Bus 1 runs to the spa from the Upper station, while the Lower station is within walking distance of the Tržnice, the central city bus interchange. Buses 2 and 13 go to the spa. Coaches from Prague arrive at the Lower station.

Beyond Karlovy Vary

Jáchymov • Mount Klínovec
Loket • **Karlovy Vary**
Františkovy Lázně

Mountains riddled with mines, fairy tale castles, radioactive spas and lots of opportunities to enjoy the great outdoors – that's the Karlovy Vary region.

In summer you can grow palm trees outdoors in fairly low-altitude Karlovy Vary, but north of the town rise the cold, mysterious and almost tourist-free Krušné Mountains (known as the Erzgebirge on the German side of the nearby border), which culminate at Mount Klínovec.

The last Czech mountain range to be 'discovered', this is a harsh but magical place to hike and cross-country ski, but another attraction here are the Unesco-listed mines and the town of Jáchymov which often leaves visitors in baffled wonderment. Also lost among the forested peaks is spectacular Loket castle, one of Czechia's finest. The third point of the West Bohemian Spa Triangle is the prim little town of Františkovy Lázně, a worthwhile half-day trip.

TOP TIP

The sparsely inhabited Karlovy Vary region has good transport links but hire a car to get the most out of the area.

Jáchymov

BABETKA/SHUTTERSTOCK ©

RICHARD SEMIK/SHUTTERSTOCK ©

WHERE TO GET A BEER IN THE KRUŠNÉ MOUNTAINS

Ryžovna
The lonely Ryžovna Brewery, 25km north of KV, produces three types of beer; the restaurant is a welcome place to eat.

Červený Vlk
In Boží Dar, the Red Wolf brews five different beers served in a 21st-century dining area.

Krušnohor
Based in Tisová near Kraslice, Krušnohor brews the Krušné Mountain's best beers, which occasionally pop up elsewhere in Czechia.

Loket Castle

Loket Castle

SPECTACULAR MEDIEVAL HILLTOP CASTLE

The town of Loket, a cluster of houses in pinks, greens and blues huddled around a fairy tale castle, stands on a loop in the Ohře River. The loop is so extreme it almost makes an island (loket means 'elbow' in Czech, a reference to the river bend). 'JW Goethe's favourite town' (as tourism brochures describe it) is so pretty, if you saw it in a film you'd think it was a painted backdrop. Loket's German name is Elbogen (which also means 'elbow'), and it's been famous by that name since 1815 for the manufacture of porcelain, as have the neighbouring towns of Horní Slavkov (Schlackenwald) and Chodov (Chodan). Loket's impressive castle was built on the site of a Romanesque fort, of which only the tall square tower and fragments of a rotunda and palace remain. Its present late-Gothic look dates from the 14th century. The nearly impregnable castle has played an important role in Bohemian history. Young Wenceslas, the future Holy Roman Emperor Charles IV, was imprisoned here as a child around the year 1320. From 1788 until 1947, the castle was used (and abused) as a local prison.

Jáchymov and the Mountains

MINES, MOUNTAINS AND DOLLARS

Defining the border between Saxony and Bohemia, the Krušné Mountains extend across the north of the country in a thousand forested peaks. It's paradise for hikers, berry pickers, mushroomers, cross-country skiers and those just looking to escape the 21st century. The hiking possibilities in par-

GETTING AROUND

Loket is served by fairly regular bus from Karlovy Vary, as is Jáchymov. For other places in the Krušné Mountains you'll need a car. To get to Františkovy Lázně, take the train to Cheb and change.

UNESCO SPAS & MINES

Until recently, the Karlovy Vary region could not boast a single Unesco-listed site. But in the space of two years, a whopping eight were added.

In 2019 Unesco recognised the significance of the mining industry in the Krušné Mountains, bringing five mines and mining-related sites under its wing.

In 2021 the long-awaited decision was made to add **Mariánské Lázně** (p127), **Karlovy Vary** (p120) and **Františkovy Lázně**, the so-called West Bohemian Spa Triangle, to the World Cultural Heritage list, along with eight other spa towns across Europe in a joint nomination.

The COVID-19 pandemic put a slight dampener on celebrations, but these Unesco listings could make an important contribution to tourism in what is Czechia's poorest region.

Františkovy Lázně

ticular are endless, with hundreds of kilometres of marked trails. There are countless places of interest across the range, but the town of Jáchymov is particularly fascinating. In the 16th century, the silver mines here led to the foundation of a mint that produced coins called Talers (from the town's German name, Joachimstal). This word went on to become 'dollar'. Also found in these hills is uranium, the same uranium that Marie Curie used to isolate the element radium and which political prisoners extracted at great personal cost in the 1950s for shipment to the USSR. The town's third wow factor is Europe's only radioactive spa, with clients bathing in mildly radioactive water (considered to be perfectly safe) at the Radium Palace spa complex.

Františkovy Lázně

THE THIRD SPA TOWN IN THE SPA TRIANGLE

The region's third spa town is Františkovy Lázně, a much more sedate affair than Karlovy Vary and Mariánské Lázně. It's a place of well-tended parks with statues and springs, the centre so perfectly renovated it hardly feels like Czechia at all. The town was listed by Unesco in 2021 along with its bigger cousins. The key sights are the **Church of the Ascension of the Cross** (kostel Povýšení sv Kříže) on Ruská, and the town's central spring, the **Františkův pramen**, at the southern end of Národní. To get a better understanding of the spa's history, drop by the **Municipal Museum**. The big draw for families from both sides of the border is the excellent **Aquaforum** water park with its indoor and outdoor pools.

MARIÁNSKÉ LÁZNĚ

Mariánské Lázně ● ✪ PRAGUE

Just over two centuries ago, enterprising monks from **Teplá Monastery** (p131) decided to make a little extra cash by building a spa in a swampy, inhospitable valley amid the dense Slavkovský Forest. What started out as a few timber guesthouses around a muddy hole quickly turned into one of Europe's most fashionable spa towns, attracting the great and good (and not so good) of the 19th and early 20th centuries. Returned almost to its former glory since the days of communist workers' recreation, today Mariánské Lázně is arguably Czechia's most relaxing, attractive and user-friendly spa town. Known affectionately as Mariánky among locals, Unesco recognised this grand old spa's significance, listing the town as a World Heritage Site in 2021.

TOP TIP

The bus or train stations are 2.5km south of the spa zone. Trolleybus 7 leaves regularly from near both terminals. Once in the spa, you can easily get around on foot. As parking is limited, having a car here is more trouble than it's worth.

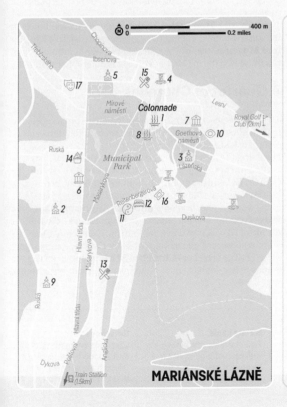

MARIÁNSKÉ LÁZNĚ

HIGHLIGHTS
1 Colonnade

SIGHTS
2 Anglican Chapel
3 Church of the Assumption of the Virgin Mary
4 Cross Spring
5 Evangelical Church
6 Fryderyk Chopin Memorial Museum
7 Municipal Museum
8 Singing Fountain
9 St Vladimír Church
10 Weimar Hotel

ACTIVITIES
11 Ensana Health Spa Resort Nové Lázně

SLEEPING
12 Hotel Nové Lázně

EATING
13 Česká Hospůdka
14 Modrá cukrárna
15 U Zlaté Koule

DRINKING & NIGHTLIFE
see 12 Vídeňská kavárna

ENTERTAINMENT
16 Casino concert hall
17 Městské Divadlo

Julia Malyk, a Ukrainian refugee currently living in Mariánské Lázně, shares her favourite spots in the town.

Mariánské Lázně for me is a cozy, small town with good people and a pleasant atmosphere.

Hamelika Tower
My favourite place is this tower, in the forest. It offers a stunning view of the forested landscape and it is a piece of the past.

Prelát Park
This is an attractive place where we can relax with family and enjoy mineral water. The park is full of attractions for children; there is an obstacle course where I like to go with my friends.

Boheminium
Another interesting place is this park with miniature models of famous Czech buildings. A horse farm is located nearby and there are roe deer and goats that you can feed.

The Spa
MARIÁNSKÉ LÁZNĚ'S UNESCO-LISTED SITE

Occupying the northern end of town, the spa zone is one of Europe's grandest. Aimless wandering is the best way to explore – for orientation, arrow-straight **Hlavní třída** (Main Street) runs the length of the neighbourhood.

Anchoring the spa is the cast-iron **Colonnade**, built in neo-baroque style in 1889, an instantly recognisable piece of architecture for most Czechs. It was actually made at the other end of the country (in Blansko, Moravia), taken to pieces, brought by train and bolted back together again in situ. Its gently curving length reminds many of a Victorian train station. It's a lovely place to stroll with a cup of mineral water, a spa wafer (a filled wafer biscuit) or an ice cream. In a neo-Classical pavillion of its own at the northern end of the Colonnade is the **Cross Spring** (Křížový pramen), the spa's first water source.

At the southern end is the famous 1980s **Singing Fountain**: 240 water jets that perform every two hours between May and October to popular tracks and classical pieces. Come after dark to watch the show with added lights. From the fountain, head uphill to sloping **Goethe Square**, dominated by the **Church of the Assumption of St Mary**. To your left is a chain of interconnected hotels belonging to the Ensana Resort, the main spa treatment providers.

The five-star **Hotel Nové Lázně** is the town's top hotel. In the top left-hand corner of the square is the excellent **Municipal Museum**, one of the oldest surviving buildings where Goethe stayed during his last visit to Mariánské Lázně in 1823.

A Quartet of Churches
PRAYER AT THE SPA

The road names in central Europe's spa towns often reflect the nationalities of the guests who stayed there in the 19th century – Mariánské Lázně has a Russian Street (Ruská třída) and English Street (Anglická ulice) for instance. And this is also true of the churches in the town. Aptly, in Ruská Street we find the Orthdox **St Vladimír Church**, built in 1901 in the neo-Byzantine style. Inside stands one of the largest ceramic iconostases in the world. A few steps north lurks the **Anglican Chapel**, the work of obscure London architect William Burges from 1879. At the top of Hlavní, on Mírové náměstí, the Evangelical Church is wedged between other buildings while the Catholic spa guests are served by the octagonal **Church of St Mary** (p128) on Goethe Square. This doubles up as a summer classical music venue.

 WHERE TO EAT

Česká Hospůdka
A cosy Czech pub with a wood fire and excellent, inventive local cooking. €

U Zlaté koule
Five-star class combines with cosy informality and a game-rich menu at this spa favourite. €€

Swisshouse
Czech and international dishes, the best food in ML, served at this intimate wellness hotel in the spa park. Phone ahead. €€

Royal Cabin at the Nové Lázně

WHY I LOVE MARIÁNSKÉ LÁZNĚ

Marc Di Duca, co-author of Prague & Czechia

I'll come clean – Mariánské Lázně is my home town and for me there is no better place to live. Strolling through the spa on a crisp winter morning, the kaisergelb facades contrasting with the freshly fallen snow – it's like living in a fairy tale. The air is some of the cleanest in Europe, the architecture some of its most evocative. And that water! There are 40 mineral-rich springs in town with another 60 rising in the forests around. And if Edward VII liked it here, that's good enough for me.

British Royal Connections
EDWARD VII IN MARIÁNSKÉ LÁZNĚ

The most illustrious visitor ever to take the waters at Mariánské Lázně was **Edward VII, King of England**. The most powerful man of the era, the son of Queen Victoria – who was related to almost every head of state in Europe – came here a total of nine times as Prince of Wales and king. Pretty young Mizzi the hatmaker of Hlavní Street may have been his main focus of interest at first, but later he described Mariánské Lázně as the most beautiful place he had visited

The biggest event that took place in the town was the meeting between Edward VII and Emperor Franz Joseph of Austria in 1904 at the Kursaal, now the Casino concert hall adjoining the Nové Lázně Hotel. Home to the West Bohemian Symphony Orchestra, it's well worth asking the receptionists if you can take a look inside. In the Nové Lázně is the **Royal Cabin**, a spa room built specially for Edward VII. Apart from leaving behind lots of gunned down-deer and one sad Sudeten hatmaker, the king bequeathed the town one of its main draws – the Royal Golf Club, a tricky course set almost 800m above sea level.

A WALKING TOWN

Mariánské Lázně can be tackled on foot as the spa area is compact. Trolley buses run to other parts of the town.

WHERE TO GET A COFFEE

Vídeňská kavárna
Elegant Viennese coffeehouse at the Nové Lázně with polite service and desserts made on the premises.

Modrá cukrárna
ML's oldest cafe on Hlavní with a traditional cake and coffee section and a more expensive modern cafe.

Café Pohoda
In Kamenný dvůr, this is a hidden gem of a coffee spot south of the spa.

Beyond Mariánské Lázně

If you enjoy wild natural beauty, uninhabited landscapes, romantic castles and winter nights by log fires, you'll love the area around Mariánské Lázně.

The Mariánské Lázně micro-region is all about the forest, getting out into nature and feeling the earth under your feet. To the north is the huge **Slavkovský Forest** (p131), and to the south and west the Bohemian Forest, a virtually unpopulated protected landscape that extends south until it merges with the **Šumava** (p135). Characterful **Bečov nad Teplou** is the only town of size on the rail line and road between Mariánské Lázně and Karlovy Vary, its castle safekeeping one of the country's most precious objects. **Kladská**, just north of Mariánské Lázně, is a popular day trip, as is the ancient monastery at **Teplá**.

TOP TIP

Transport links are poor in the Slavkovský Forest. Hire a bike to get the most out of the area.

SKYWORKER/SHUTTERSTOCK ©

Bečov nad Teplou

Slavkovský Forest

MAGICAL, ANCIENT FORESTS

Extending between Mariánské Lázně and Karlovy Vary, the Slavkovský Forest is a largely untouristed, largely undiscovered 640 sq km of thick forest, hiking, cycling and cross-country skiing trails and tiny under-inhabited villages. The forest starts on the northern edge of the spa but it's an 8km hike or ride until you reach the first village, the beauty spot of **Kladská** with its Tyrolean chalets and protected peat bog. Other highlights of the forest include the dramatic **Tři kříže** (three crosses set high on a rocky promontory), the oddly spiralling Krásno viewing tower, the castle at **Bečov nad Teplou**, and the pretty little spa town of Lázně Kynžvart with its spa houses and chateaux where you can view Austrian Chancellor Metternich's collection of curios. The area is crisscrossed with Czech Hiking Club–marked trails and official cycle trails marked with yellow signs.

Bečov nad Teplou

DRAMATIC HILLTOP CASTLE

The de facto capital of the Slavkovský Forest area is the gritty little town of Bečov nad Teplou (Bečov for short), a railway junction in a sweeping forested valley with one stellar attraction – an impressive castle and adjoining chateau clamped to the rock of a high promontory above the Teplá River. Though interesting in itself, the highlight of the castle is the second-most valuable object in all of Czechia: the dazzling **Reliquary of St Maurus**. It was brought here by the last owners of the castle, the Beauforts, Nazi collaborators who were expelled from Czechoslovakia in 1945. The last thing they did was hide the reliquary, never to return. In 1984 a mysterious US businessman called Danny Douglas offered the Czechoslovak state US$250,000 to export a secret object (the hidden reliquary). Using snippets of info they gleaned, the Communist secret police (the StB) were able to locate the precious casket before Douglas could, and St Maurus remained at Bečov.

Recently relocated to a special wing, security is tight as you are ushered into the dark room, the golden casket containing the bones of St Maurus illuminated before you. The rest of Bečov is worth an hour's exploration. Its high-perched square is lined with restaurants, cosy pensions, antique shops and a few private museums. The train and road journey to Bečov is dramatic, ducking and weaving along the winding, thickly forested valley of the Teplá River. In 2019 the journey was rated as one of Europe's top 10 most scenic rail routes by British newspaper the Guardian.

TEPLÁ MONASTERY

Situated 18km east of Mariánské Lázně, the monastery that gave birth to a spa industry still stands in the town of the same name, Teplá. Belonging to the Premonstratensian Order, the definite highlight of the 800-year-old monastery is the astounding baroque library, one of the finest in Central Europe. Buses from Mariánské Lázně stop nearby and tours are with a guide.

THE GUIDE

SOUTH & WEST BOHEMIA

SCENIC ROUTES

Bečov and Teplá are on a very scenic rail line running between ML and KV and Teplá can be reached by bus. Other places in the Slavkovský Forest have limited transport links and you will need your own transport.

WHERE TO EAT

Pension Kladská
One of Czechia's top 100 restaurants with gourmet local fare. In Kladská. €€€

U Tetřeva
Meet the creatures of the surrounding forest – on a plate. Hunting-trophy-bedecked dining room. In Kladská. €€

Hradní Bašta
Cosy restaurant serving Czech classics at the gates of Bečov castle. €€

PLZEŇ

⭐ PRAGUE

● Plzeň

Bohemia's second city Plzeň (Pilsen) is a grainy, industrial place with three stellar attractions that make it worth a trip from Prague or the spas to the north. The Pilsner Urquell Brewery and the Brewery Museum provide the most fascinating beer experience in the country, while Techmania is possibly Czechia's top kids attraction. The Great Synagogue is one of Europe's premier Jewish heritage sites, where size does matter. Otherwise the city has some light sightseeing possibilities around a pretty medieval square as well as a few atmospheric pubs that pack out with students from the University of West Bohemia. But life in Plzeň is really all about heavy engineering, with the Škoda works occupying a massive area to the southwest of the centre, churning out trams and trains for export across Eurasia. If you are weary of 21st-century hip, Plzeň is refreshingly lacking in it.

TOP TIP

The centre is just small enough to explore on foot. Only to reach Techmania will you need to use the city's public transport system – take trolleybus 15 from the train station or get off the train at Plzeň Jižní Předměstí.

BEST EVENTS IN PLZEŇ

Christmas Markets
Prague it ain't, but fewer visitors and lower prices are a big plus.

Liberation Festival
'Thanks America!', cry the locals in May as they celebrate the 1945 liberation of their city.

Pilsner Fest
The city's beer festival is held in early October.

Riegrovka Live Music Festival
All summer central Riegrova echoes to dozens of music events.

TUTO Jídlo
Food festival over the first weekend in September featuring top-quality Czech and international cuisine.

Bottoms up to Plzeň!
PLZEŇ'S HOP-INFUSED HERITAGE

The number one reason people come to Plzeň is to visit the famous Pilsner Urquell Brewery (Prazdroj in Czech) where Pilsner lager was invented in 1842. Arguably Czechia's best known and most copied beer, it was 'invented' when a Bavarian brewer named Groll, whose task it was to upgrade the unpopular brew the locals were forced to drink, came up with a new way of brewing. The drink – pils lager – quickly spread to Prague's pubs and the world. Entry to the brewery is by guided tour. Highlights include the old cellars (dress warmly) and a glass of unpasteurised nectar (tasting far better than the Urquell you get in pubs). Get beer merch at the brewery shop.

A Stroll Through Plzeň
DISCOVER PLZEŇ'S CITY CENTRE

Plzeň's epicentre is **náměstí Republiky** (Republic Square), the obvious place to launch a walking tour. It is watched over by the towering St Bartholomew's Cathedral. There are 301 steps to the top and the view is worth it. Take ulice Františkánská in the southeast corner to reach the **Museum of West Bohemia**, Plzeň's impressive main museum where you'll find an enthralling presentation of the city's history from the 10th to 19th century. From the museum it's a short walk through pleasant **Smetana Gardens** to the rather abstract General Patton Monument, a permanent reminder that it was the US

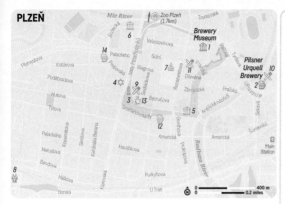

PLZEŇ

HIGHLIGHTS
1 Brewery Museum
2 Pilsner Urquell Brewery

SIGHTS
3 General Patton Monument
4 Great Synagogue
5 Museum of West Bohemia
6 Patton Memorial Pilsen
7 St Bartholomew Cathedral
8 Techmania Science Centre
see 1 Underground Plzeň

EATING
9 Lokál Pod Divadlem
10 Na Spilce
11 U Salzmannů

DRINKING & NIGHTLIFE
12 Měšťanská Beseda
13 Walter
14 Zach's Pub

army and not the Red Army who liberated West Bohemia in May 1945 (the communists used to say it was Soviet troops in US uniforms). In early May the city throws a huge party, Slavnosti Svobody (Liberation Festival).

The monument is on a thundering thoroughfare (sady Pětatřicátníků), almost opposite Plzeň's finest slab of architecture, the Great Synagogue, the second-largest Jewish place of worship in Europe and the third-largest in the world. It dates from the 1880s and was built in neo-Romanesque style.

Getting Technical
THE WEST'S TOP KIDS' ATTRACTION

Techmania is arguably the best way to entertain the kids in the entire country – it's even worth a day trip from Prague. Based in one of Škoda's huge heavy-engineering workshops, kids are free to roam all day, trying out myriad experiments as they go. The concept fits in with Komenský's idea that learning should be fun. Sit back and relax as your little ones mess about with magnets, splash around in the water world, see if they can outrun a cheetah and build towers out of thousands of wooden blocks. There are also excellent science demonstrations, a 3D planetarium and full-sized historic trains manufactured at the Škoda engineering works.

PLZEŇ'S INDUSTRIAL HERITAGE

Škoda Family Museum
Dedicated to the Škoda family of car and engineering fame.

DEPO2015
Art centre in an old tram depo – it's all about start-ups, exhibitions and ideas.

Bohemia Sekt
Take a tour of the Czechs' biggest winery, Bohemia Sekt in Starý Plzenec.

Paper Mill
Another old industrial facility transformed into a cultural centre.

 WHERE TO EAT

Lokál pod Divadlem
The Plzeň branch of a popular pub-restaurant serving Czech standards and good beer. €

Na Spilce
The pub-restaurant at the Urquell Brewery is a great place to end the day in Plzeň. €€

Salzmannů
Plzeň's oldest tavern with a proud tradition of serving well-chilled Urquell and belly-filling Bohemian cuisine. €€

Beyond Plzeň

The Plzeň Region is a diverse area of gently wooded hills, pretty baroque towns and the rounded peaks of the Šumava.

Plzeň is the capital of a large region that extends up into the mountains that form the border in the south and west with Bavaria and Austria. Apart from the frontier-defining peaks of the Šumava and Bohemian Forest, this is an area known for its baroque architecture and Bohemian folk traditions. The Šumava is one of the best places in the country for light hiking and skiing, though it can be crowded with Prague locals in summer. Domažlice is where most of the folk action is concentrated. It's well worth taking time out to discover this surprisingly interesting region, one that attracts very few foreign tourists.

TOP TIP

In July or August, book accommodation well in advance. There are seven free campsites in the national park; see the park website, www.npsumava.cz

Domažlice

PYTY/SHUTTERSTOCK ©

Šumava

THE GREEN ROOF OF EUROPE

Shared between the Plzeň and South Bohemian regions, the mysterious Šumava mountain range – sometimes called the Green Roof of Europe – is a magnet for backcountry hikers, skiers of all types, holidaying Czech families and nature lovers. The hills rising to over 1300m along the border are carpeted in thick forest, much of which is a national park and firmly out of bounds. Hiking trails, maintained by the Czech Hiking Club (Klub českých turistů, KČT), will lead you to alpine lakes, high peaks, waterfalls, peat bogs, fast-flowing rivers and areas of virgin forest. KČT hiking maps 64 to 67 cover the region in superb detail.

Domažlice

FOLK CUSTOMS AND TRADITIONAL ARCHITECTURE

Around 50km southwest of Plzeň, the oft-overlooked town of Domažlice is one of Czechia's prettiest and most interesting to those in search of folksy Slavic colour. Top attraction here is náměstí Míru, a very wide, cobbled street with Gothic arcading topped with colourful baroque gables. Beyond the arches lurk tiny shops, some having changed little since communist days. The town has two superb museums – the Chodsko Museum (Museum Chodska, in the castle) has exhibitions on local Chod traditions and other aspects of the region, while the Jindřich Jindřich Museum (Muzeum Jindřicha Jindřicha) focuses firmly on the ethnography of the Chodsko Region. The annual Chod Festival is in August though Domažlice is a wonderfully off-the-beaten-track place to explore all year round.

Chodsko & The Chods

SLAVIC TRIBE

Chodsko is the border region where the Bohemian Forest (Český les) and Šumava ranges meet. The Chods, a sturdy, independent Slavic tribe, were entrusted with patrolling the Bavarian border by King John of Luxembourg in 1325, in return for exemption from feudal servitude. After the Thirty Years' War, the new overlords refused to honour the old agreements, the Chods briefly and disastrously rebelled, losing their rights completely as a result. Their colourfully traditional way of life survives in unique customs and speech, although only on special occasions – like the annual Chod Festival (Chodské slavnosti) in mid-August – are you likely to hear Chod dudy (bagpipes) or catch sight of Chod women's long printed dresses.

SLAVIC TRIBE

The **Chods**, a sturdy, independent Slavic tribe, were entrusted with patrolling the Bavarian border in return for exemption from feudal servitude

GETTING AROUND

The easiest way to reach Domažlice is by train from Plzeň. The Šumava is served by bus and train, though the bus is often the better option.

ČESKÝ KRUMLOV

⊕ PRAGUE

Český Krumlov •

Český Krumlov, in Bohemia's deep south, is one of the most picturesque towns in Europe. It's a little like Prague – a Unesco World Heritage Site with a stunning castle above the Vltava River, an old town square, Renaissance and baroque architecture, and hordes of tourists milling through the streets – but all on a smaller scale. You can walk from one end of town to the other in 20 minutes. There are plenty of lively bars and riverside picnic spots. In summer it's a popular hang-out for backpackers and in winter, when the crowds are gone and the castle is blanketed in snow, it's a magical place. Before the pandemic struck, Český Krumlov had become synonymous with overtourism. The crowds are yet to return to those levels but when they do, it's easy to escape on a hike or bike ride into the surrounding hills.

TOP TIP

Sadly, the special beauty of Český Krumlov is no longer the secret it once was, and from April to October overtourism is the word that comes to mind. This is one destination where it pays to visit in the off season.

Exploring Český Krumlov

FAIRY TALE BOHEMIAN TOWN

Wandering Český Krumlov on foot on a winter Wednesday, the snow falling silently, the cosy cafes beckoning you in, the churches bedecked in seasonal decoration and the scent of mulled wine in the air, must be one of the most magical experiences in Czechia.

BEAUTY BY DESIGN

Český Krumlov town hall rests on six Gothic arches on the square's northeast flank

Most begin their exploration at the huge castle occupying a promontory high above the town. The guided tours run only from April to October and are worth it, but part of the fun here is getting lost in the passages, arcading and gangways on the south side which lead to the bridge 'na plášti' (the Cloak Bridge) – an amazing Renaissance structure rising incredibly high above the gorge.

Other highlights include the beautifully painted **Round Tower** dominating the scene, and the baroque theatre, one of only two in Europe preserved in its original state.

The area to the southeast of the castle is **Latrán**, the main street through it (bearing the same name) starting at the **Budějovice Gate** (Budějovická brána) and ending at the **Lazebnický Bridge** dating from the early 19th century, the gateway to the Inner Town (Vnitřní město) which rises on what is essentially an island created by a tight loop in the Vltava River.

Pass through the narrow streets packed with tiny shops and

ČESKÝ KRUMLOV

BEST EVENTS IN ČESKÝ KRUMLOV

Festival of Baroque Art
Baroque music and opera performed around the town and most notably at the castle's baroque theatre (September).

Advent Markets On Svornosti Square
This must be Central Europe's most intimate Christmas market.

Five-Petalled Rose Celebrations
Renaissance bash in June with jousting knights and many a silly costume.

Český Krumlov International Music Festival
A real hotchpotch of a music festival held over the summer.

St Wenceslas Celebrations
Held on 28 September, Český Krumlov marks St Wenceslas Day, the Czech patron saint, with much merrymaking.

cafes to reach **Svornosti Square**, a small, painfully pretty piazza where there's always something going on. The town hall rests on six Gothic arches on the square's northeast flank. Leave the square at the southwest corner to find the Egon Schiele Art Centrum, the town's top gallery. Loop around the south of the Inner Town to reach the large Church of St Vitus (Kostel sv Víta), the biggest in Krumlov, where classical music concerts sometimes take place.

Egon Schiele & Český Krumlov

SCHIELE'S TIME IN KRUMLOV

The Austrian expressionist painter Egon Schiele's (1890–1918) connection to Český Krumlov comes through his mother, Marie Soukupová, who was born here.

Schiele himself lived in Krumlov in 1911, spending most of his time here painting his Dead Towns pictures, a far cry from the explicit nudes for which he is famous. However, things did not go well when he returned to those naked female forms – he raised the ire of the townsfolk by hiring underage girls as nude models and was eventually chased out of town.

The excellent, private **Egon Schiele Art Centrum** houses a small retrospective of the celebrated and controversial

WHERE TO GET A COFFEE

Egon Schiele Café
Characterful old cafe at the Schiele Art Centrum.

Zapa Cafe
Great spot on the main tourist oute for a coffee or ice cream.

Ideál
Small roastery and cafe with the freshest brews in town and tasty cakes.

BEST EXPERIENCES IN ČESKÝ KRUMLOV

Graphite Mine
Don a hard hat for a tour of the country's last graphite mine, only recently abandoned.

Krumlov Brewery
Take a tour of the local brewery to learn about beer traditions going back 700 years.

Magic Herb Garden
Savour the aroma of 26 herb beds at this tranquil herb garden south of the centre.

Carriage Rides
Take a horse and carriage around the town or out into the surrounding countryside.

Canoe Trips
The Vltava River at Krumlov is ideal for trips in canoes and on rafts, which can be hired in town.

KACA SKOKANOVA/SHUTTERSTOCK ©

Egon Schiele Art Centrum

Viennese painter, but the institution's main activity is organising world-class exhibitions by artists from across the globe.

One of Krumlov's best cafes is on the premises. The other Schiele attraction in town is the Egon Schiele Garden Studio, a hillside house that served as residence and studio in 1911. Schiele created several important works here, including *Dead Town* and *Krumlov by Night*.

The house has been restored to look like the old studio and is used by contemporary artists, who work and exhibit their paintings here.

Krumlov's Overtourism Problem

CHANGE MANAGEMENT

Until 1990, few had heard of this pretty town in Bohemia's south. If you had visited in those days you would have found few foreign tourists, just locals dwelling among a soot-cracked jumble of crumbling medieval buildings. Things began to change in 1992 when Krumlov was one of the first places in the country to be declared a World Heritage Site by Unesco, kicking off a tourist industry that peaked in 2018, when 412,000 overnight stays were recorded. Possibly put off by over-

WHERE TO EAT

Krčma v Šatlavské
Medieval cellar with meat-heavy menu. Reservations essential. €€

U Dwau Maryí
Old Bohemian recipes washed down with mead and ale. €€

Hospoda Na Louži
Old-fashioned tavern serving meat-and-dumpling combos and local beer. €€

tourism itself, the summer before COVID saw a slight drop. With its trdelník (Hungarian chimney cake) sellers, Thai massage shops and gift shops stocked high with cannabis sweets and matryoshka dolls, Krumlov was a place locals had evidently begun to avoid.

Short Trips from Český Krumlov

ESCAPING THE CROWDS

Possibly the best escape on foot from Krumlov's tourism is up **Mount Kleť** (1084m), a green marked trail running for around 7.5km from Krumlov castle to the top. There you'll find a viewing tower, a restaurant, various shelters and picnic tables.

A 23km drive north, the tiny village of Holašovice well deserved its Unesco listing for a unique collection of folk baroque gables ringing a pretty village green. On the southeast edge of the village is a prehistoric stone ring, one of the most impressive in the country and sometimes dubbed the South Bohemian Stonehenge.

Top billing for a day trip is **Rožmberk**, 25km to the south, another wonderfully picturesque town on a tight bend in the Vltava River. The castle here is surrounded on three sides by the Vltava and once belonged to the Rožmberk family who dominated the whole of the south Bohemian area in the 13th century. Zlatá Koruna Monastery, in another river bend 7.5km north, makes for a superb day hike. There's a choice of tours to take once you get there.

The impressive castle ruins of **Dívčí Kámen** – rising high above the Vltava around 15km north – is a magical overnight hiking destination. A red trail runs here from Zlatá Koruna or take the train.

HOLAŠOVICE

On the southeast edge of the village is a prehistoric stone ring, one of the most impressive in the country and sometimes dubbed the **South Bohemian Stonehenge**

GETTING AROUND

Český Krumlov can only really be explored on foot. The only time you might need the town's buses is if your hotel is out of town. A car might be useful for day trips but not at all essential.

ČESKÉ BUDĚJOVICE

⚙ PRAGUE

České
Budějovice
•

The provincial capital of the South Bohemia region, this oft-ig-nored city of almost 100,000 people comes as a surprise to many. It's known locally for its huge, arcade-bordered piaz-za (náměstí Přemysla Otakara II), a precious bit of 14th-cen-tury town planning by the Přemsyl dynasty of the day after whom it is named. However, Budějovice's German name is Budweis, of US beer fame – the city's state-owned brewery fought a long legal battle (settled amicably) with the American drinks giant over the brand as the brewery in České Budějo-vice produces Budweiser Budvar, the original beer. Once you have spent a day or so wandering the square, taking a trip to Hluboká Castle and sampling the real Budweiser, you'll be ready to move on to Krumlov or elsewhere.

TOP TIP

If you're travelling during the ice-hockey season (September to March) catch the home team ČEZ Motor České Budějovice in action at Budvar Arena. Tickets can be bought at the arena on game days.

CZECHIA'S LONGEST RIVER

That river flowing through České Budějovice is the Vltava, the same watercourse under those rafts in Český Krumlov and home of the swans you can feed from Charles Bridge. For the Czechs the Vltava isn't a river, but *the* river, the longest in the country at a whopping 430km. (How does it all fit?) It rises in a boggy valley 6km south of the Šumava town of Kvilda. By the time it is swallowed by the Labe (Elbe) at Mělník, it has drained all of south and west Bohemia and swelled to a major, navigable waterway.

Exploring České Budějovice

STROLLING BUDĚJOVICE'S MEDIEVAL CENTRE

The place to start in České Budějovice to get your bearings is náměstí Přemysla Otakara II, the square named after the city's founding monarch. It's the biggest town square in the country, with attractive arcaded buildings grouped around the 1727 **Samson's Fountain** (Samsonova kašna). And when they say square they mean it – its exactly 133m on all four sides. Among the architectural treats around the edge is the 1555 **Renaissance town hall** (Radnice), which received a ba-roque facelift in 1731. The figures on the balustrade – Justice, Wisdom, Courage and Prudence – are matched by an exotic quartet of bronze gargoyles.

Just off the square to the northeast is the Černá věž, the Gothic-Renaissance **Black Tower**. It's 72m tall and was built in 1553. Climb its 225 steps (yep, we counted them) for fine views. The tower's two bells – Marta (1723) and Budvar (1995; a gift from the brewery) – are rung daily at noon. Beside the tower is the **Cathedral of St Nicholas** (Katedrála sv Mi-kuláše), built as a church in the 13th century, rebuilt in 1649, then made a cathedral in 1784.

The main indoor attraction in the centre is the **Museum of South Bohemia** (Jihočeské muzeum) to the square's southeast. Founded in 1877, it holds an enormous collection of historic books, coins, military objects, folk art and displays on natu-ral history and archaeology, with a focus on the local region.

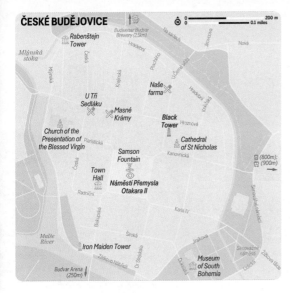

ČESKÉ BUDĚJOVICE

POKING AROUND THE OLD TOWN

Part of the fun of a trip to České Budějovice is the chance to poke around the tiny alleyways that radiate from gigantic náměstí Přemysla Otakara II, the town's famous square. The original Old Town is almost entirely surrounded by a picturesque canal (Mlýnská stoka) and the Malše River, as well as extensive gardens where the town walls once stood, great places to chill out on the grass or let the kids play. Only a few bits of Gothic fortifications remain, including Rabenštejn Tower, and 15th-century Iron Maiden Tower, a crumbling former prison. Along Hroznová, on Piaristické náměstí, is the Church of the Presentation of the Blessed Virgin with a former Dominican monastery, which has a splendid pulpit.

One of the highlights of a trip to České Budějovice is see-ign where the original Budweiser beer was born, at the Bud-weiser **Budvar Brewery**. The tour highlights modern pro-duction methods, with the reward being a glass of Budvar in the brewery's chilly cellars. The brewery is 2km north of the main square.

Hluboká nad Vltavou

CZECHIA'S MOST FAMOUS NEO-GOTHIC PILE

One of the most celebrated chateaux in the country, **Hluboká** draws visitors from across the country as well as people on half-day trips from České Budějovice. It was built by Přemys-lid rulers in the 13th century and the building changed own-ership several times until it was acquired by the Schwarzen-bergs in the 17th century. They gave the castle its English Tudor makeover, modelled on Britain's Windsor Castle, in 1871. Entry is by guided tour only and there are four routes to choose from, though the vast majority choose tour 1. Housed in a former riding school next to **Hluboká Chateau**, the exhibition of the **South Bohemian Aleš Gallery** mixes modern and historical art concepts, highlighting Czech religious art from the 14th to 16th centuries as well as 17th-century Dutch masters.

 **WHERE TO EAT**

Naše farma
Offers dishes made from fresh local produce grown on organic farms in the surrounding region. €€

Masné Krámy
Czech food and cold Budvar beer in a České Budějovice institution. €

U Tří Sedláků
The traditional Czech food here – think rabbit, venison, dumplings – is among the best in town. €€

MICHAELA JILKOVA/SHUTTERSTOCK ©

The Czech Switzerland (p156)

NORTH & EAST BOHEMIA

★PRAGUE

SANDSTONE ROCKS & BONE CHURCHES

Mountain ranges rise in the northeast of Prague, punctuated by wonderful rock formations – ideal hiking country. Human-made structures come in the form of fairy-tale castles and one rather spooky church.

Though joined at the hip, Bohemia's north and east differ from one another quite significantly, the northern border areas are all rugged mountain ranges (including the country's highest peak **Sněžka**) and outdoor adventure, while east of Prague extend the low, fertile plains along the **River Labe** (Elbe), an area peppered with the cultural heritage of the Czech heartlands.

If you are towing tots, then **Liberec** is arguably the country's most entertaining city for you. It has attractions galore, including **iQLANDIA** (p148) science centre, which will stimulate developing minds all day long.

They'll even enjoy the cable-car ride up to the **Ještěd Tower**. If hiking boots are weighing down your luggage, set them free on the trails of the **Czech Switzerland National Park** or through the Elbe Sandstone Rocks. This is some of the most memorable hiking in the country. A very popular day trip from Prague is **Kutná Hora**, best know for its ossuary or 'bone church' . The town was once the silver capital of Europe, and the local mint and mines are the real story here. **Little Litomyšl** in the far east of Bohemia boasts one of the finest chateaux north of the Alps.

GRISHA BRUEV/SHUTTERSTOCK ©

THE MAIN AREAS

LIBEREC	**THE CZECH SWITZERLAND**	**KUTNÁ HORA**	**LITOMYŠL**
Possibly Czechia's top city for kids	A national park that's perfect for hiking	Macabre bone church and silver-mining heritage	A Renaissance gem of the east
p148	**p156**	**p163**	**p168**

Find Your Way

This part of the country is well-served by public transport, with buses taking over where the trains can't reach. However, having a car is a big advantage in the more remote mountainous areas.

GERMANY

THE CZECH SWITZERLAND, p156
A national park and perfect for hiking

Hřensko

České Švýcarsko

Děčín

Ústí nad Labem

Most

Terezín

Chomutov

Lake River

Mělník

Kladno

PRAGUE

Vltava

CAR

The D10 motorway runs from Prague almost all the way to Liberec and is the main access route for the far north. Take the D8 to reach Děčín, the D11 east towards Kutná Hora and Litomyšl.

BUS

Bus is best to Litomyšl, though the train is better for other cities. Local buses are good for reaching trailheads but are timetabled to ferry schoolchildren and workers from rural areas to the towns in the morning and back again in the afternoon.

TRAIN

Liberec, Děčín and Kutná Hora are all well-served by train from Prague. However hardly any places in the mountains have rail service – there you'll have to rely on local buses.

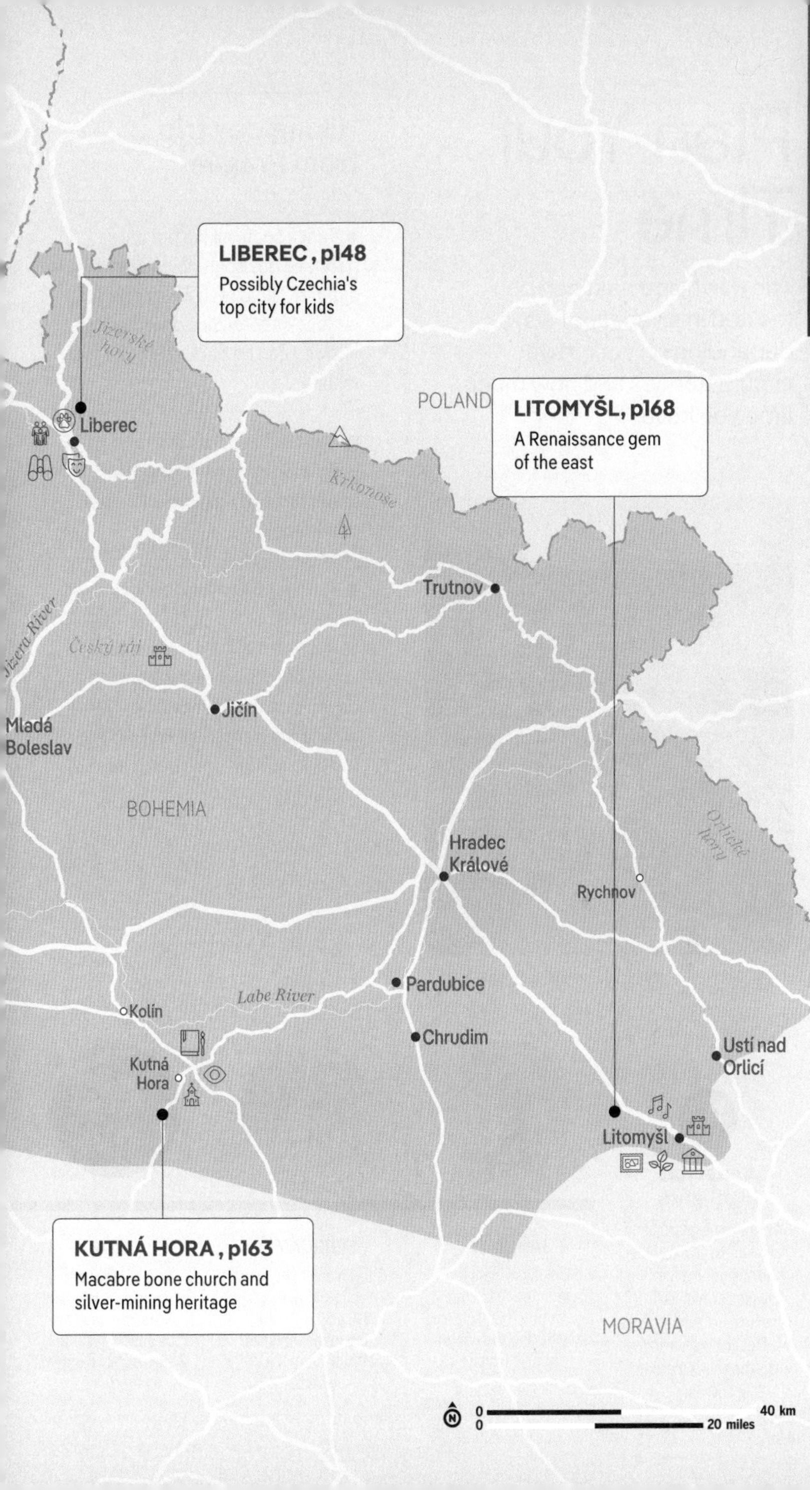

LIBEREC , p148
Possibly Czechia's
top city for kids

POLAND

LITOMYŠL, p168
A Renaissance gem
of the east

*Jizerské
hory*

Liberec

Krkonoše

Jizera River

Trutnov

Český ráj

Jičín

Mladá
Boleslav

BOHEMIA

Hradec
Králové

Rychnov

*Orlické
hory*

Labe River

Pardubice

Kolín

Chrudim

Kutná
Hora

Ústí nad
Orlicí

Litomyšl

KUTNÁ HORA , p163
Macabre bone church and
silver-mining heritage

MORAVIA

N
0   0   40 km
0   20 miles   **145**

Plan Your Time

The north and east can be tackled in a variety of ways, depending on your travel circumstances and how much time you have.

The Czech Switzerland (p156)

Hiking day trip from Prague

● Fancy some hiking but only have one day spare to escape the capital? The **Czech Switzerland** is close enough for a one-day trek and you can be back in Prague for dinner.

● You could approach a tour company that runs **hiking trips** (p158) but a DIY excursion is easy to arrange.

● An early train from Prague (change to bus in Děčín) can see you on the main red trail in Mezní Louka by 9am. That gives you all day to take in the **Pravčická Gate** and/or the **Kamenice Gorge**. The last connection back from Hřensko is after 7pm.

Seasonal highlights

Anytime is a good time to head to the Czech mountains. Arriving in low season in Kutná Hora and Litomyšl gives a different perspective on these historical towns.

JANUARY

Ski season gets into gear in the Krkonoše – book early if you plan to stay during the winter-sports frenzy.

FEBRUARY

Clip on cross-country skis to join the **Jizerská 50**, a 50km skiing race in the Jizerské Mountains. Or just watch...

JUNE

The best time for classical-music fans who can head to the Litomyšl for the **Smetana's Litomyšl** festival.

FOTO-MIGAWKI MD/SHUTTERSTOCK ©

ITOMM/SHUTTERSTOCK ©; CTK/ALAMY STOCK PHOTO ©; CUM OKOLO/ALAMY STOCK PHOTO ©

Czech mountain odyssey

● The **Stezka Českem** (Czechia Trail) is a relatively new initiative with a hiking trail (using existing paths) created around the entire circumference of Czechia.

● One of the most challenging sections is the northern stretch between the **Labské pískovce** protected area and the eastern reaches of the **Krkonoše**, a distance of around 200km. This route starts in Tisá and ends in Žacléř, taking 10 days to three weeks, and including the **Czech Switzerland**, the Jizerské Mountains around Liberec and the Krkonoše range.

● The **Stezka Českem** is currently one of the most talked-about challenges among the Czech outdoor community.

A Long weekend

● Kutná Hora and Litomyšl form the ideal double act for a weekend away from the capital.

● Head first to **Kutná Hora** some 75km east of Prague where a full day is enough to explore the Sedlec Ossuary, the town's rich mining heritage and the **Cathedral of St Barbora**, the finest church outside the capital.

● On Sunday morning it's a 90km drive, or two-hour train journey east to **Litomyšl** where you can enjoy lunch at a local restaurant, before joining a tour of the chateau. Prague is then a two-hour evening trip away.

JULY
The last weekend of July sees Liberec's **Benátská!** festival, a musical extravaganza featuring big names on the Czech music scene.

AUGUST
Mushrooming is a national sport in Czechia. August is the first month you might spot basket-wielding Czechs scouring the forests.

OCTOBER
Arguably the best time to hit the Czech Switzerland trails as autumn gets into its full, multi-hued swing.

DECEMBER
Every Sunday throughout Advent, **Litomyšl** holds an atmospheric Christmas market in and around the chateau.

LIBEREC

Two decades ago, few foreign visitors ever found their way to this northern city, but how things have changed. The capital of the Liberec Region and a city of over 100,000 means there are now several good reasons for getting on the train from Prague. Though the city itself could never be described as the country's most fetching, it makes a great base for exploring a region of mountains, castles and glass workshops, as well as its own few big-name sights. The iQLANDIA science centre is only rivalled by Pilsen's Techmania, if you find yourself in Czechia with children. You could also spend an entire weekend at the Babylon Centre without ever venturing outside. However, the city's main attraction rises high above even the tallest communist block – the 1970s, space-age Ještěd TV tower is one of the country's most instantly recognisable structures and essential viewing if in the region.

TOP TIP

A fairly large city by Czech standards, Liberec has a comprehensive transport system of buses and trams. Apart from the Ještěd cable car, almost all the city's attractions are within walking distance of the train station.

WHY I LOVE LIBEREC

Marc Di Duca,
co-author Prague & Czechia

As a father of two, I love that Liberec has more to do for families than any other regional capital by a Habsburg furlong. You could keep the kids entertained here for many days on end, iQLANDIA and the Babylon Centre the obvious attractions but the zoo, Dino Park and the surrounding castles also in the mix.
And then there's Ještěd, a surefire hit with kiddies who will enjoy the ride up and the fixed telescopes at the top they can use to find your hotel back in Liberec far below.

iQLANDIA
THE NORTH'S TOP KIDDIE ATTRACTION

For many this is the country's top attraction for the young – engaging iQLANDIA is a great day out for kids. This science centre is packed with experiments, demonstrations, exhibitions and fascinating facts, all totally hands-on and commendably kid-proof. Stealth learning has never been such fun!

The centre has six levels, the top five linked by a spiralling walkway. The ground floor is all about water. Kids are encouraged to splash around in specially designed water features, inside and out, and program the interactive fountain which dominates the central atrium. One level up the spiral brings you to the elements-themed section, where you can learn about the weather and experience a hurricane.

The next floor up exhibits the human body and the senses – experience what it's like to be blind and test your strength and stamina. The most popular floor is the next level where things get technical – see a car cut in half, ride a Mars rover simulator and test your braking skills in an interactive driving game. Here also is the planetarium (additional ticket required). The top-floor roof terrace has several musical instruments for children to bash and hammer.

Below the ground floor is a fascinating, very much hands-off exhibition of obsolete technology, most of it chunky, nostalgia-inducing, communist-era junk.

Kids will wonder at 1980s landline telephones and typewriters, while older Czechs walk around exclaiming 'we still have one of those' at the less antiquated stuff.

LIBEREC & AROUND

Ještěd
CZECH BUILDING OF THE CENTURY

That odd thing pointing into the sky to the southwest around Liberec is Ještěd, a 1012m-tall peak topped with a 1970s TV tower that *Thunderbirds* or a James Bond Villain would be proud of. Czech architect Karel Hubáček won the coveted Perret prize in 1969 for the design of this 100m-tall pinnacle that rises from a 33m-wide circular base containing a restaurant and hotel. In 2000 it was declared 'Czech building of the 20th century'.

It's the region's top sight and well worth the effort to reach it, if only for the stupendous views on all sides (it's said you can see Prague 100km away when visibility is good). The tower, bristling with telecommunications aerials and disks, is a real timepiece, the whole building a retro experience taking visitors back to 1970s Czechoslovakia. The bistro is relatively inexpensive, the hotel usually hopelessly booked up.

Getting up to the **Ještěd Tower** is half the fun and there are several ways to reach the top. The easiest and most boring is to drive there and park in the car park next to the tower. However, even on quieter days this fills quickly and space is tight, so if you drive, leave the car at the Výpřež car park and

CRYSTAL VALLEY

Liberec is by far the best base for exploring the so-called Crystal Valley, a loose association of glass-themed attractions (the largest on earth) that stretch across the north of Bohemia, from Kamenický Šenov in the west to Harrachov in the east. At over 60 sites across the region you can watch glass being blown, twisted, cut and polished by master craftspeople, sometimes one-person operations. There are also glass museums to visit, students to chat with, jewellery to admire and countless glass souvenirs to buy. At smaller workshops and studios it is best to call ahead so they know you are coming – few are open at the weekend. See www.crystalvalley.cz for a comprehensive list of places to visit.

GETTING AROUND

By far the best way to reach Liberec from Prague is by bus. These leave regularly from Florenc and Černý Most stations and pull in at the main bus station next to the train station in the city centre.

PYTY/SHUTTERSTOCK ©

Ještěd Tower

either walk up the road (2.8km) or through the forest (1.7km), the latter steep and rough in places. Most people take the cable car, which leaves from near the end of tram line No 3. In winter this serves skiers visiting Ještěd's slopes.

An accident in 2022 brought the service to a halt, but it should be up and running again by the time you visit. Obviously the most strenuous but rewarding way to summit is on foot – take the blue marked hiking trail from the tram terminus. The 3.4km-long walk is uphill and rough underfoot all the way.

Liberec's Other Top Sights

A STROLL THROUGH THE CITY

Besides the big-ticket experiences, Liberec has some light sightseeing. The city's fourth big attraction is its **zoo**, one of the best-known within Bohemia. The layout means you don't have to walk too much to admire the 160 species.

Another attraction for children is the **DinoPark** within the Liberec Plaza shopping mall where you can admire scale models of dinosaurs and watch a 3D dino film. Liberec's FX Šalda Theatre dates from 1883 and is one of the

 **WHERE TO STAY**

Pytloun City Boutique Hotel
Fresh and central, this luxurious four-star number is part of the local Pytloun hotel empire. €€

Hotel Radnice
Traditional, centrally located hotel within walking distance of the sights. €

Pytloun Design Hotel
Best price-to-quality ratio in town – 3.5km south of the centre. Lots of parking. €

most attractive in the country. Inside is original decoration by the Klimt brothers.

The **Museum of North Bohemia** underwent comprehensive renovation in 2020 and now exhibits its collections in spruced-up interiors. The most interesting is arguably the decorative-arts section with glass, porcelain, ceramics and woodcarvings. It also houses the world's longest glass ladder (where are the others with which it so fiercely competes?) measuring 24m and made locally in 2022.

Top Castles of the Liberec Region

FIVE TRIP-STOPPING CASTLES

Liberec is a great starting point for exploring the wider region and that exploration should definitely include a castle or two. Top of the list must be **Bezděz**, a massive, unfiltered Gothic fortress that sits atop an impossibly high mountain around 40km southeast. Views of the surrounding forests are some of the best from any Czech castle.

A dominant feature of the Czech Paradise area, **Trosky Castle** is possibly the country's most famous ruin, its two towers rising high above the forested landscape. Some 16km south of Liberec stands the monster that is **Sychrov**, a vast palace in every 'neo' style in the architectural textbook. Near Turnov, the **Hrubý Rohozec chateau** has stood on the site since the 13th century but was rebuilt into a neoclassical residence in the 19th century.

Another massive pile is **Frýdlant** to the north of Liberec, made up of a Renaissance chateau and a medieval castle, both set high on a basalt promontory.

WHERE TO GET A DRINK IN LIBEREC

Kavárna Bez Konceptu

The place in town for a morning-after breakfast, brunch or just a cuppa Joe.

Ztráty a Nálezy

Very cosy tavern in the backstreets of Liberec serving local beer.

Barvírna
Best craft beer in town and lots of soak-up material.

FAMOUS FORTRESSES

Trosky Castle is possibly the country's most famous ruin, its two towers rising high above the forested landscape

WHERE TO EAT

Radniční Sklípek
Cheap and filling Czech food in cellars beneath the town hall. €

bistRAWveg
Raw vegan food at the Plaza shopping mall. €

Balada
Long-established, central restaurant serving traditional Czech food. €€

Jízerské Mountains

Liberec

Krkonoše Mountains

Český ráj

Beyond Liberec

Beyond Liberec in almost every direction you'll
discover places of exquisite natural beauty,
many off the tourist trail.

If you are into hiking, biking or skiing, then the wider area
around Liberec is one of the best places in the country to lace
up or click on. To the north are the little-visited **Jizerské
Mountains** with their lonely hiking trails and 1000m peaks.
To the south is the **Český ráj** (literally meaning Czech Paradise) which, as the name suggests, is one of the most alluring parts of Bohemia.

However, the real treat is in the east where the highest
peaks in the country – the **Krkonoše Mountains** – draw
all kinds of adrenalin-sports enthusiasts. This is where you'll
find **Sněžka**, the highest mountain in Czechia and the country's biggest ski resorts.

TOP TIP

Late spring and autumn
are the best times to hike
the northern mountains.
The ski season runs from
December to March/April.

Mount Sněžka (p155)

PYTY/SHUTTERSTOCK ©

Skiing on the Krkonoše Mountains

Krkonoše Mountains

CZECHIA'S HIGHEST PEAKS

Around 30km by car from Liberec is the country's most frequented national park (especially during the winter-sports season): the Krkonoše Mountains (sometimes called the Giant Mountains in English). These rise up against the Polish border, their slopes and deep-cut valleys swathed in spruce forests. Most Czechs associate the area with skiing – the main ski centres are Špindlerův Mlýn, Harrachov and Pec pod Sněžkou – the last in the list sitting in the shadow of Mount Sněžka, Czechia's highest peak at 1602m.

All of these resorts get hopelessly booked out and crowded from December through to March (the traffic situation here can be dire), mostly by Škoda-loads of Praguers hitting the nearest serious slopes to the capital.

TAKE TO THE SLOPES

The main ski centres are **Špindlerův Mlýn**, **Harrachov** and **Pec pod Sněžkou,** sitting in the shadow of **Mount Sněžka**

JIZERSKÉ MOUNTAINS

Rising immediately to the north of Liberec, the Jizerské Mountains are the antidote to the oft-overcrowded Krkonoše which they adjoin.

Riddled with easygoing hiking and cycling trails and with only one summer-only road, this is a place to truly escape into unpopulated backcountry. The highest point is **Mount Jizera** (1122m) from which there are great views, but there are many other destinations to choose from.

Start in **Liberec** near the zoo or head to a trailhead by public transport. The Czech Hiking Club (KČT) map 20-21 covers the area in detail. The Jizerské Mountains are known for one of the biggest winter-sports events – the **Jizerská 50**, a 50km cross-country-skiing endurance race that traverses the entire range and attracts around 7000 skiers.

WHERE TO STAY IN A MOUNTAIN CHALET

Lučni Bouda
The Krkonoše's oldest ridge chalet and one of Europe's largest. €€

Labská Bouda
Controversial communist-era mega-project jutting out into thin alpine air at 1312m. €

Martinova Bouda
Pretty chalet named after Czech tennis player Martina Navrátilová who spent some of her childhood here. €

BEARFOTOS/SHUTTERSTOCK ©

Český Ráj

When the snow melts, hikers take over – there are countless routes to choose from but the most spectacular is the red ridge trail that traces the border with Poland. Like in the Alps, there are high-perched chalets (called bouda) to stay at (book these several days in advance), some basic affairs, others offering a certain level of three-star comfort. All offer meals.

Whether trekking or mountain biking, you can easily cross over into Poland where the considerably smaller Karkonoski Park Narodowy protects the northern side of the range. Be sure to take your passport. Despite the relatively modest altitudes of these mountains, it's usually windy and cold year-round at the higher elevations. Even in summer, mountain fog creates a hypothermia risk. Flip-flops at 1600m, even in summer, are not a good idea.

Český Ráj

ROCK FORMATIONS & DRAMATIC CASTLES

Spectacular landscapes dotted with the ruins of audaciously located castles make this maze of sandstone 'rock towns' and basalt volcanic fingers a fairy-tale place to explore, espe-

 GETTING AROUND

To get the most out of this mountainous region you really need your own car. While the Krkonoše resorts and the Český ráj area are well-served by public transport, more remote parts of the Jizerské Mountains are trickier to reach.

cially on foot. Walking trails weave through the bizarre protected landscape, as the Czech Paradise ascends gently to morph into the foothills of the Krkonoše Mountains. During the Czech National Revival, poets, sculptors and painters were inspired by the compelling panoramas, and today the collages of weirdly shaped sandstone and basalt attracts hikers and climbers. Summer (June to August) gets exceptionally busy so come in spring or autumn to get the most out of the area.

Highlights include Trosky, Valdštejn and Kost castles and the rock formations at Hrubá Skála and Prachovské skály – the last in the list is the largest so-called 'rock town' and the only one in the area where you have to pay admission to hike the trails. Turnov, Jičín and Železný Brod are good bases for exploring the area but it is also easily reached from Liberec, 25km to the north.

Climbing Sněžka

CZECHIA'S HIGHEST PEAK

There are several ways to hike to the top of Sněžka, a fairly easy climb whichever way you go. The most direct and shortest route is along a blue trail directly north out of Pec along Obří důl. However, this is tarmac for the first 3km before the path climbs steeply.

For a better outdoor experience, take the red marked trail then the green west to Výrovka, then red and blue routes to the top via Luční bouda – 10.5km in total. You can then descend via the blue trail (or take the cable car). Another option is to follow a green trail to Růžohorky, then the yellow path that runs underneath the cable car.

THE CZECH SWITZERLAND

Czech Switzerland

⭐ PRAGUE

Almost at the northernmost point of the country, the **Czech Switzerland** (České Švýcarsko) is a real treat for anyone looking to hike while in Czechia. Declared a national park in 2000, this is an area of gargantuan stone towers, cliffs, rock fingers, arches and caves that often rise horizontally from the trails and surrounding forests. These natural features provide gob-smacking views across the landscape, making every hike a rather stop-start but memorable affair.

Most visitors head straight for the **Pravčická Gate** (Pravčická brána), Europe's largest natural stone arch, but there are countless other places of equally dramatic natural beauty further along the trails. In the long, very dry summer of 2022 the Czech Switzerland suffered one of the biggest forest fires Czechia has ever witnessed, with firefighters drafted in from across the country to extinguish the flames.

TOP TIP

A full day on the trails is perfectly feasible as a trip from Prague, just 1½ hours to the south. Several Prague-based tour companies run trips to the national park. However, staying overnight enables you to go further than the day-tripper experience.

FAST FACTS

Website
www.ceskesvycarsko.cz

Information Centre
Dům Českého Švýcarska in the village of Krásná Lípa

Date established
1 January 2000

Best Time to Come
Autumn and late spring/early summer

Area 79.23 sq km

Total area covered in forest 97%

Map KČT hiking map sheet 12

Area affected by 2022 fire 1600 hectares

Highest point
Růžovský vrch (619m)

Classic Hiking Loop

THE CLASSIC CZECH SWITZERLAND HIKE

From **Hřensko** village, a pretty though touristy place where the wide River Elbe flows into Saxony, head to the trailhead 2.5km east. Follow the red marked trail along the road, hitch or take a taxi. Start at **Tři prameny** from where it's a 2km climb to the **Pravčická Gate**, a mammoth, natural rock arch under which sits a restaurant and refreshments kiosk. It's the symbol of the region and one of the country's most impressive sights. You must pay to get under the arch (you can no long clamber over it) but the best photos are from a distance.

From the arch the red trail bucks and weaves between stone pinnacles and rock formations with imaginative names like Fortress (Pevnost), Chinese Wall (Čínská zeď) and Cone (Homole), until you reach the hamlet of **Mezní Louka** 4.8km later. Between November and March, you have to take the green trail through Mezná, then a yellow path back to Tři prameny. From April to October you can take the blue trail and a short stretch of road to **Divoká soutěska** for one of the most unusual hiking experiences in Czechia.

The **Kamenice River** cannot be hiked all the way, with two very narrow gorges (Divoká soutěska and Edmundova soutěska) blocking the path. Instead, small ferry boats carry hikers along the river, the forest and cliffs rising high above. It's an experience that will live long in the memory, especially if here in au-

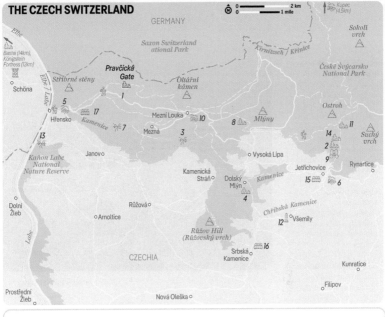

THE CZECH SWITZERLAND

HIGHLIGHTS	**4** Ferdinandova soutěska	**9** Mariina vyhlídka	**14** Vilemínina stěna
1 Pravčická Gate	**5** Hřensko	**10** Mezní Louka	SLEEPING
SIGHTS	**6** Jetřichovice	**11** Rudolfův kámen	**15** Na Výšinkách
2 Balzerovo ležení	**7** Kamenice Gorge	**12** Skalní kaple	**16** Penzion Pod Kaštany
3 Divoká soutěska	**8** Malá Pravčická brána	**13** Suchá Kamenice	**17** Penzion Soutěsky

tumn. From the last ferry, it's a 2.5km amble back into Hřensko. This fairly easy hike has refreshments along the way. From November to March bring winter gear and extra food.

Hike from Jetřichovice

INVIGORATING HIKING CIRCUIT

If you've done the classic loop via the Pravčická Gate and are hungry for more, there's good news. This often quieter 8km circuit from Jetřichovice village is one of the most exciting hikes in the Czech mountains. Try this in autumn for a truly special outdoor experience. Buses operate between Děčín, Hřensko and Jetřichovice, so

 WHERE TO STAY

Penzion Soutěsky
Wonderfully restored, timber guesthouse at the end of the gorge in Hřensko. €

Na Výšinkách
Comfortable rooms in a family-run farmhouse pension in Jetřichovice. €€

Penzion Pod Kaštany
Basic guesthouse in Srbská Kamenice with a trek-launching breakfast and warm, cosy rooms. €

KAROLSXII/SHUTTERSTOCK ©

Pravčická Gate (p157)

MORE BEAUTY SPOTS

Away from the most frequented trails, the Czech Switzerland has countless other beauty spots few foreign visitors have time to see. Here are just some of them.

Ferdinandova soutěska
Another gorge on the Kamenice between Srbská Kamenice and Dolský mlýn.

Malá Pravčická brána
The famous rock arch has a little brother, the Little Pravčická Gate on the main red trail.

Kopec
Visit this village to see why the region is called the Czech Switzerland.

Suchá Kamenice
Short walk up a picturesque valley near Hřensko with a winter-only stream.

it's easy to reach the trailhead. Taking the red trail north out of the village, it's a 1km climb to the first stop, Mariina vyhlídka (Marie's Viewpoint), a carved timber pergola perched high atop a rock tower and reached by stone and metal steps. Views of the surrounding mountainscape are stupendous.

Passing Balzerovo ležení, a huge overhang protecting carved benches and a firepit, it's then less than a kilometre to your next photo op, the **Vilemínina stěna** (Vilemína's Wall), where a side path leads to a viewing point. The red path twists through tall formations to Rudolfův kámen (Rudolf's Rock). At the top is another hut reached by more precariously narrow paths, ladders and steps. The view from the top, arguably the best in the national park, makes the slightly challenging climb worth the effort. The going is easier after Rudolf's Rock, another 2.8km taking you

OFF THE BEATEN TRACK

This often quieter 8km circuit f **Jetřichovice village** is one the most exciting hikes in th Czech mountains

BEST TOURS TO THE CZECH SWITZERLAND

Bohemian Adventures
Best outfit specialising in hikes in the national park. Picks up in Prague.

Northern Hikes
Activity tours to the region from Prague.

Prague Active
Year-round, easy hiking tours starting in the capital.

to **Skalní kaple** (Rock Chapel), a tiny shrine cut from a boulder. There you part company with the red trail and switch to blue which leads you back down to Jetřichovice.

National park Saxon Switzerland

INVIGORATING HIKING CIRCUIT

The rock revelry doesn't stop at the border with Saxony – the smaller Saxon Switzerland (Sächsische Schweiz in German) mirrors the Czech Switzerland and has some equally good hiking and awe-inspiring natural features.

Coach parties almost always lay siege to the **Bastei**, a huge rock formation rising almost 200m above the River Elbe, accessed by bridges and walkways. However, the rest of the park has fantastic hiking with countless trails, rock formations, waterfalls and gorges that you could spend weeks traversing.

Unfortunately, few trails on the Czech side link with those in the German park. One human-made attraction – **Königstein Fortress** – lies around 15km from the Czech border. This is said to be the largest fortress in Europe, sitting atop a massive rock bluff high above the River Elbe. The offline map app mapy.cz will guide you along the paths on both the Czech and Saxon sides of the border. Alternatively the Kompass Elbsandsteingebirge map does a good job, too.

CZECH HIKING CLUB TRAILS

Czechia has some of the densest and best organised system of hiking trails in the world, a fact you will certainly appreciate when rambling through the Czech Switzerland. The entire national network of over 44,000km is overseen by the Czech Hiking Club (Klub českých turistů - KČT) which sends out an army of volunteers on a rolling basis equipped with paint pots and brushes. Trails are marked in four colours - red, blue, green and yellow - any others you see are local markers. Red trails are long distance paths. The same system is used to a large extent in Slovakia, the Carpathian Mountains in Ukraine and some parts of Croatia.

See the club's website (www.kct.cz) to learn more about this remarkable organisation.

Königstein Fortress

IVAN KRAVTSOV/GETTY IMAGES ©

 GETTING AROUND

Regular trains run from Prague's main train station to Děčín where you can change onto buses to Hřensko, Mezní Louka and Jetřichovice.

The Czech Switzerland

Hřensko

Labské Pískovce

Děčín

Beyond the Czech Switzerland

The Czech Switzerland National Park is only one precious kernel in a vast area of rock formations.

To the north and west of the Czech Switzerland the rock formations continue to thrust their towers and cliffs into the crisp, pine-scented air. The main body of the Labské Pískovce (Elbe Sandstone Rocks) Protected Area lies to the west of the Elbe and the city of Děčín, a worthwhile stop if only to visit the castle and stock up on hiking supplies. Far less visited than the Czech Switzerland National Park, the Labské Pískovce reserve is a superb place to escape the day-tripping crowds and tour groups with some parts no less idyllic than the more celebrated national park. For a different perspective on the area, take a mini river cruise along the Elbe to Hřensko.

TOP TIP

The sandstone rocks continue over the border in Saxony with many more hiking options to choose from.

Labské Pískovce

RICHARD SEVCIK/SHUTTERSTOCK ©

Děčín Chateau

Děčín

TOWN WEDGED AMONG THE ROCKS

The largest town in the area (just 12km by road from Hřensko), Děčín is a workaday sort of place sitting astride the wide Elbe as it hurries the combined waters of Bohemia towards the border. You may find yourself here with time to spare when changing stops on public transport. The town has a few attractions worthy of your time.

Top draw is Děčín Chateau which towers high above the Elbe. It was in the ownership of the Thun-Hohensteins until 1932 and they transformed the complex over the centuries from a Renaissance chateau to a neoclassical residence. Tours explore the grand interiors.

Interestingly, the chateau was used as a military barracks during the Cold War, including Soviet troops from 1968 until 1991, who left it in a sorry state. Opposite the chateau looms the Paštýrská stěna (Shepherd's Wall), a sandstone cliff with wonderful views from the top. Up here you'll also find Děčín Zoo, a restaurant and the beginning of a marked trail into the Labské Pískovce.

TOP HIKES IN THE LABSKÉ PÍSKOVCE

Děčínský Sněžník
Take the red trail from Děčín's Paštýrská stěna to the stone-built Děčínský Sněžník viewing tower. 19km (round trip)

Labe Loop
Head along the yellow trail from Děčín's Tyršův Bridge up into the protected area looping back along a green trail. 14km

Tanečnice
In the part of the protected area north of the national park, make a loop along the blue trail to the Tanečnice viewing tower. 23km

Zschirnstein Loop
Make a circuit of the Zschirnstein rock towers on the Saxon side of the border. Around 10km exta.

WHERE TO EAT

Coffee & Books
Sandwiches, cakes, books and a cosy atmosphere – what more could you wish for? €

Arrigo
Surprisingly flash Italian job for these parts with excellent Czech dishes, too. €€

Cafe Prostoru
Cool hangout that moved some years ago from Prague with smooth coffees and light meals. €

REAL-LIFE NARNIA

The 2005 Disney hit *The Chronicles of Narnia* was partly shot in a part of the Labské Pískovce called the **Tiské stěny** (Tisá cliffs) near the village of Tisá. Director Andrew Adamson chose Tisá as the backdrop thanks to its fairy-tale atmosphere, as close to Narnia as any place could probably get. Another local feature also appears in the film – the **Pravčická Gate** in the Czech Switzerland National Park. Narnia is just one of countless blockbuster movies to be shot on location in Bohemia.

BORIS STROJNIKO/SHUTTERSTOCK ©

The Elbe River

Cruising the Elbe
RELAXING ELBE BOAT TRIPS

The Elbe is navigable all the way between Prague and Dresden and away from the trails, one of the best ways to spend a day or longer in these parts is to take a cruise along the river. The small boats are operated by Labská Plavební (www.labska-plavebni.cz) and run between Děčín and Dresden (Dražďany in Czech) via Hřensko, Bad Schandau, Königstein and Pillnitz.

If you don't have the time to go all the way, just a mini-cruise to Hřensko is a great way to combine a boat trip with a bit of hiking. The journey takes 50 minutes and passes along the picturesque Elbe Valley with its high cliffs and pretty houses – and, there's a bar on board. Departure is usually in the morning, returning in the afternoon, giving you time to make it up to the Pravčická Gate at the very least.

GETTING AROUND

There are regular train connections between Děčín and Prague. In Děčín change onto buses for all destinations across the region.

To reach Tisá, a change in Libouchec is required and it is far easier to make the trip by car.

KUTNÁ HORA

PRAGUE ★ • Kutná Hora

Enriched by the silver ore that once veined the surrounding hills, the medieval city of Kutná Hora became the seat of Wenceslas II's royal mint in 1308, producing silver groschen that were then the hard currency of central Europe. Boom-time Kutná Hora rivalled Prague in importance, but by the 16th century the mines began to run dry, and its demise was hastened by the Thirty Years' War and a devastating fire in 1770. The town became a Unesco World Heritage Site in 1996, luring visitors with a smorgasbord of historic sights. One of those sights is the reason most make the short journey from Prague – the Sedlec Ossuary, known to most day-trippers as the Bone Church. An eeriest spectacle in the land, this chapel is decorated with thousands of stacked and arranged human bones.

TOP TIP

The 'Bone church' is in the suburb of Sedlec. City buses run half-hourly between the train station and the bus station 700m north of the main square. Alight at the Sedlec Tabák stop for the Sedlec Ossuary. Otherwise it's a 30-min walk (2.5km).

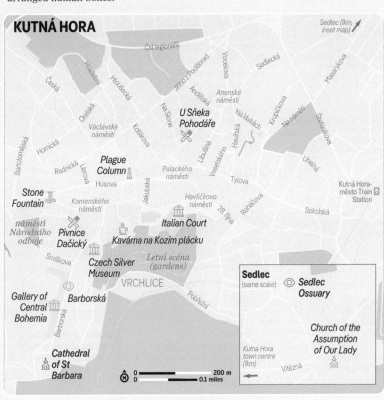

KUTNÁ HORA

Sedlec (1km, inset map)

Čsl.legionářů
Hradební
Hlouská
Jiřího z Poděbrad
Vocelova
Sedlecká
Masarykova
Anenské náměstí
Česká
Orelská
Na lávkách
Krupiková
Na náměstí
Šefaříkova
Václavské náměstí
Na Slone
U Sňeka Pohodáře
Andělská
Havlíčká
Libušina
Veselského
Bartoloměská
Hornická
Radnická
Jerova
Kollárova
Jakubská
Plague Column
Palackého náměstí
Tylova
Uhelná
Husova
Rohačova
Kutná Hora-město Train Station
Stone Fountain
Komenského náměstí
Havlíčkovo náměstí
28 Října
Sokolská
náměstí Národního odboje
Pivnice Dačický
Kavárna na Kozím plácku
Italian Court
Smíškova
Czech Silver Museum
Letní scéna (gardens)
VRCHLICE
Pobřežní
Gallery of Central Bohemia
Barborská
Barborská
Cathedral of St Barbara

Sedlec (same scale)   ◎ Sedlec Ossuary

Church of the Assumption of Our Lady

Kutná Hora town centre (1km)

Vítězná

🇳 0 _____ 200 m
0 _____ 0.1 miles

Sedlec Ossuary

CZECHIA'S MOST GHOULISH SPECTACLE

When the Schwarzenbergs purchased **Sedlec monastery** (2.5km northeast of the town centre) in 1870 they allowed local woodcarver František Rint to get creative with the bones in the crypt (the remains of an estimated 40,000 people), resulting in this remarkable 'bone church'. The skeletons found their way into the church when the surrounding cemetery was reduced in size.

The human remains here are mostly plague victims and those who perished in the Hussite wars. Garlands of skulls and femurs are strung from the vaulted ceiling like the Addams Family's Christmas decorations, while in the centre dangles a vast chandelier containing each bone in the human body.

Four giant pyramids of stacked bones squat in the corner chapels, and crosses, chalices and monstrances of bone adorn the altar. There's even a Schwarzenberg coat-of-arms made from bones, and Rint signed his name in bones at the foot of the stairs. Disappointingly photography is not officially permitted in the ossuary.

Cathedral of St Barbora

GREATEST CATHEDRAL OUTSIDE PRAGUE

Kutná Hora's greatest monument is the Gothic Cathedral of St Barbora. Rivalling Prague's St Vitus in size and magnificence, its soaring nave culminates in elegant, six-petalled ribbed vaulting, and the ambulatory chapels preserve original 15th-century frescoes, some of them showing miners at work. Take a walk around the outside of the church; the terrace at the eastern end enjoys the finest view in town.

Construction was begun in 1380, interrupted during the Hussite Wars and abandoned in 1558 when the silver began to run out. The cathedral was finally completed in neo-Gothic style at the end of the 19th century.

Other Places of Interest

PROBING FURTHER

Away from the big-ticket sights, there are several other worthwhile attractions scattered across town. The oversize Plague Column on Šultysova St reminds us that 6000 people died of the plague here while another XXL feature comes in the shape of the Gothic Stone Fountain, the work of Matěj Rejsek, the architect who designed the Cathedral of St Barbora. This

CZECH SILVER MUSEUM

Originally part of the town's fortifications, the Hrádek (Little Castle) was rebuilt in the 15th century as the residence of Jan Smíšek, administrator of the royal mines, who grew rich from silver mined illegally under the building. It now houses the Czech Silver Museum. There are two guided tours; the second includes a visit down an ancient silver mine.

Tour 1 (one hour) leads through the main part of the museum where the exhibits examine the mines that made Kutná Hora wealthy, including a huge wooden device once used to lift huge loads from the 200m-deep shafts.

Tour 2 (1½ hours) allows you to don a miner's helmet and explore 500m of medieval mine shafts beneath the town.

 WHERE TO EAT

Dačický
Old Bohemian, wood-panelled beer hall with lager and dumplings galore. €€

U Šneka Pohodáře
Enjoy a pizza and a Bernard beer at the 'Easy-going Snail'. €

Kavárna na Kozím plácku
Cute cafe with big timber beams and mismatched 1950s furniture. €

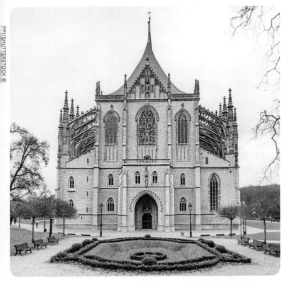

Cathedral of St Barbora

ITALIAN COURT

East of St James Church (kostel sv Jakuba; 1330) lies the **Italian Court**, the former Royal Mint. It gets its name from the master craftsmen from Florence brought in by Wenceslas II to kick-start the business. They began stamping silver coins here in 1300, the famous Prague groschen, which in the 14th century were the currency across Europe (a bit like a medieval euro). This remained the royal Bohemian mint until 1727 and the original treasury rooms hold an exhibit on coins and minting.

The tour then continues to the Royal Audience Hall with its murals depicting the election of Vladislav Jagiellon Czech king and the Chapel of Sts Wenceslas and Vladislav, decorated in bright Art Nouveau style.

huge piece of infrastructure provided water to the town until 1890. The 17th-century former Jesuit College has been restored and now houses the Gallery of Central Bohemia which is devoted to 20th- and 21st-century art.

There's also a gallery shop that showcases the work of young Czech artists and designers. Opposite the Sedlec Ossuray is the Cathedral of Assumption of Our Lady & St John the Baptist, a Unesco-listed basilica which was rebuilt in the 18th century in the rare Gothic-baroque style by the architect Jan Blažej Santini-Aichl (another of his creations – the Church of St Nepomuk on the Green Mountain near Žďár nad Sázavou, 80km east – is also a Unesco site).

REMINDERS OF THE PAST

The oversize Plague Column on Šultysova St reminds us that 6000 people died of the plague here

GETTING AROUND

Hourly buses leave Prague's Háje station. There are direct trains from Prague's main train station to Kutná Hora-hlavní nádraží about every two hours.

Beyond Kutná Hora

Kutná Hora

Český Šternberk

Church of St Nepomuk

The tranquil Sázava River, a tributary of the Vltava, flows from Žďár nad Sázavou to the southern outskirts of Prague.

As it gathers strength before it is consumed by the mighty Vltava, the River Sázava cuts a deep valley, hemmed by ancient, rounded hills and thick forests. Popular among Czechs for summer rafting and canoe trips, the Sázava runs through many pretty provincial towns, most overlooked by visitors on their way elsewhere, lending its name to many. Of the many sights along its length, Český Šternberk Castle and the Church of St Nepomuk on the Green Mountain just outside Žďár nad Sázavou are the most worthwhile, though you could spend a week exploring the valley.

TOP TIP

Žďár nad Sázavou is an interesting place to break the journey between Prague and Moravia, well away from mainstream tourism (except for the Unesco trail) where you can observe everyday Czech life up close.

River Sázava

SAMO461/SHUTTERSTOCK ©

Český Šternberk

Český Šternberk

MASSIVE FORTRESS HIGH ABOVE THE SÁZAVA

Some 40km southwest of Kutná Hora, Český Šternberk is one of the oldest castles in the country and still in the ownership of the Sternberg family who established it in 1241. This Gothic pile towers over the slow-moving waters of the River Sázava, and were it nearer Prague it would be a major attraction in the Czech lands. Inside, the early baroque alterations were added to in the 20th century when central heating and electricity were installed. For visitors there is just one guided tour which takes in 15 rooms on the 2nd floor. Highlights include the Knights Hall with its baroque stucco decoration and the study of the current owner's father, Jiří Sternberg. After the tour, be sure to visit the Hladomorna tower which was designed to protect the castle from attack. In addition to the interiors, the views of and from the castle are commendably photogenic, its hulk rising over a picturesque bend in the river.

CHURCH OF ST NEPOMUK ON THE GREEN MOUNTAIN

The Unesco-listed **Church of St Nepomuk** on the Green Mountain is the reason the vast majority of visitors alight at the unpretentious town of Žďár nad Sázavou. Around 4km north of the train station, Santini-Aichl's zany Gothic-baroque church rises atop a hill and is built in the shape of a five-pointed star surrounded by a decagonal cloister. Five stars are said to have appeared over the spot where Nepomuk was cast into the Vltava in Prague by Václav IV for refusing to divulge the confessional secrets of the queen. The church is full of symbolism in the shape of stars, multiples of five and tongues, another symbol of St Nepomuk. For the time, the design was a daring and outrageous architectural statement.

GETTING AROUND

The main railway line from Prague to Moravia follows the River Sázava religiously all the way to Žďár nad Sázavou making places along the valley easily accessible.

THE GUIDE

NORTH & EAST BOHEMIA

LP PRODUCTION/SHUTTERSTOCK ©

LITOMYŠL

PRAGUE

Litomyšl

A strong contender for the title of East Bohemia's prettiest town, little Litomyšl lies 50km southeast of the regional capital Pardubice. The main reason to come here is for Czechia's most eye-catching and best-preserved renaissance chateau, one of the finest north of the Alps. Listed by Unesco in 1999, it's been in the ownership of the Czech state since the end of WWII. Litomyšl is also the birthplace of one of the Czechs' most beloved composers, Bedřich Smetana (1824–84) who was actually born at the chateau brewery and lived there until he was six. The Smetana's Litomyšl classical-music festival is one of the highpoints of the Czech cultural calendar. Throw in one of the country's prettiest Gothic-baroque-Renaissance squares, a couple of rewarding art galleries and some sugary baroque religious heritage, and you have some very good reasons to head to this corner of Bohemia.

TOP TIP

Litomyšl is a small place and the compact historical centre where you will find both the square and the chateau can be crossed in minutes on foot. The train station is just to the north of the square, buses pull in at the station south of the square.

SMETANA'S LITOMYŠL

The 19th-century composer Bedřich Smetana is by far Litomyšl's most illustrious son and the town knows how to celebrate the fact. The Smetana's Litomyšl classical-music festival is the second oldest such event in the country and takes place annually in the last two weeks of June. One of the best features of the festival is that the main stage is located within the chateau, in the second courtyard to be exact, which is said to have superb acoustics. A sliding roof has been installed in recent years meaning the essentially open-air festival can take place no matter what the East Bohemian weather is doing.

Litomyšl Chateau

CZECHIA'S FINEST RENAISSANCE PALACE

Northeast of the main **Smetanovo Square** stands Litomyšl's spectacular **zámek** (chateau), a glorious feat of architectural artistry commissioned by the Pernštejn family in the 16th century and left virtually untouched, at least on the outside, since those times.

Before you rush inside for the tour, take note of some features of the exterior. Most notable is the sgraffito 'envelope' decoration on the facade – it's claimed no two motifs are repeated across its entirety, a feat of virtuosity indeed. The triple-tier loggia is also quite unique in Czech lands.

Entry is by guided tour only and there are two tours to choose from. The main route takes you through the grand rooms used by the Valdštejns in the early 19th century, part of the chateau that underwent extensive renovation in 2021. This includes the highlight of the interiors, the incredibly well-preserved, private family theatre dating from 1797 which still sports most of its original features.

The decoration of the theatre is the work of Josef Platzer who also adorned the Estates Theatre in Prague and Vienna's court theatre. An optional tour explores the wing occupied by the Thurn-Taxis family, the last owners of the chateau who were forced to leave in 1945.

Interestingly, the Thurn-Taxis had a monopoly on the imperial Austrian postal and transport system and from their surname we get the word 'taxi'. Bedřich Smetana was born in the former castle brewery in

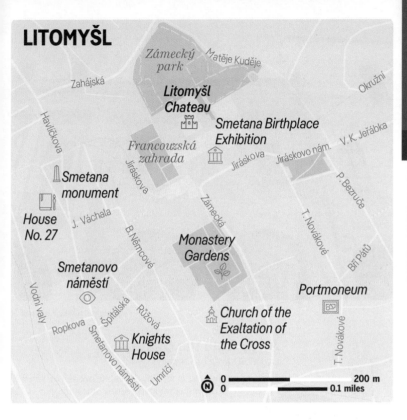

the grounds of the chateau and the building now houses the Smetana Birthplace Exhibition (Rodný Byt Bedřicha Smetany), a modest museum examining the composer's early childhood in Litomyšl. It's part of the Litomyšl Regional Museum (as is the **Portmoneum**, p171).

After the tour, be sure to take those aching feet to the Monastery Gardens on the southwest side of the chateau lying between two churches. The small space to the south is Václav Havel Square, surprisingly one of only a handful of public areas in the entire country named after the Czechs' most famous president.

 WHERE TO EAT

Restaurace Bohém
In the Hotel Aplaus, Bohém has the tastiest food in Litomyšl and a prime location near the chateau. €€

Restaurace U Kolji
A clean, Scandi-style interior and light cuisine makes this a good lunch option. €€

Veselka
Litomyšl's best traditional pub with chequered tablecloths, cold beer and a no-nonsense menu of filling fare. €

RUDNITSKAYA, ANNA/SHUTTERSTOCK ©

The Knights' House, Litomysl

Away from the Chateau

LAYER ON LAYER OF HISTORY

The rest of Litomyšl is well worth exploring and as you will discover, the amazing architecture does not end at the chateau. Smetanovo náměstí, the town's main square, is a slender procession of burghers' houses with baroque and neoclassical facades, most of them resting on Gothic arcading.

SMETANOVO NÁMĚSTÍ

House No 27, near the Smetana statue, is where the most famous Czech female writer, **Božena Němcová**, lived between 1839 and 1840

The oldest and most impressive house on the square is the **Knights' House** (dům u Rytířů) dating from the 1540s. The richly decorated facade stands out among the pastel fronts of the others, the upstairs windows a riot of motifs. Today it houses Litomyšl's municipal gallery which has temporary exhibitions running on a rolling basis, meaning you can enter the house all year round to see the unique Renaissance interiors.

WHERE TO DRINK

Muuza
21st-century cafe-bar at the Hotel Aplaus with a food menu by day and cocktails by night.

Chocco Cafe
The best coffee-and-cake halt on the main square.

Veselka
Brews its very own beer called Bedřich, after the composer.

At the northern end of the square rises the Smetana monument which was erected in 1924 to mark a century since the composer's birth.

It depicts Smetana himself, standing hands on hips, turning to look at something. Oddly enough, the square on which it stands only acquired its name in 1990 – during the communist years it unhappily bore the name of post-war Stalinist leader Klement Gottwald. House No 27, near the Smetana statue, is where the most famous Czech female writer, Božena Němcová, lived between 1839 and 1840 and where she gave birth to her son Karel.

The Church of the Exaltation of the Cross (kostel Povýšení sv Kříže) near the chateau is an impressive wedge of baroque. Fully restored, inside you'll find a huge organ – this is one of the venues for the Smetana's Litomyšl Festival. Litomyšl once had a thriving Jewish community and some fragments of their culture remain today, most notably the Jewish cemetery 2km north of the centre. The tourist information centre on Smetanovo náměstí organises guided Jewish-themed tours.

Portmoneum

WONDERFULLY WEIRD

In stark contrast to the restrained Renaissance splendour on display in town, to the southeast of the chateau, in a nondescript bungalow on a quiet residential street, stands the wondrous Portmoneum where the walls, ceilings and furniture are covered in the hyper-real paintings of idiosyncratic **Josef Váchal** (1884–1969).

Váchal completed the paintings from 1920 to 1924 for the house owner, Josef Portman, and the proto-psychedelic images blend Christian iconography and Hindu inscriptions with a deliciously ghoulish bent. It's wonderfully weird like some forgotten album cover from an obscure 1970s rock band.

Váchal is a slightly forgotten Czech artist who excelled in many disciplines, from painting to woodcarving, poetry to graphic art. He was a Renaissance man, a suitable accolade in this town.

BEST TRIPS FROM LITOMYŠL

Poličkal
Fascinatingly beautiful and almost tourist-free town with some of the best-preserved medieval fortifications in Europe.

Žďárské vrchy
Protected hills rising over 800m in places offer lots of hiking 40km southwest.

Hike to Kozlovský kopec
Day hike (around 25km) west out of Litomyšl following a red trail to the Kozlovský kopec viewing tower.

Pardubicel
A full day trip to the regional capital with its castle and gingerbread traditions.

Bikepark Peklák
Near Česká Třebová, 12km northeast, hire a bike to bomb myriad downhill trails.

 GETTING AROUND

If you don't have a car, getting to Litomyšl can be a mini adventure. From Prague a change is always necessary whether you come by bus or train. Major express trains heading to all points east stop in Česká Třebová from where there are buses to Litomyšl. Other buses leave from Svitavy, Choceň, Pradubice and Hradec Králové.

Vineyards, Moravia

MORAVIA
VINEYARDS & ROLLING HILLS

Long, warm autumns of wine and song, fruit ripening in
the hazy sun, multi-hued folk traditions and easygoing
locals – Moravia is the antidote to Prague's hustle.

Czechia's easternmost province, Moravia,
is yin to Bohemia's yang. If Bohemians are
disciples of the hop, then Moravians are
devoted followers of the grape. If
Bohemia is all about towns and
mountains, Moravia is mainly
villages and bucolic landscapes. The provincial
capital, Brno, has the
museums and a grow-
ing collection of fash-
ionable bars and ca-
fes, but the northern
city of Olomouc, once
a former capital itself,
has the captivating ar-
chitecture and religious
heritage of a pious region.
Tiny Telč, with its miraculous-
ly preserved Renaissance and baroque town square, is also no slouch when
it comes to pretty buildings. The more rural south is dominated by vineyards and,
naturally, wine-drinking day-tipplers. This

was the former stomping ground of some
of the wealthiest noble families of the Austro-Hungarian empire, and you can still
see the glint of old money at former aristocratic piles in Mikulov, Valtice
and Lednice.

Mostly fertile plains hem-
ming rivers such as
the Morava and the
Odra, Moravia is less
about the great out-
doors than the more
mountainous Bohe-
mia (though there are
some substantial peaks
in Moravia's north and
west). The flatter land-
scape means better cycling
possibilities, no more so than
around the wine producing areas
of the south. There's decent hiking in the
Podyjí National Park along the border with
Austria, in the Chřiby Hills near Kroměříž
and in the Lednice-Valtice area.

ROSTIK924/SHUTTERSTOCK ©

THE MAIN AREAS

BRNO	MIKULOV	OLOMOUC	TELČ	KROMĚŘÍŽ
Moravia's energetic capital city. **p178**	Epicentre of Czechia's winemaking industry. **p185**	Moravia's undiscovered gem. **p192**	Pretty, historical square and chateau. **p194**	Sumptuous chateau and baroque gardens. **p196**

Find Your Way

Moravia is just as well served by buses and trains as the rest of the country, and most places have direct links with Brno. Hiring a car is only worth it if you intend to tour more outlying southern areas.

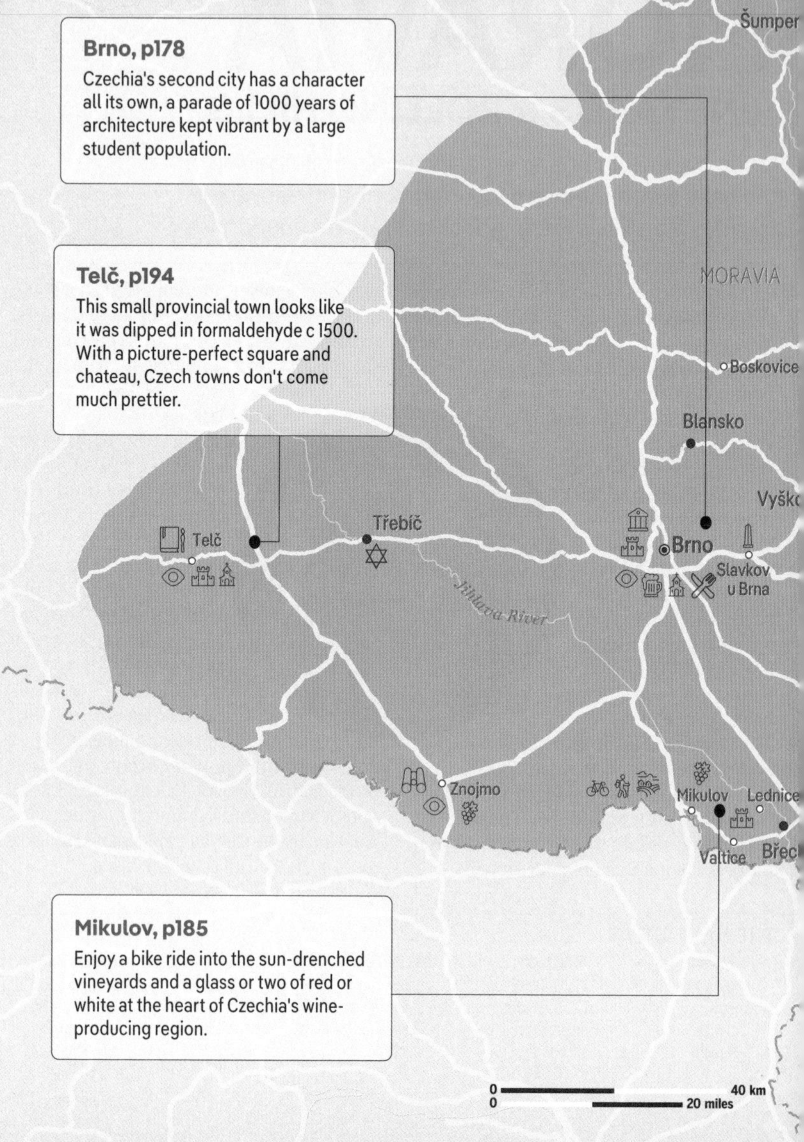

Šumper

Brno, p178

Czechia's second city has a character all its own, a parade of 1000 years of architecture kept vibrant by a large student population.

Telč, p194

This small provincial town looks like it was dipped in formaldehyde c 1500. With a picture-perfect square and chateau, Czech towns don't come much prettier.

MORAVIA

Boskovice

Blansko

Telč   Třebíč   Vyško

Jihlava River   Brno

Slavkov
u Brna

Znojmo   Mikulov   Lednice

Valtice   Břec

Mikulov, p185

Enjoy a bike ride into the sun-drenched vineyards and a glass or two of red or white at the heart of Czechia's wine-producing region.

0   40 km
0   20 miles

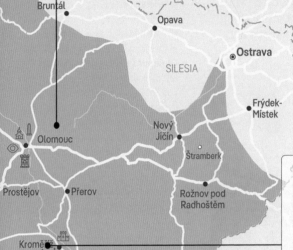

Olomouc, p192

This large and mostly ignored gem is one for architecture and art lovers, with its baroque fountains, multi-style churches and Unesco-protected Trinity Column.

Bruntál

Opava

SILESIA

◉ Ostrava

Frýdek-Místek

Nový Jičín

Štramberk

Olomouc

Prostějov ● Přerov

Rožnov pod Radhoštěm

Kroměříž

Zlín

Kroměříž, p196

Quiet and easygoing, this town of around 28,000 boasts a blockbuster chateau and some of the finest formal gardens outside Prague.

Uherské Hradiště

Morava River

odonín

TRAIN

The main train lines through Moravia run between Břeclav and Brno then on to Prague, between Břeclav and Ostrava via Zlín and between Břeclav and Olomouc. Countless branch lines serve minor towns such as Slavkov, Znojmo, Rožnov pod Radhoštěm, Mikulov and Lednice.

CAR

The D1 motorway links Prague with Ostrava and runs the entire length of Moravia. Having a car is definitely an advantage if you want to tour the southern vineyards but a pain to park in Brno where there is good public transport.

BUS

Bus probably just wins out over train in Moravia with most places linked to Brno and other larger cities by this mode of transport. As across the country, the service is skeletal on Saturday afternoons and most of Sunday.

175

Plan Your Time

Moravia is relatively small and transport links are good so you should have no problem touring the province by public bus and train.

Znojmo (p190)

Weekend Break

● A weekend away from the capital will give you a taste for the region and may have you planning for a longer stay later.

● If we had to choose just two places for a Moravian weekend, **Olomouc** (p192) and **Mikulov** (p185) would get our vote. Spend Saturday admiring Olomouc's exquisite fountains and Unesco-listed **Trinity Column** (p185), then the Entree Restaurant (with prior reservation) for a memorable dinner.

● Sunday should be about hiking a wine trail, sipping Moravian whites in tiny wine cellars in the vineyards of the **Pálava area** (p189) and sampling some of the region's sun-ripened fare in Mikulov's wine restaurants.

Seasonal highlights

The Moravian calendar is all about folk, food and music events with some of the best known in the entire country taking place in this eastern province.

MARCH/APRIL

Easter remains a popular holiday in Czechia. Good Friday and Easter Monday are public holidays.

MAY

In late May, **Vlčnov's Ride of the Kings (Jízda králů)** is the best known folk event in Moravia.

JULY

The **Colours of Ostrava** festival is probably the music festival best known outside the borders of Czechia.

MICHAELA JILKOVA/SHUTTERSTOCK ©, PHOTOBON/ALAMY STOCK PHOTO/CREDIT ©, HAAK78/ SHUTTERSTOCK ©

Wine Tour of the South

● You could spend a week or two visiting South Moravia's wine-producing areas, but three days should to do justice to the **Pálava area** (p189) and **Znojmo** (p190).

● Start in **Mikulov** (p185) with a tour of the town's chateau and Jewish sites, then hop on a bike to pedal the Pálava area just to the north with its endless vineyards and wineries.

● Next day head to relaxing Znojmo for more wine tasting. Spend the third day sobering up on the trails of the **Podyjí National Park** (p190). Don't forget to buy some bottles of the local vino before you leave.

Moravian Full Monty

● With a week or so to spare, you can easily explore the whole eastern province.

● The obvious starting point is the capital **Brno** (p178) where (if you've made reservations) Villa Tugendhat should be your first stop. Take in a museum or two and perhaps a trip out to see the battlefield in Slavkov (Austerlitz; p185) or the **Moravian karst area**.

● Next head south to the **South Moravia vineyards** (p186) basing yourself in **Mikulov** (p185) or **Znojmo** (p190). Hike in the **Pálava area** (p189) or in the **Podyjí National Park** (p190) before travelling north again to see pretty Olomouc and the open-air museum at **Rožnov pod Radhoštěm** (p183).

AUGUST	SEPTEMBER	OCTOBER	DECEMBER
Telč explodes into life during a two-week festival of the best of Czech folk music called **Prázdniny v Telči**.	The **Znojmo Wine Festival** and the Pálavské vinobraní are the two biggest wine festivals in the country.	**Burčák** is strong, young wine sold and consumed between August and late November. This is the time to try it.	Brno's **Advent** market is the best in the region and is held at various locations across the city centre.

BRNO

⊗ PRAGUE

Brno
◉

'Prague is the Brno of Bohemia', we've heard Moravians cheek-ily say of the national capital. Alas, Brno is not the Prague of Moravia and those expecting such will be disappointed. More a workaday sort of place, things are kept lively by thou-sands of university students who ensure a decent club, bar and entertainment scene. Another reason some come here is architecture – the city has some wonderful old churches and a few intriguing examples of daring modern architecture from the early 20th century, such as the Unesco-protected Villa Tugendhat, arguably the best-known functionalist vil-la outside the capital. The city also has several worthwhile museums and a few quirky ones thrown in the mix, dealing with a range of unusual subjects. But the main reason to head here is to use centrally located Brno as a base for other plac-es in the province.

TOP TIP

Brno is linked by public transport to the vast majority of places in Moravia, and many in Bohemia, and makes for a superb base. You can be in Prague in two hours from here, in Bratislava (Slovakia's capital) in 90 minutes.

WHERE TO STAY IN BRNO

Barceló Brno Palace
Five-star heritage luxury on the edge of Brno's Old Town.
€€€

Hotel Omega Brno
Well-kept, midrange hotel offering best price-to-quality ratio in town.
€€

Wake Up Wellness Hostel
Central hostel with design elements and good, clean facilities.
€

Brno Off the Beaten Track

DIGGING DEEP IN BRNO

Brno is a city of almost 400,000 and has many more attrac-tions outside the city centre, as you would expect for a city of that size. Here are some of Brno's more off-beat sights.

Brno Reservoir
This is a major leisure area for the city's residents with beach-es and watersports galore.

Starobrno Brewery
Yes, in addition to wine those Moravians also brew pretty good beer. Take a tour of Brno brewery.

Brno Zoo
Not one of the best known in the country, but still a worth-while excursion, especially if you have children to entertain.

Ossuary at St James
Discovered in 2001, the crypt of the Church of St James holds the bones of around 50,000 people.

Zetor Gallery
Say the word 'Zetor' to any Czech and a smile of recognition will come over their face. This museum has a display of his-torical and current models of Zetor tractor, a fan shop (yes, you read that right) and temporary exhibitions.

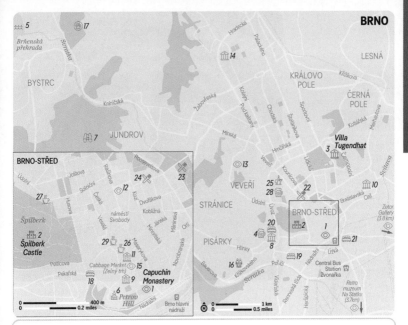

HIGHLIGHTS
1 Capuchin Monastery
2 Špilberk Castle
3 Villa Tugendhat

SIGHTS
4 Starobrno Brewery
5 Brno Reservoir
6 Cathedral of
Sts Peter & Paul
7 Holedná Viewing Tower

8 Mendel Museum
9 Moravian Museum
10 Museum of
Romani Culture
11 Old Town Hall
12 Ossuary at St James
13 Planetarium
14 Technical Museum
15 Underground labyrinth
under the Cabbage
Market

16 Vida Science Centre
17 Zoo

SLEEPING
18 Barceló Brno Palace
19 Hotel Omega
20 Penzion Na
Starém Brně
21 Wake Up
Wellness Hostel

EATING
22 Bistro Franz
23 Pavillon
24 Soul Bistro

**DRINKING &
NIGHTLIFE**
25 Bar Naproti
26 Café Mitte
27 Cafe Podnebi
28 JBM Brew Lab
29 SKØG Urban Hub

Villa Tugendhat

BRNO'S UNESCO-LISTED FUNCTIONALIST VILLA

Brno had a reputation in the 1920s as a centre for modern architecture in the Bauhaus style. Arguably the finest example is this family villa, designed by modern master Mies van der Rohe for Greta and Fritz Tugendhat in 1930. The house was the inspiration for British author Simon Mawer in his 2009 bestseller The Glass Room. Entry is by guided tour, booked

 WHERE TO EAT

Bistro Franz
Colourfully retro Bistro Franz focuses on locally sourced, organic ingredients. €

Pavillon
High-end steakhouse in an elegant, functionalist space. €€€

Soul Bistro
Bright, cheery bistro with an eclectic seasonal menu including several vegetarian choices. €€

179

AHEAD OF THEIR TIME

The bells of the **Cathedral of Sts Peter & Paul** disconcertingly ring noon an hour early, at 11am. Legend has it that the practice dates to when Swedish soldiers laid siege to the city during the Thirty Years' War in 1645. Their commander, General Torstenson, who had been frustrated by Brno's defences for more than a week, decided to launch a final attack, with one caveat: if his troops could not prevail by noon, he would throw in his hand. By 11am the Swedes were making headway, but the cathedral's tower-keeper had the inspired idea to ring noon early. The bells struck 12, the Swedes withdrew, and the city was saved.

POSZTOS/SHUTTERSTOCK ©

Cabbage Market cellar

in advance by phone or email. Two tours are available: basic (one hour) and extended (1½ hours). Because of the high demand for tickets, it's recommended to book at least two months in advance. If you can't book a tour, the front of the house is still worth a look for how sharply it contrasts with many of the other contemporaneous buildings in the neighbourhood. To find the villa, take the tram from Moravské náměstí up Milady Horákové to the Dětská nemocnice stop, then walk 300m north.

Brno With Kids

ENTERTAINING LITTLE 'UNS IN BRNO

Brno will be a tough sell for kids. After the charms of the Brno 'dragon' and the wagon wheel in the Old Town Hall have worn off, you'll have to come up with some more inspired ideas. Both smaller kids and teens will enjoy the Vida Science Centre and its dazzling array of hands-on, interactive exhibitions on the human body, planet earth and technology. Another possibility is the Planetarium, where projections sometimes feature

WHERE TO GET A COFFEE

Cafe Podnebi
Studenty hangout with coffee, desserts and a hidden oasis summer garden.

SKØG Urban Hub
Urban coffee halt, gallery, performance space and bistro.

Cafe Mitte
Superb Arabica and best outdoor seating of any cafe in town.

simultaneous English commentary. Brno's Zoo, on the outskirts of town, occupies a lovely setting and has a wide variety of animals. The Technical Museum is also a lot of fun. Don't miss the panopticon on the 1st floor; this huge wooden stereoscope allows up to 20 viewers to look at 3D images from antique glass slides that are changed on a regular basis.

Brno's Quirky Town Hall

BRNO'S BEST-KNOWN MYTHS & LEGENDS

No visit to Brno would be complete without a peek inside the city's medieval **Old Town Hall**, parts of which date to the 13th century. The oddities start right at the entrance on Radnická. Take a look at the Gothic portal made by Anton Pilgram in 1510 and notice the crooked middle turret. According to legend, this was intentional: Pilgram was not paid the agreed amount by the council so, in revenge, he left the turret more than slightly bent.

Take a stroll inside to see the corpse of the legendary Brno dragon that supposedly once terrorised the city's waterways. The animal, in fact (well, at least we've been told), is an Amazon River crocodile, donated by Archprince Matyáš in 1608.

Near the dragon, you'll see a wooden wagon wheel hanging on the wall. It was apparently crafted by an enterprising cartwright from Lednice. In 1636 he bet a mate that he could fell a tree, build a wheel and roll it 50km to Brno – all before dusk. He was successful, and the hastily made and quickly rolled wheel has been on display ever since.

Unfortunately, someone started the dodgy rumour that the cartwright had received assistance from the devil and he died penniless when his customers went elsewhere.

Underground Brno

UNDER THE CITY'S SKIN

Over the last decade, the city has opened several sections of extensive underground tunnels (Brněnské podzemí) to the general public. The tour from the Cabbage Market (Zelný trh) takes around 60 minutes to explore several cellars situated 6m to 8m below the square, which has served as a food market for centuries. The almost kilometre of subterranean rooms and passageways were built for several purposes, including to store goods (including beer and wine) and to hide in during wars.

BRNO'S TOP MUSEUMS

Moravian Museum
Natural history and ethnographic museum with some six million pieces. The country's second-largest.

Museum of Romani Culture
Excellent museum providing an overdue positive showcase of Romany culture.

Retro muzeum na Statku
In the far southern suburbs, this is the biggest museum of communist-era junk in the land. Apr to Oct.

Technical Museum
Classic technical museum packed with yesteryear technology and vintage vehicles.

Špilberk Castle
Brno's most visible landmark is now a huge museum.

GETTING AROUND

The train station is just off the south side of the Old Town while coaches pull in the Zvonářka bus station and at the Grandhotel Brno. Brno also has an international airport (Tuřany BRQ) with direct budget flights from several cities across Europe and London. The city has a comprehensive public transport network of buses and trams which you will need if you want to visit any attractions outside the medieval core.

Beyond Brno

Use Brno as a base to reach an incredibly varied collection of towns and other attractions across Moravia

Rožnov
pod Radhoštěm
Moravský Kras
Třebíč   Zlín
Brno   Slavkov u Brna

Robust public transport links from the regional capital means day trips into the Moravian hinterland are easy and enjoyable – you'll always be back in Brno for a good dinner. And it's not all felt hats and wine tasting out there! The region is incredibly varied, from the limestone caves and subterranean rivers of the Moravian Karst to the folksy timber architecture of Rožnov nad Radhoštěm, from the functionalist architecture of Zlín to the eerie battlefield know abroad as Austerlitz (Slavkov in Czech). With a bit more time to spare you can take a trip to Třebíč to view its Unesco-listed splendour. Friendlier locals than in Prague and tastier, sun-ripened produce often make Moravia side trips unexpected highlights.

TOP TIP

Having a car is an obvious plus, but make sure you have a hotel in Brno with parking.

Macocha Abyss

Moravian Karst Area

UNDERGROUND ADVENTURES IN MORAVIA

Brno's immediate north has some of Czechia's best caving in a region known as the **Moravian Karst** (Moravský kras). Carved with canyons and some 400 caves, the landscape is pretty, with woods and hills.

The karst formations resulted from the seepage of mildly acidic rainwater through limestone, which over millions of years slowly dissolves it, creating hollows and fissures. In the caves, the slowly dripping water has produced extraordinary stalagmites and stalactites.

The centre for caving expeditions is the town of **Blansko**, which has a good tourist information office that sells maps and advance tickets to two of the main caves: **Punkva** and **Kateřinská**. On weekends, particularly in July and August, tickets sell out in advance, so book ahead.

The most popular tour is through the **Punkva Cave**, a 1km walk through limestone caverns to the bottom of the **Macocha Abyss**, a 140m-deep sinkhole. Small, electric-powered boats then cruise along the underground river back to the entrance. Also popular is the **Kateřinská Cave**, usually a little less crowded than Punkva. The 30-minute tour explores two massive chambers, including the humungous Main Dome.

Zlín

BAŤA'S INTERWAR URBAN EXPERIMENT

In the early 20th century, Moravia was a hotbed of groundbreaking modern architecture. Small industrial town Zlín was home to some radical and fascinating experimentation in functionalist town planning, following the vision of philanthropist shoe millionaire **Tomáš Baťa**.

Adhering to Baťa's plan, factories, offices, shopping centres and houses all used lookalike red bricks and a functionalist template to provide a total environment to house, feed and entertain workers at Baťa's massive shoe factory.

For a taste of the importance of Bat'a and his ideas, stop by **Building 14|15** of the Baťa Complex for the Baťa Principle: *Today Fantasy, Tomorrow Reality* exhibition. There are tons of interesting and interactive displays on the history of Zlín and the Bat'a shoe company, filled with old photos, machinery and maps (and, of course, lots of shoes).

OPEN-AIR FOLK MUSEUM

Less than two hours' drive from Brno, the **open-air folk museum** (Valašské muzeum v přírodě) in the small town of **Rožnov pod Radhoštěm** is arguably the best of its kind in Czechia.

It's made up of pieces of timber architecture from across the country, but mostly from Moravia, dismantled, brought to Rožnov and reassembled for future generations to admire. Folksy cottages, sawmills, bakeries, churches and countless other structures contain period inventory and often locals in costume demonstrating traditional crafts.

The museum was established in 1925 and has been added to over the decades. Somewhat randomly, the museum also contains the grave of Czech long-distance runner **Emil Zátopek**, who won three golds at the 1952 Helsinki Olympics.⬚

WHERE TO EAT

Restaurace U Johana
The gingerbread house interiors distract little from the excellent local and internationally flavoured dishes. €€

La Villa
Michelin-star-standard tasting menus and impeccable service. €€€

Kafec
Modern cafe, and great breakfast and brunch spot. €

Třebíč Jewish Quarter

SLAVKOV U BRNA

Slavkov (Austerlitz) and its surrounds are almost as significant players in the Napoleonic wars as the Frenchman himself. As the setting for the pivotal **Battle of the Three Emperors** in 1805, it was here that Napoleon defeated the combined forces of Austrian Emperor Ferdinand I and Russian Tsar Alexander I. Napoleon stayed for several days at **Slavkov Chateau** where the treaty with Austria was signed. You can tour the chateau, or experience the 'Virtual Battle' which gives you a good handle on the surrounding terrain the battle was fought on. Complete the **Austerlitz circuit** with a trip to Pracký kopec, a hill 12km east of Slavkov where the battle was decided. At the site is the **Cairn of Peace** (Mohyla míru).

Třebíč
UNESCO-LISTED ARCHITECTURE

Small Moravian town Třebíč made it onto travellers' itineraries in 2003 when Unesco placed its nearly perfectly preserved former Jewish Quarter on its World Heritage List.

Dating from 1669, the Renaissance Rear Synagogue is the highlight of the quarter with beautifully restored frescoes and a wonderful historical model of the ghetto as it appeared in the mid-19th century. Entry is by 30-minute guided tour.

The 17th-century Jewish Cemetery on Hrádek, 600m north of the Jewish Quarter, is the largest in the country, with more than 11,000 graves. The oldest dates to 1641.

Třebíč's other Unesco site is the incredible Basilica of St Procopius, a Romano-Gothic church that visually demonstrates the transition between the Romanesque and Gothic styles in the mid-13th century.

GETTING AROUND

If you don't have a car, the decision whether to go by bus or train will be the issue. Train is best for the karst area and Třebíč, bus for Slavkov and Zlín. For Rožnov it's best to have a car.

MIKULOV

★ PRAGUE

Mikulov

Synonymous among Czechs with the country's small but vocal wine industry, Mikulov is arguably the most alluring of the southern Moravian wine towns, surrounded by white, chalky hills and adorned with an impressive hilltop Renaissance chateau, visible for kilometres around. The surrounding area was the only part of the Czech lands to fall within the Roman Empire and it is said that legionnaires introduced vines to the Moravian soil almost 2000 years ago.

Mikulov was once a thriving cultural centre for Moravia's Jewish community, and the former Jewish Quarter is slowly being rebuilt. It has one of the country's largest and most atmospheric Jewish cemeteries. Once you've had your fill of history, the next best thing to do is set out on a hike or bike to explore the surrounding wine cellars and bucolic landscapes or simply relax with a glass of local white.

TOP TIP

The tourist office at Náměstí 1 is a good place to start if you are thinking about getting out into the countryside to discover the local viticulture. The friendly and helpful staff have hiking and cycling maps of the area and can give recommendations.

MIKULOV

Brno (50km)

Jewish Cemetery

Goat Hill

Brněnská

Pavlovská

Najáme

Mlýnská

Koněvova

Boutique Hotel Tanzberg

Poštovní

22 dubna

Husova

High Synagogue

Náměstí

Česká

Mikulov Chateau

Dobrý Ročník

Dietrichstein Burial Vault

Zámecká

Pension Baltazar

Vinařské Centrum

Mikulov Wine Trail

Kapucínská

Koněvova

Novokopečná

Hotel Templ

Alfonse Muchy

Svobody

Vídeňská

Vinařství Šílová

Way of the Cross

Sacret Hill

Purkyňova

U parku (150m); (1km)

Pianstů

22 dubna

Vídeňská

N

0   200 m
0   0.1 miles

Sights of Mikulov

EXPLORING MIKULOV'S ATTRACTIONS

The best place in Mikulov to get your bearings is the central **náměstí** (an imaginative name just meaning The Square). The town hall (containing the tourist office) prevails on the northern side, pretty pastel houses line the rest of the cobbled expanse. A gap in the stucco beyond the Holy Trinity Column leads to the **Dietrichstein Burial Vault** (Dietrichštejnská hrobka), a family mausoleum occupying the former St Anne's Church. The front of the building features a remarkable early-18th-century baroque facade, the work of Austrian master **Johann Bernhard Fischer von Erlach**. The tombs, dating from 1617 to 1852, hold the remains of 45 of the local lords of the manor and their family members.

Few Czech towns are dominated to such an extent by a chateau as Mikulov, the hilltop palace's apricot facades and round towers rising over the scene from a rocky vantage point. This was the seat of the **Dietrichstein** family from 1575 to 1945, and played an important role in the 19th century, hosting on separate occasions French Emperor Napoleon, Russia's Tsar Alexander and Prussia's King Frederick. Much of the castle was destroyed by German forces in February 1945: the lavish interiors are the result of a painstaking reconstruction. The castle is accessible by guided tour only. The standard tour takes around 1½ hours and visits significant castle rooms as well as exhibitions on viticulture and archaeology.

After visiting the castle and perhaps reviving legs with a bistro lunch, it's time for a climb, an ascent of **Sacred Hill** (Svatý kopeček) to be exact, a huge, barren limestone mound east of the chateau, an old pagan ritual site until the arrival of Christianity. A blue marked trail heads from the lower section of the náměstí and follows the **Way of Cross** to the top. There you'll discover the whitewashed **Chapel of St Sebastian** and a photogenic panorama of Mikulov and the chateau.

MIKULOV'S JEWISH HERITAGE

Apart from luring visitors to its wine bottles and chateau, in recent decades Mikulov has also joined the Jewish heritage trail. The High Synagogue (Horní synagoga) on Husova St dates from around 1550 and is said to be the only synagogue in Moravia of the 'Polish' style. It was rebuilt after a fire in 1719 and renovated several times since. Today it houses a small exhibition on the Jews of Mikulov. The size of the forlorn 4000-tombstone Jewish cemetery (Židovský hřbitov) north of the town is a testament to the importance of the community to Mikulov over the centuries. The oldest surviving headstone dates to 1605. Enter through the former Ceremonial Hall, which holds a small exhibition on Jewish history and burial traditions.

Discovering Moravian Wine

SOUTH MORAVIA'S LITTLE-KNOWN VITICULTURE

Compared to the wine regions of France, California, Australia or New Zealand, the Moravian wine tourism experience is much more low-key and homespun. Rather than flash boutique hotels or Michelin-starred restaurants, the wine scene here is more likely to involve lazy harvest festivals and leisurely cycle touring between family-owned vineyards. South from Brno towards the borders with Austria and Slovakia, the

 WHERE TO STAY

Penzion Baltazar	**Boutique Hotel Tanzberg**	**Hotel Templ**
Nicely renovated guesthouse in the Jewish quarter with tranquil garden terrace. €€	Recently revamped, 17-bedroom hotel with well-maintained, rather un-boutique quarters. €€	Beautifully reconstructed, family-run hotel with period features. €€

Mikulov main square, náměstí

CZECHIA'S TOP WINE EVENTS

Find wine events near where you're staying at www.festivalyvina.cz.

Pálavské vinobraní
Wine festival in Mikulov and around, the largest in the country.

Znojmo historické vinobraní
Biggest bash of the year in Znojmo, with hectolitres of local víno.

St Martin's Day
On 11 November restaurants across Czechia serve a specially fermented wine and roast goose to celebrate.

Karlštejnské vinobraní
Celebrates the fact that vines are cultivated around Karlštejn Castle.

Mělnické vinobraní
Bohemia's biggest wine celebration at the chateau in Mělník.

Moravian wine region accounts for 90% of the total area under vine in Czechia. Traditionally, robust red wines were part of the Moravian rural diet, but in recent decades, late-ripening white wines have taken centre stage. With grape ripening occurring at a slower pace, the emphasis is on full-bodied, aromatic and often spicy wines

The Mikulov subregion is characterised by the proximity of the **Pavlovské hills**, creating a local terrain rich in limestone and sand. Wines to look for during your visit include the mineral-rich white varietals of **Rulandské šedé, Ryzlink vlašský** (better known in German as Welschriesling) and **Veltlínské zelené** (Grüner Veltliner). Müller-Thurgau and Chardonnay grapes also do well.

WINE TASTING THE CZECH WAY

The wine scene here is likely to involve lazy harvest festivals and leisurely cycle touring between family-owned vineyards

Further west, the **Znojmo** subregion is situated in the rain shadow of the Bohemian and Moravian highlands, and the soils are more likely to be studded with gravel and stones.

WHERE TO DRINK WINE

Dobrý Ročník
Small wine and coffee bar, serving local wines by the glass or the bottle.

Vinařské Centrum
Wine-tasting centre on the main square.

Vinařství Šílová
Minimalist wine restaurant with reds and whites from its own winery.

Aromatic white wines including **Sauvignon**, **Pálava** and **Ryzling rýnský** (Riesling) are of notable quality, and red wines, especially **Frankovka** (Blaufränkisch), are also worth trying. Keep an eye out for Czech Tourism's excellent **Through the Land of Wine** brochure or see www.wineofczechrepublic.cz for details of wine-touring routes and Moravia's growing profile in international wine competitions.

Top spots to try Moravian wines include Mikulov's **Vinařské Centrum** and the **National Wine Centre** in Valtice (p190). When buying in the supermarket don't be fooled by Czech flags on bottles and make sure your seemingly Moravian Müller-Thurgau isn't cheap plonk from Slovakia or Hungary.

Mikulov Wine Trail

HIKE TO YOUR NEXT GLASS

The main activities here are hiking, cycling and wine tasting and the Mikulov Wine Trail is a pleasant way to combine them. The 82km-long circuit passes through and connects smaller, local vineyards around the rolling countryside, mostly in the **Pálava** area.

The tourist information office can recommend rides along the circuit. Many head for **Brod nad Dyjí** where there are 150 wine cellars. You can hire a bike at Cyklocentrum. Note that inebriation and cycling are a bad combination. If hiking's your thing, head along the red trail north, passing castle ruins, **Pálava Hill** and **Děvín** viewing point to **Dolní Věstonice** (11km) on the Nové Mlýny reservoir. Return by bus or loop through the vineyards around Horní Věstonice and Perná back to Mikulov.

 GETTING AROUND

Getting to Mikulov by train from anywhere always involves a change in either Břeclav or Šakvice. Buses run sporadically from Brno's Zvonařka station. The town can be explored on foot. To get out into the sticks either lace up hiking boots or hire a bicycle.

Beyond Mikulov

South Moravia is a land of wine traditions,
south-facing slopes of ripening grapes, romantic
castles and gentle hiking in wooded hills

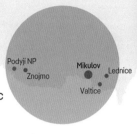

The South Moravia region, along the border with Austria, is all about the long, warm autumn that ripens those grape varieties that love the local limestone soil. The area's wine traditions have shaped the region's culture for the last two millennia and are one of the less-expected sides of Czechia for foreigners. The Pálava protected area to the north is where the best grape-based action happens. Away from the vines, there's the **Podyjí National Park**. The country's smallest national park offers easygoing hiking trails while the Unesco-listed Lednice-Valtice area has an odd collection of follies, castles and, you guessed it, more wine. Quiet Znojmo is an alternative base to Mikulov and best for the national park.

TOP TIP

In Znojmo, don't miss the breathtaking vistas out over the Thaya (Dyje) River valley from behind the Church of St Nicholas.

Podyjí National Park

Valtice-Lednice

UNESCO-PROTECTED LANDSCAPE

The Unesco-protected historic landscape of Valtice-Lednice is popular with Czechs, who hike, bike, sample the region's wines and tour the historic architecture, including two world-class royal palaces. The two towns are about 10km apart, connected by regular buses. There isn't much nightlife, so they're best visited as a day trip from Mikulov or Brno. If you have more time, either town is a perfect base for exploring the rolling hills of **southern Moravian wine country**: hundreds of kilometres of walking and cycling trails crisscross a mostly unspoiled landscape.

The massive, neo-Gothic **Lednice Chateau**, owned by the Liechtenstein family from 1582 to 1945, is one of the region's most popular weekend destinations. The crowds come for the splendid interiors and gardens, complete with an exotic-plant greenhouse, lakes with pleasure boats, and a mock Turkish minaret – architectural excess for 19th-century nobility. Entry is by guided tour, with two main tours available. One visits the chateau's major rooms, including the famous wooden spiral staircase. The other concentrates on the Liechtenstein's living quarters; the highlight is the 19th-century Chinese salon. Other tours visit the greenhouse and children's rooms.

Originally built in the 12th-century, **Valtice Castle**, the seat of the wealthy Liechtenstein family, is one of the country's finest baroque structures, the work of JB Fischer von Erlach and Italian architect Domenico Martinelli. Entry is by guided tour, and the grounds and gardens are free to explore during opening times. Tour highlights include belongings left behind when the Liechtensteins fled the advancing Soviets in 1945. Notice the walls, plastered with kilos of gold.

You can hike the area between the castles or hire a bike.

NATIONAL WINE CENTRE

The National Wine Centre's wine salon, in the cellar of Valtice Chateau, is the place to try and buy local varietals. It is dedicated to promoting Czech wines, with a full menu of wine tastings and experts on hand to guide you through your selections. Tastings by the glass are available, as well as extended tastings, lasting up to 1½ hours, where guests are invited to sample to their heart's (and head's) content.

Znojmo & the Podyjí National Park

GATEWAY TO THE WINE REGION

The border town of **Znojmo** is one of southern Moravia's most beloved day trips, particularly for travellers from neighbouring Austria. People come for the wine and to stroll the village-like alleys, linking intimate plazas with bustling main squares. Znojmo lies between Prague and Vienna and could easily be covered in a few hours as a stopover.

Alternatively, there are some nice small hotels and pensions, and Znojmo is a convenient base for exploring the southern Moravian wine region. The baroque castle is a top sight – a

 WHERE TO EAT

Na Věčnosti
Rare and long-established vegetarian place in the centre of town. €

Winebar Chatka
Tapas and more substantial hot mains accompany wine at this restaurant at the Vinařský dům (House of Wine). €

La Casa Navarra
You probably didn't come here to eat Italian, but if you did, do it here. €€

ZEDSPIDER/SHUTTERSTOCK ®

Lednice Chateau

branch of the Znojmo Museum, it's the place to discover local history. Nearby is the **Rotunda of Our Lady & St Catherine**, one of the republic's oldest Romanesque structures. It has well-preserved 11th-century frescoes depicting the life of Christ and several Přemyslid rulers.

Reaching into the city limits is the country's smallest national park, 63-sq-km **Podyjí.** It traces the River Dyje as far as the castle at **Vranov nad Dyjí**. This is gentle hiking and wildlife-spotting country. The park continues on the Austrian side of the border as even-tinier **Thayatal National Park**.

EXPLORE WINE COUNTRY

Znojmo is a convenient base for exploring the southern Moravian wine region

  GETTING AROUND

Getting around the region is best by car, but buses and trains link Znojmo and Valtice-Lednice with Brno (sometimes with a change in Břeclav). Znojmo also has rail connections to nearby Austria.

OLOMOUC

⊗ PRAGUE

Olomouc

They've been describing Olomouc as undiscovered for a decade or so – and thankfully, they still are! Practically unknown outside the Czech lands and strangely underappreciated at home, this city of 100,000 has a certain authentic majesty, the old centre an almost Italianate ambience.

Forget Brno, this is Moravia's answer to Prague (just minus the Thai massage and cannabis lollipops) The main square is among the country's grandest, ringed by historic buildings and blessed with a Unesco-protected trinity column. Olomouc boasts the second largest conservation area in the country after Prague, the evocative central streets dotted with beautiful churches, testament to the city's long history as a bastion of the Catholic church. When you're done with sightseeing, head for a pub or microbrewery frequented by the thousands of students who attend classes here. Oh, and don't forget to try the cheese, Olomoucké tvarůžky, the only authentically Czech cheese and the smelliest in the land.

TOP TIP

If you arrive in town in late May or early June you'll be just in time for the Festival of Songs (Svátek písní), a five-day international choir event that takes place on the squares and in the churches of the old centre.

UNESCO-LISTED COLUMN

Chiselled into baroque perfection between 1716 and 1754, Olomouc's pride and joy is this 35m-high **Trinity Column** that dominates Horní náměstí. These columns can be found across central Europe but the Olomouc version is outstanding. It is claimed to be the biggest single baroque sculpture in the region. It's no wonder that in 2000 the column was added to Unesco's World Heritage Site list. The individual statues depict a bewildering array of Catholic religious motifs, including the Holy Trinity and some of the best-known saints. There's a chapel at the base.

Olomouc's Piazzas

WANDERING OLOMOUC'S PRETTY SQUARES

Most sights are in the historic centre, with two great central squares that fan out below the Town Hall. Everything is fairly close together and within easy walking distance. Olomouc's main square, Horní náměstí (Upper Square), has the Town Hall and the city's most important sight: the gargantuan **trinity column**. The square also contains two of the city's **six baroque fountains**. Dolní náměstí (Lower Square) runs south of Horní náměstí, and is lined by shops and restaurants.

Václavské náměstí (Wenceslas Square) northeast of the centre, was where Olomouc began. A thousand years ago, it was the site of Olomouc Castle, and you can still see the castle foundations in the lower levels of the **Archdiocesan Museum**. This is the city's most worthwhile museum and traces the history of Olomouc back 1000 years. The area still holds Olomouc's most venerable buildings and darkest secrets; Czech King Wenceslas III (Václav III) was murdered here in 1306.

Churches Galore

CHURCHES, CHAPELS AND CATHEDRALS

Reflecting Olomouc's position as the seat of an Archbishop (only Prague is on the same level as far as the Catholic church hierarchy is concerned), Olomouc has more than its fair share of ecclesiastical attractions. The 1685 **Archbishop's Palace** is still the headquarters of the Olomouc Archbishopric. Entry to see the lavish interiors is by guided tour only (there's a free audio

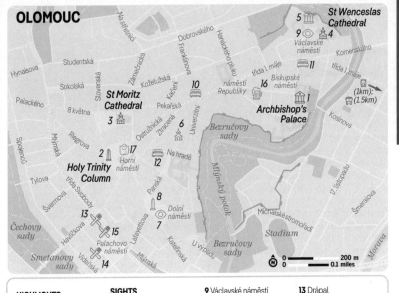

HIGHLIGHTS
1 Archbishop's Palace
2 Holy Trinity Column
3 St Moritz Cathedral
4 St Wenceslas Cathedral

SIGHTS
5 Archdiocesan Museum
6 Chapel of St Jan Sarkander
7 Dolní náměstí
8 Marian Plague Column
9 Václavské náměstí

SLEEPING
10 Miss Sophie's Olomouc
11 Pension Royal
12 Penzión Na Hradě

EATING
13 Drápal
14 Plan B
15 Plan B
16 Svatováclavský Pivovar

SHOPPING
17 Horní náměstí

guide in English). It was here that Franz Josef I was crowned Emperor of Austria in 1848 aged just 18.

Olomouc has no less than two cathedrals. The **Cathedral of St Moritz** (Chrám sv Mořice) is a vast Gothic affair though inside you'll find baroque 'improvements' and the country's largest organ with huge, drainpipe-size tubes. The Archbishopric's **Cathedral of St Wenceslas** (Katedrála sv Václava) was first consecrated in 1131. An adjoining house is where King Wenceslas III was murdered in 1306, an act that essentially brought the Přemyslid dynasty to an end.

In contrast to the bombast of Olomouc's cathedrals, the rotund, 1909 **Chapel of St Jan Sarkander** (kaple sv Jana Sarkandra) is a tiny affair. Sarkander was a local priest who died under torture in 1620 for refusing to divulge confessions and the chapel sits on the site of his prison. He had to wait until 1995 for canonisation, which was declared by Pope John Paul II himself.

WHERE TO STAY

Miss Sophie's Olomouc
Olomouc branch of the popular Prague boutique hotel. €€

Penzion Na Hradě
Olomouc's best deal with sleek rooms and a small garden. €€

Pension Royal
A spacious, splurge-worthy romantic getaway. €€

 GETTING AROUND

Olomouc has excellent rail links to the rest of the country with the Bohumín-Prague-Karlovy Vary express stopping here two or three times a day. Trains and buses run to/from Brno several times an hour. In the city, everything in the old centre can be seen on foot.

TELČ

⊙ PRAGUE

◦Telč

The tranquil little town of Telč, perched on the border between Bohemia and Moravia, possesses one of the country's prettiest and best-preserved historic squares. The main attraction here is the beauty of the square itself, lined by Renaissance and baroque burgers' houses, with their brightly coloured yellow, pink and green facades like an open-air museum of 16th-century architecture. Created by an enterprising lord of the manor named Zachariáš z Hradce, it has changed little since then. Spend part of your visit simply ambling about, taking in the classic Renaissance chateau on the square's northwestern end and the parklands and ponds that surround the square on all sides. In 1992, the historical centre was one of the first sites in the country listed by Unesco. Telč can be approached as a day trip from Brno or overnight from Prague

TOP TIP

The best time to visit Telč is in late July and early August, when the town explodes into life during the Prázdniny v Telči music festival. This runs from late July to mid August and involves countless performances, discussions, concerts and exhibitions.

TELČ CHATEAU

Telč's sumptuous Renaissance chateau guards the northern end of the Telč peninsula. It was rebuilt from the original Gothic structure in the 16th century and has immaculately tended lawns and beautiful interiors. In the ornate Chapel of St George are the remains of the chateau's builder, nobleman Zachariáš z Hradce. Entry to the chateau is by guided tour only. Two main tours are available. Route A (about 50 minutes) passes through the Renaissance halls and the Golden Hall. Route B (around 40 minutes) explores the castle's residence rooms on the 1st floor.

Telč's Historical Centre

EXPLORING TINY TELČ

The obvious place to begin your exploration is on Telč's drop-dead gorgeous town square, **náměstí Zachariáše z Hradce**, with its long row of townhouses sporting street-level arcades and high gables, all painted in a palette of pastel shades. Famous houses on the square include **No 15**, which shows the characteristic Renaissance sgraffito. The house at **No 48** was given a baroque facade in the 18th century. **No 61** has a lively Renaissance facade rich in sgraffito. The square is almost bookended by two gates, the pretty, **Renaissance Upper Gate** (Horní brána) and the hefty **Lower Gate** (Dolní brána). Pass through the former to arrive at the **Ulický & Staroměstský lakes**, through the latter to access Štěpnický Lake.

The **Church of St James'** (kostel sv Jakuba) impressive 60m-high Gothic tower dominates the central square and affords beautiful views out over the countryside. The **Church of the Holy Spirit** (kostel sv Ducha) and adjoining tower date from the late-Romanesque period of the early 13th century. The church has been rebuilt several times over the centuries, but the 49m tower is original and the town's oldest surviving building. Telč's third church is the twin-towered, baroque **Name of Jesus** (kostel Jména Ježíš) completed in 1667 as part of the surrounding Jesuit college.

An oft-neglected visitor attraction in Telč is the **Technical Museum**, a warehouse stuffed with all manner of classic cars, machinery, household goods, prams and machines. The text is mainly in Czech, but language isn't a hindrance as the real attraction is the stuff on display.

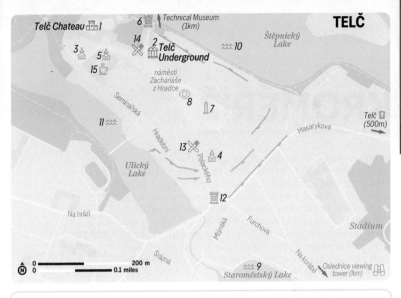

TELČ

HIGHLIGHTS
1 Telč Chateau
2 Telč Underground

SIGHTS
3 Church of St James
4 Church of
the Holy Spirit

5 Holy Name of
Jesus Church
6 Lower Gate
7 Marian Column
8 Náměstí Zachariáše
z Hradce
9 Staroměstský Lake

10 Štěpnický Lake
11 Ulický Lake
12 Upper Gate

EATING
13 Bistro Cafe Friends
14 Švejk
Restaurant Telč

**DRINKING &
NIGHTLIFE**
15 Cukrárna-
Kavárna Haas

Telč Underground

EXPLORE A MEDIEVAL TUNNELLING SYSTEM

Around 250m of the extensive medieval tunnelling system below
the main square and the chateau complex have been opened to
visitors to explore and learn about the history of the town. They
were mostly used as stores and as a place to hide for the locals
when enemies were at the gate. More sections are being opened
up so the experience may have changed by the time you arrive.
Guided tours lead groups through the various channels, and the
exhibitions are comprised of multimedia and 3D video displays.
Tours operate through the day. Book ahead through the tourist
office website (www.telc.eu). Bring a jacket and wear sturdy shoes.

WHERE TO EAT

Bistro Cafe Friends
Modern urban bistro
sophistication. €

Švejk Restaurant Telč
Classic Czech
cooking in a pub-like
setting. €€

**Cukrárna-Kavárna
Haas**
Delicious chocolates,
cakes and coffee, just
a few steps from the
main square. €

 GETTING AROUND

Getting to Telč from anywhere (Brno and
Prague) usually involves a change of bus or
train in Jihlava. To get around Telč you will only
need what is at the end of your legs, preferably
with some sturdy cobble-proof shoes attached.

KROMĚŘÍŽ

✪ PRAGUE

Kroměříž

For those on the Unesco trail, sleepy Kroměříž is worth a day trip if you happen to be in this part of the country. The main draw is the sumptuous baroque Archbishop's Palace, with its commanding tower, rococo interiors and even a certifiable masterpiece: Titian's The Flaying of Marsyas. The palace is a World Heritage Site and a great place to while away a few hours. Outside the palace, there are some attractive Renaissance and baroque churches and other buildings scattered about, and two lovely gardens: the formal Flower Garden and a sprawling park below the chateau itself. Kroměříž is also home to an excellent microbrewery, an essential retreat once you've taken in the sights.

TOP TIP

When visiting Kroměříž, you might want to keep an eye on the weather as the gardens are closed during periods of rain and snow.

MAX ŠVABINSKÝ & KROMĚŘÍŽ

The biggest draw at Kroměříž' municipal museum is a collection of the works of Czech artist **Max Švabinský**, who was born in Kroměříž in 1873. Several rooms of Švabinský's work are located on the 1st floor, while the top floor is dedicated to wildlife. Also worth seeing are Švabinský's lunettes (arched paintings) on the walls of the Franciscan monastery that now houses the **Hotel Octárna**. The paintings were originally intended for Prague's National Theatre. The house where the artist was born is on **Jánská St,** opposite the Church of John the Baptist.

The Archbishop's Palace

UNESCO-LISTED GRANDEUR

Listed by Unesco in 1998, the town's **Archbishop's Chateau** dates from the late 17th century and is Kroměříž's big-ticket sight. Established as a fortress as early as the Great Moravian Empire era, it was rebuilt in the Gothic and then Renaissance styles until it was destroyed by the Swedish during the Thirty Years' War. It was Bishop Karl von Liechtenstein-Kastelkorn who raised his digs from the ashes, creating the baroque residence we see today. No longer used by the Archbishops of Olomouc, the complex was nationalised by the communists in 1950 and remains in the hands of the Czech state to this day.

Its 84m-high **baroque tower**, visible for kilometres around, is the main attraction, along with impressive interiors boasting baroque and rococo murals, an art gallery with works by the Venetian master Titian (including *The Flaying of Marsyas*) and other luminaries, as well as the castle grounds. The highlight of the interiors is without doubt the **Sněmovní sál** (Assembly Hall) which hosted the imperial assembly which sat in mammoth session between 1848 and 1849, temporarily shunning Vienna after the 1848 revolution. The hall also served as the backdrop for some scenes in Miloš Forman's Oscar-winning 1984 film *Amadeus*.

Entry is by guided tour only, and several different tours are available. Most visitors will be satisfied with the 90-minute main tour of the historic rooms, the 'Reprezentační sály a Zámecká věž' tour. The beautiful gardens below the castle are open year-round and free to visit.

KROMĚŘÍŽ

WHERE TO STAY IN KROMĚŘÍŽ

Hotel La Fresca
Modern urban bistro sophistication in sleepy Telč. **€**

Švejk Restaurant Telč
Classic Czech cooking in a pub-like setting next to the castle. **€€**

Cukrárna-Kavárna Haas
Delicious chocolates, cakes, sweets and coffee, just a few steps from the main square. **€**

Baroque Gardens

KROMĚŘÍŽ' EXQUISITE FORMAL GARDENS

Established by the Chotek family, archbishops in the 1830s, the **Podzámecká zahrada** (Chateau Garden) extends behind the chateau to the Morava River. Originally the chateau vegetable garden, it boasts some well-trimmed topiary and is dotted with lakes, follies and pavilions. Peacocks strut their stuff here and there's an aviary to enjoy. Most are surprised that it is free to enter year-round.

The smaller, 17th-century baroque **Květná zahrada** (flower garden; enter from Gen Svobody St) is managed by the Archbishop's Palace, but is located on the opposite side of town, about a 15-minute trek on foot west of the chateau. The appeal is an immaculately kept formal garden, laid out in perfect geometrical order by the chateau gardeners. The main sights are a frequently photographed colonnade and the rotunda, which houses an interesting piece of tech. The **Foucaultovo kyvadlo** (Foucalt Pendulum) was suspended here by schoolteacher František Nábělek in 1906 and is a copy of an original hung by the French physicist Léon Foucalt in the Pantheon in Paris in 1852 as an experiment to demonstrate the Earth's rotation.

GETTING AROUND

Buses run regularly from Brno's Zvonařka station and from Zlín directly to Kroměříž. To reach the town from anywhere by train requires a change in Hulín 6km away. Once in town, the whole of Kroměříž can be easily tackled on foot.

TOOLKIT

The chapters in this section cover the most important topics you'll need to know about in Czechia. They're full of nuts-and-bolts information and valuable insights to help you understand and navigate Czechia and get the most out of your trip.

Arriving
p200

Getting around
p201

Money
p202

Accommodation
p203

Family Travel
p204

Health & Safe Travel
p205

Food, Drink & Nightlife
p206

Responsible Travel
p208

LGBTiQ+ Travel
p210

Accessible Travel
p211

How to Enjoy Winter Sports
p212

Nuts & Bolts
p213

Language
p214

Chapel of St Lawrence, Mount Snezka (p155)
EVA PRUCHOVA/SHUTTERSTOCK ©

✈ Arriving

Prague is the obvious gateway for anyone arriving in Czechia. Václav Havel Airport is by far the country's largest and is located 15km by road from the city centre. There are two terminals – Terminal 1 is for flights outside the Schengen zone, while Terminal 2 handles flights to/from all other destinations.

Visas

EU nationals don't require a visa for any length of stay. Travellers from the UK, Canada, New Zealand, the US and Australia can stay for up to 90 days in any six-month period without a visa.

SIM Cards

Cards for unlocked phones can be purchased at the 24-hour Vodafone shop in Terminal 2. EU phones will work here as they do at home.

Wi-Fi

Free wi-fi is available at both terminals and is fairly reliable, if slow. Elsewhere in Czechia, wi-fi access is better than in some Western European countries.

Cash

It's good to have a little cash when heading into the city centre and there are ordinary ATMs belonging to Czech banks (not fee-charging Euronet) at both terminals issuing Czech crowns

Public transport from airport to city centre

Prague

METRO — 30 mins **40Kč**

BUS — 30 mins **100Kč**

TAXI — 30 mins **700Kč**

PRAGUE AIRPORT TAXI

One of the Czech travel experiences you'll want to avoid is being ripped off by a taxi driver within the first hour of arriving in Prague (although it's now more common on your way back to the airport). The authorities have done everything they can to stamp out foreigners being wildly overcharged for the 700Kč ride to or from the city centre, but the problem persists. To avoid this scam, always use Taxi.eu (svez.se), the official airport taxi company for the journey to and from the airport (book online). Their white cars line up 24 hours a day in front of both terminals and all take cards.

Getting Around

Prague has one of the best public transport systems in the world. The rest of the country also has excellent links. Motorways are a work in progress

TRAVEL COSTS

Prague–Karlovy Vary
170Kč

Train Ticket Prague–Brno
from 260Kč

Petrol
Approx
40Kč/l

10-Day Motorway e-sticker
310Kč

Hiring a Car

Cars can be hired at Prague Airport. Hire points in the regions are not so common. Vehicles are usually of a good standard. All cars and vans come with an e-sticker, which allows you to use the motorway system.

Czech Roads

Czech motorways are new but all too often unfinished. There is a charge for using them, which is paid online. Other roads are a mixed bag with anything between decent, European-standard tarmac and potholed communist-era asphalt.

OTHER MODES OF TRANSPORT

Apart from the buses, trains and trams mentioned here, the only other ways you might find yourself being transported are cable car and boat. The former climb mountains such as Sněžka and Ještěd, taking skiers in winter and hikers in summer. Boats ply some lakes and reservoirs as ferries and the navigable Vltava and Elbe as cruise liners. Only Prague has a metro system. There are no scheduled domestic flights within Czechia.

TIP

The website www. idos.idnes.cz is a one-stop shop for all transport timetables and information across Czechia.

DRIVING ESSENTIALS

Drive on the right

50

Speed limit is 50km/h in urban areas, 90km/h on secondary roads and 130km/h on motorways

0

Blood alcohol limit is 0g/Litre

Bus

Buses go where the trains don't, usually linking district and regional capitals to outlying villages and small towns. Express coaches operate from Prague to major population centres. Buses are often cheaper than trains and are sometimes the faster option.

Train

Czechia has one of the densest train networks in the world, with trains running to surprisingly small villages and along mountain valleys. Big cities are linked by express trains though journey times can be slow. České Dráhy is the national rail company but many services are run by others.

City Transport

Every town with a population of over around 10,000 people has some kind of city transport, usually buses, but often trams and trolleybuses. These are cheap to use and run regularly throughout the day, though rarely at night except in very big cities (Prague, Pilsen, Brno).

Money

CURRENCY: CZECH CROWN (KČ)

Euros

Increasingly it is possible to pay with euros in Czechia though not common. Some supermarkets take euros but the exchange rate will be lower than at a bank. Your change will come in crowns. US dollars are not accepted.

Card payments

COVID-19 pushed the majority of businesses towards card payment systems. All large hotels, shops and restaurants take cards, as does Prague's public transport machines. In small shops and cafes cash is still used.

Tipping

Tipping is not really expected in Czechia and adding 10% to the bill as a gratuity will be met with a dumbfounded (or overjoyed) reaction. Here, people round up the bill to the nearest 100Kč. It's common practice but not necessarily expected. Don't reward huffy service.

HOW MUCH FOR A...

Coffee
60Kč

Beer 0.5L
50Kč

Bottled Water
20Kč

90-minute Prague Public Transport Ticket
40Kč

HOW TO... Save on Currency

Never change your local currency into crowns before arriving in Czechia. Exchange rates are lousy in Western Europe, never mind the rest of the world. Withdraw money from ATMs in Czechia. Never use free-standing Euronet ATMs that charge a fortune, and when asked by machines about conversion, always choose your own bank/without conversion.

ROUNDING UP & DOWN

Price tags in shops don't always correspond with the price you actually pay at the till. This is because the crown is divided into 100 hallers (halér̆), which do not physically exist.

(These worthless coins were phased out two decades ago.) However, prices are still quoted in hallers but rounded up or down at the checkout. Something priced 9.90Kč actually

costs 10Kč. An item costing 8.40Kč is 8Kč. Two items that together would cost 17.70Kč will come to total 18Kč. These days, prices in hallers only seem to appear in supermarkets.

LOCAL TIP

Never change money on the street in Prague. Unsuspecting tourists have been handed Bulgarian Lei and Mongolian Tögrög instead of Czech crowns, or a criminal exchange rate. Always use banks.

Accommodation

Haughty Habsburg Hotels

Prague, the spa towns and the odd large city have some very special historical hotels with olde-worlde, five-star traditions going back to the days of the Austrian Empire. The Pupp in Karlovy Vary is the country's most illustrious hotel, but the Nové Lázně in Mariánské Lázně and the Paříž in Prague are not far behind.

Be My Guest

The humble penzion (guesthouse) can be anything from a family-run B&B to a small hotel. These often have breakfast rooms, if not a small restaurant. Some larger hotels have co-opted the word to sound homey, but in general pensions have more character and are smaller than hotels. Often they are the best choice of accommodation in large towns.

Sleep High

In the Krkonoše Mountains and some other ranges, mountain chalets – more often than not boasting a decent restaurant – are some of the most characterful places to stay in the country. Accommodation ranges from three-star rooms to space on a floor for your camping mat. Book well ahead in July and August.

HOW MUCH FOR A NIGHT IN...

a hostel
450Kč

a pension (for two)
1700Kč

a campsite pitch
400Kč

Bunking Down

A hostel here can offer anything from a bunk bed in a room of 12 to a double room with shower, the common factor being that you pay by the bed (if you want a double to yourself, you have to pay for two beds). Outside Prague and Český Krumlov there aren't a lot of backpacker-style hostels.

Under the Stars

Campsites are normally fields with basic facilities, tents pitched randomly in a big open field in the centre and cabins arranged around the edge. Most have some food service. The Czech climate means most camping grounds are open from May to October only, though there are exceptions. Wild camping is kinda tolerated but avoid making fires.

SHORT-TERM RENTALS

Booking websites such as Airbnb and Booking.com are very much part of the Prague overtourism problem. Whole streets in the city centre have been bought up for short-term rentals, turning blocks into ghost towns and playing havoc with municipal planning. Noisy guests and lampposts bristling with key safes have led to crusading locals lobbying the city council to have these services either banned or heavily taxed. It's all got rather nasty so, if possible, try to avoid booking through these websites – reserve direct with a hotel or guesthouse instead.

Family Travel

Czechia is a relatively family-friendly destination and you should have few issues travelling with children. Locals are often sympathetic to families with kids and, outside Prague, may even go out of their way to assist. Children's facilities are often excellent and baby products widely available, though probably more expensive than back home.

Sights

The maximum age for child discounts on admission fees varies from 12 to 18; children under six often get in for free. An ever-increasing number of museums have interactive elements in their exhibitions as well as hands-on displays. However, it has to be said that many sights lag way behind Western Europe when it comes to making things interesting for kids.

Facilities

Rough pavements, non-existent changing facilities, missing lifts and lack of highchairs in restaurants are just some of the issues you may encounter. That said, playgrounds are usually new and of a high standard, a kids' corner can be found in even cheap accommodation and Czechs are generally very accommodating to families. Some hiking routes have been made pram friendly.

Getting Around

All children up to the age of 18 receive a discount of 50% on all public transport. To receive this discount, all children should have photo ID with them. Under-15-year-olds pay nothing on Prague's public transport.

Eating Out

Many (though definitely not most) restaurants offer a dětský jídelníček (children's menu) – usually fried cheese or a chicken schnitzel, served with chips. Highchairs and kids cutlery are quite rare. Typical cafe bakeries called cukrárny are great places for kids.

KID-FRIENDLY PICKS

iQLANDIA (p148)
Hands-on science centre that is probably Czechia's top for tots.

Techmania (p133)
The west's most kid-centric attraction with huge workshop's worth of science-based experiments, hands-on exhibits and interactive attractions; in Plzeň.

Prague Zoo (p94)
Czechia's best zoo is a must for Prague-bound little ones.

National Technical Museum (p89)
The country's best classic museum for children with countless bits of old tech and yesteryear vehicles.

GET THEM OUTDOORS

A trip to Czechia is a wonderful opportunity to get those kids off their devices and out breathing really fresh air.

Hitting a trail, scavenging for berries, having a snowball fight on a mountainside or splashing around in a lake – this country has options galore for family fun days out in the open. Take a cable car ride up a peak and hike down, hunt mushrooms in the forest, have a pine cone battle, get your kids skiing lessons, spot deer in a remote valley or just find the nearest playground – the possibilities are truly endless.

LEFT: ZHAKYAROSLAV/SHUTTERSTOCK ©, TOP RIGHT: ALLIANCE IMAGES/SHUTTERSTOCK ©

Health & Safe Travel

INSURANCE

Insurance is not compulsory to travel to Czechia but it's good to have. Consider a policy that covers flight cancellation and medical care. Alternatively, or additionally, EU travellers can apply for the European Health Insurance Card (EHIC) that covers emergency medical treatment free of charge.

RACISM

Czech society remains largely intolerant of foreign cultures, especially when it comes to people of different skin colour and Muslim visitors. Prague is the least problematic Czech city, but some locals' reactions to foreigners in smaller towns can be shocking.

SAFETY EIGHTH

Welcome to one of the safest places on earth! The Global Peace Index 2022 rated Czechia as the 8th-safest country on earth, and when you consider that the vast majority of misdemeanors are committed in Prague, it leaves the rest of the country with one of the lowest crime rates in the world.

SOLO TRAVEL

Czechia is one of the safest places in the world – women travelling solo are unlikely to encounter hassle.

WOMEN TRAVELLERS

Czech men are generally very respectful of women and you should have no problem in their company. Marauding Brits and Scandinavians on stag trips are a different matter. Avoid these guys if you can.

Mountain Safety

The Czech mountain rescue service are called out on a daily basis to save people who have set out on hikes without sufficient knowledge of the terrain or the right equipment. Google the conditions you might encounter and dress accordingly, carry emergency food and water, and tell someone where you are going.

Forest Fires

Climate change seems to be making Czech forests more prone to summer blazes. These occasionally happen after prolonged dry and very hot periods. If a fire breaks out in your location, evacuate immediately. These are far more destructive events than most can imagine.

Ticks

The most dangerous creature in the forest? Wolves or crazed wild boars? No, the tiniest of them all – the tick. These guys can carry two diseases – tick-borne encephalitis and Lyme disease. The latter can be treated with antibiotics, the former is rarer but can only be avoided by prior vaccination. Use repellents and cover up.

Food, Drink & Nightlife

Czech Mealtimes

Snídaně (breakfast, 7am–9am) At home a quick slice of bread with something; in hotels a lavish German-style spread.

Svačina (mid-morning snack, 10am) By mid-morning Czechs are peckish for pastries, sandwiches and coffee.

Oběd (lunch, 11.30am–2pm) Main meal of the day, often three courses. Most restaurants offer cheap set menus.

Where to Eat

Restaurace (restaurant) This can be anything from a Michelin-starred spot to a grotty station pub.

Hospoda (pub) Those from English-speaking countries will be surprised to find sitting room only in Czech pubs, places to drink beer and eat simply dishes.

Cukrárna (cafe bakery) These typically Czech cafes have largely disappeared from Prague's centre but every self-respecting town has a couple, serving cakes, strudel, coffee and even wine.

Jídelna (canteen) Cheap, quick, often stand-up affairs.

MENU DECODER

Jídelní lístek menu	**Hovězí** beef
...dle denní nabídky ...of the day	**Jelení/srnčí/dančí** venison
Předkrm starter	**Kachna** duck
Polévka soup	**Smažený** fried
Vývar broth	**Vařený** boiled
Salát salad	**Pečený** roasted
Hlavní chod main course	**Grilovaný** grilled
	Míchaný mixed
Moučník/Dezert dessert	**Přílohy** sides
Maso meat	**Hranolky** chips/fries
Kuřecí/kuře chicken	**Brambory** potatoes
Vepřový pork	**Rýže** rice
Ryba fish	**Knedlík** dumpling

HOW TO... Eat Out in Czechia

The etiquette around eating out probably differs from your home country so here's how to do it. First of all, it has to be said that wait staff in Prague (nowadays often not Czech themselves) are used to foreign quirks and aren't too finicky about following the rigid norms of acceptable Czech behaviour, but beyond the end of Prague's metro lines things are different. Menus in the capital are always in English, but don't count on this anywhere else. Attracting the waiter's attention isn't usually the ordeal it once was but clicking fingers and waving is a real no-no. Mains often don't come with sides, which must be ordered separately. Since COVID, paying by card has become normal, though you may be asked to go to the bar to do so. Round up the bill to the nearest 100Kč.

HOW MUCH FOR A...

Cinema Ticket
200Kč

Espresso
60Kč

Slice of Gateau
30–50Kč

Restaurant Main
Course
150–250Kč

Weekday Lunch
Menu
100–200Kč

Beer
50Kč

Glass of Wine
50–80Kč

HOW TO...

Survive a Czech Pub

So you've chosen a pub and entered the building. Already the locals are staring in your direction suspiciously. So what should you do in order to avoid more disapproving looks from the regulars? Pub etiquette is an important part of the whole beer-imbibing process.

First off, don't barge in and start rearranging chairs – if you want to share a table or take a spare seat, first ask je tu volno? (is this free?). It's normal practice in crowded Czech pubs to share tables with strangers.

Take a beer mat from the rack, put it in front of you, and wait for the staff to come to you; waving for service is guaranteed to get you ignored. When the waiter approaches, just raise your thumb for one beer, thumb and index finger for two etc – it's automatically assumed that you're here for the beer. Waiters keep track of your order by marking a slip of paper that stays on your table; don't write on it or lose it.

When the level of beer in your glass falls to within an inch of the bottom, an eagle-eyed waiter will be on their way with another. If you don't want any more, place a beer mat on top of your glass. To pay, just say zaplatím (I'll pay). The marks on your slip of paper are added up, and you pay the bill.

Beer Champions

Did you know that the Czechs have by far the largest per capita beer consumption in the world at 140L per person per year? Lager-loving Germany is 4th with 99L, and boozy Britain drinks half what the Czechs do (70L).

GOING OUT

In Prague, a daily and nightly onslaught of classical music, ballet, opera, theatre, rock, jazz, musicals, exhibition openings and festivals keeps locals and tourists entertained. Classical music is of international standard while large venues in Prague are often on the tour schedule of some of the world's biggest pop and rock stars.

One strange phenomenon is catching a show by a forgotten 1970s or '80s US or UK stars, still touring unbeknownst to all but diehard fans. (Jethro Tull played Loket amphitheatre in 2022.) Opera is another big draw though theatre and musicals (the latter often recycled Broadway and West End shows) are in Czech only. Clubbing is big in Prague and perhaps Pilsen, Brno and Ostrava –

the rest of the country is quieter in the evenings.

A night out in small towns usually involves a meal in a restaurant, a theatre performance or a visit to the cinema. The spas are pretty much dead in the evenings, elderly spa guests tucked up in bed by 8pm.

There's a small gay scene in Prague, centred around the Vinohrady neighbourhood. Czech pubs have been falling in number in recent years for a whole host of reasons (mainly financial) but on Friday and Saturday nights they are still places to head for a truly local experience. Sports bars are great places to go when the Czechs are playing ice hockey, less so these days when there's football on TV.

Responsible Travel

Climate change & travel

It's impossible to ignore the impact we have when travelling, and the importance of making changes where we can. Lonely Planet urges all travellers to engage with their travel carbon footprint. There are many carbon calculators online that allow travellers to estimate the carbon emissions generated by their journey; try resurgence. org/resources/carbon-calculator.html. Many airlines and booking sites off er travellers the option of off setting the impact of greenhouse gas emissions by contributing to climate-friendly initiatives around the world. We continue to off set the carbon footprint of all Lonely Planet staff travel, while recognising this is a mitigation more than a solution.

Recycle

In the EU, the Czechs are second behind Germany when it comes to recycling. So help them in their admirable efforts by throwing all rubbish into special bins which can be found literally on every street corner.

Hiking Etiquette

COVID brought many people to the Czech mountains and forests who had never been there before. The result was beauty spots littered with tissue paper, nappies, face masks and worse. This is not acceptable behaviour.

Take It With You

If you see plastic bottles or anything else that doesn't belong in pristine natural surroundings, take it out with you and bin it (put it in a recycling bin in the next village).

Forest Food

When eating out, choose Czech venison, duck and wild boar over Danish/Polish pork and German beef. The former live freely as wild animals, the latter are artificially fattened and/or pumped with hormones or antibiotics.

Souvenirs

Avoid the mass-produced souvenir shops of Prague and the spas, those selling Russian dolls, cannabis lollipops and fake communist paraphernalia. Source local items instead from shops such as Botanicus and Manufaktura.

For a variety of reasons, Czechia has an energy crisis that is more acute than most other countries. Hotels are particularly affected. Turn down radiators, reuse towels and switch off lights to help them survive.

Prague has one of the world's best public transport systems – so use it. You may be used to jumping in an Uber back home, but metro and trams are much cheaper and quicker here.

Ukrainian Refugees

Support any initiative you may notice helping Ukrainian refugees. No one knows exactly how many Ukrainians there are in Czechia, but this country has done more than most to help its war-torn neighbour.

Go Meat-Free

Meat production is one of the most environmentally unfriendly activities of all. Czechs may love their schnitzels and goulash, but perhaps you might want to choose at least one meat-free meal a day.

In summer, avoid all open flames in the countryside, especially in tinder-dry forests.

Prague's farmer's markets are a superb alternative to the big German supermarket chains.

High grade?

The Global Sustainability Index ranks Czechia a surprisingly high 13th place worldwide. This seems rather odd for a country whose sustainability and green policies lag behind those of most Western European countries.

Overtourism

Prague's overtourism problem is certainly set to return in the next few years. Airbnb, Uber, scam exchange offices, Serbian trdelník (chimney cake) sellers, Thai massage, British stag groups – just don't do it, guys.

RESOURCES

uklidmecesko.cz
In early April Czechs clean up their country.

mzp.cz
Website of the Czech Ministry for the Environment.

kct.cz
The Czech Hiking Club often organises forest clean-ups and other group initiatives.

LGBTIQ+ Travellers

For a former communist country, the Czechs are surprisingly tolerant of same-sex relationships. Prague is the most open-minded city. The industrial areas of north Bohemia and north Moravia have the most conservative views, but rarely will gay couples experience any kind of negative reaction. Same-sex registered partnerships have existed since 2006. Marriage for gay couples is likely to become reality in the next few years.

Prague Pride

Mid August sees the biggest openly gay event take place in the capital – Prague Pride (www.praguepride.cz). Attracting members of the LGBTIQ+ community from across the world, this bash has taken place annually since 2010. The main stages are at Letná, across the river from the Old Town, but there is also a procession on Wenceslas Square. Many non-gay Praguers and tourists attend simply for the great street party atmosphere.

STUD

STUD (www.stud.cz) is one of the biggest NGOs promoting gay rights in the Czech Lands. The group has been active in lobbying the government and in assisting the gay community since 1996. This group holds events in the country, including the popular Queerball and Mezipatra. They also operate an online library of 500 publications on a gay theme.

QUEER BALL

Held since 2012, Queer Ball (www.queerball.cz) takes place in September in Prague and Brno and is exactly what the name suggests. Each year the organisers give the event a theme, with participants turning up in fancy dress accordingly.

Mezipatra

Every November, Brno hosts Mezipatra, an international gay and lesbian film festival focusing on movies with a gay, lesbian and transgender theme. The screenings are accompanied by countless side events including discussions, theatre events and lots of partying. Find out more at www.mezipatra.cz

Czech Railway Ad

Illustrating just how non-judgemental the Czechs are about homosexuality, in the summer of 2022, Czech Railways ran a national ad featuring an openly lesbian couple, unthinkable a couple of decades ago.

RESOURCES

Three good online sources of information include **Travel Gay Europe** (www.travelgay.com), **Prague Gay Travel Guide** (www.patroc.com/gay/prague) and **Prague Pride** (www.praguepride.cz). The first two maintain up-to-date lists of the best bars and clubs, the last in the list is more about events. **Prague City Tourism** (www.prague.eu) maintains a list of gay- and lesbian-friendly hotels and pensions.

Accessible Travel

Sadly, progress is slow when it comes to making Czechia accessible to all. Challenges remain and often accessibility is a low priority, despite legal requirements.

Steps

For visitors with any sort of mobility or sight issues, steps are the biggest problem everywhere in Eastern Europe. Lifts are becoming more common, but don't count on them, even in Prague.

Airport

Prague airport has a full assistance service for those with mobility or sight problems. See www.prg. aero/en/persons-reduced-mobility-and-orientation for full details. There are 20 points around the airport from which you can call for assistance.

Accommodation

Choose your accommodation carefully, as very few have fully accessible facilities. Only the most expensive (and/ or recently built) hotels have fully barrier-free rooms. Out in the sticks this is virtually unheard of.

MINES & CASTLES

Making some visitor attractions accessible to all is simply beyond the abilities of even the most determined engineers. Mines, viewing towers with steps and crumbing fortresses probably aren't accessible in any country.

Travel in Prague

The official public transport website lists all of the metro stations that can be used by visitors with a disability. See https://www.dpp.cz/cestovani/bezbarierove-cestovani/metro. The vast majority of stations now have lifts.

Pensioner Discounts

All people over 65, Czech or not, are eligible to 50% off public transport fares across the country. Drivers and ticket sellers should offer you the saving. Carry your passport as proof of age.

RESOURCES

Prague Wheelchair Users *(www.presbariery.cz)* works to promote barrier-free architecture and improve the lives of people with disablities.

Czech Blind United *(www.sons.cz)* represents the vision-impaired; provides information but no services.

VozejkMap *(www.vozejkmap.cz)* provides maps of accessible places for people with mobility issues.

Kudyznudy *(www.kudyznudy.cz)* is the official domestic tourism website, in Czech; it lists many places open to handicapped visitors.

MSNOBODY/SHUTTERSTOCK ©

Cross-country skiers, Jizera Mountains

HOW TO...

Enjoy Winter Sports in Czechia

Czechia may not be the first place most think of when they are looking for a winter sports destination, but this largely mountainous country has lots of under-the-radar snow fun to be had, especially if you are into cross-country skiing and snow-shoeing. Some of the Czech resorts can be favourably compared with the smaller ski centres in the Alps. For kids, the Czech mountains have lots of low-key slopes where little ones can learn.

Downhill Skiing

The Krkonoše resorts of Harrachov, Pec pod Sněžkou and Špindlerův Mlýn are the stars of the Czech skiing scene with the full range of hire centres, apres-ski options and luxury accommodation available. But there are tens of other ski slopes and resorts across the north of the country and the Šumava. Klínovec is the largest centre in the Krušné Mountains while Špičák and Zadov rule the Šumava. Deštné is top resort in the Orlické Mountains, Bedřichov is the place to snap on skis in the Jizerské Mountains. For kids, the very underrated slopes of the Krušné Mountains - places like Pernink, Bublava and Potůčky - are superb places for them to learn on gently slopes for a few euros a day.

Cross-country Skiing

Cross-country skiing (běžkování in Czech) is a hugely popular sport in

Czechia. When the downhill slopes were closed during the Covid pandemic, half the country seemed to head for the cross-country skiing trails. Great places for a day out on the 'stopa' (the grooves in the snow formed by a special snow plough) include the Jizerské Mountains, the Krušné Mountains and the Slavkovský Forest. Hire costs very little and winter-only refreshment kiosks punctuate the trails which are often marked out by the Czech Hiking Club.

Other Winter Activities

Snowshoeing has gained popularity in recent years, as has snow hiking. With snow guaranteed in the mountains from December to March, Czech kids are good skaters and sledgers (skiing is part of the Czech school curriculum). Ice hockey matches on frozen lakes are a common sight. Of course, wherever you can ski, you can also snowboard.

COST

Ski passes can range from 200Kč for the day in mini resorts in the Krušné Mountains to around 600Kč in places like Harrachov. Hire (boots, skis, sticks and helmet) might set you back around 700Kč for the day, around 2000Kč for a week for adults, around two thirds of that for kids.

➕ Nuts & Bolts

OPENING HOURS

Banks 8am–5pm Monday to Friday

Bars noon–2am

Cafes 8am–5pm

Clubs 11pm–4am Thursday to Saturday

Restaurants 11am–10pm

Supermarkets 7am–10pm daily

Shops
9am–5pm Monday to Friday,
9am–1pm Saturday

Toilets

Public toilets are difficult to find, especially outside Prague. Where you do find them, they are never free, most charging between 10Kč and 20Kč.

Weights & Measures

Czechia uses the metric system. Decimals are indicated by commas, thousands by pointst

Water

Throughout Czechia, tap water is safe to drink and of very good quality.

GOOD TO KNOW

Time Zone
CET/UTC plus 1 in winter, CEST/ UTC plus 2 in summer

Country Code
42

Emergency number
112

Population
10.7 million

Electricity 230V/50Hz

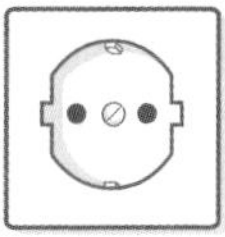

Type F
230V/50Hz

PUBLIC HOLIDAYS

There are 12 public holidays in Czechia. Some businesses and non-essential services may be closed on these days.

New Year's Day
1 January

Easter Monday
March/April

Labour Day
1 May

Liberation Day
8 May

Sts Cyril & Methodius Day
5 July

Jan Hus Day
6 July

Czech Statehood Day
28 September

Republic Day
28 October

Struggle for Freedom & Democracy Day
17 November

Christmas Eve
24 December

Christmas Day
25 December

St Stephen's Day
26 December

Language

Czech people generally have a good command of English. German and Russian are also widely spoken. Outside Prague the use of English is reduced but in tourist areas local people are very experienced in dealing with non-Czech speakers.

Basics

Hello. Ahoj. *h·hoyge.*
Goodbye. Na shledanou. *nuh·skhle·duh·noh*
Excuse me. Promiňte. *pro·min'·ten*
Sorry. Promiňte. *pro·min'·te*
Please. Prosím. *pro·seem*
Thank you. Děkuji. *dye·ku·yi*
Yes./No. Ano./Ne. *uh·no/ne*
How are you? Jak se máte? *yuhk se ma·te*
Fine. And you? Dobře. A vy? *dob·rzhe a vi*
What's your name? Jak se jmenujete? *yuhk se yme·nu·ye·te*
My name is ... Jmenuji se ... *yme·nu·yi se ...*
Do you speak English? Mluvíte anglicky? *mlu·vee·te uhn·glits·ki*
I don't understand. Nerozumím. *ne·ro·zu·meem*
One moment, please. Počkejte chvíli. *poch·key·te khvee·li*

Directions

Where's the (market)? Kde je (trh)? *gde ye (trh)*
What's the address? Jaká je adresa? *yuh·ka ye uh·dre·suh*
Can you show me (on the map)? Můžete mi to ukázat (na mapě)? *moo·zhe·te mi to u·ka·zuht (nuh muh·pye)*

Signs

Vjezd Entrance
Východ Exit
Otevřeno Open
Zavřeno Closed
Zákazáno Prohibited
Toalety/WC Toilets
Páni/Muži Men
Dámy/Ženy Women

Time

What time is it? Kolik je hodin? *ko·lik ye ho·dyin*
It's (10) o'clock. Je (deset) hodin. *ye (de·set) ho·dyin.*
Half past 10. Půl jedenácté. *pool ye·de·nats·tair* (lit: half eleven)
yesterday včera *fche·ruh*
today dnes *dnes*
tomorrow zítra *zee·truh*

Emergencies

Help! Pomoc! *po·mots*
Go away! Běžte pryč! *byezh·te prichl'm ill.*
Call ...! Zavolejte ...! *zuh·vo·ley·te ...*
  a doctor lékaře *lair·kuh·rzhe*
  the police policii *po·li·tsi·yi*

Eating & drinking

What would you recommend? Co byste doporučil *tso bis·te do·po·ru·chil*
I'll have ... Dám si ... *dam si ...*
Cheers! Na zdraví! *nuh zdruh·vee*
That was delicious! To bylo lahodné! *to bi·lo luh·hod·nair*
bill účet *oo·chet*
menu jídelníček *yee·del· nyee·chek*

NUMBERS

1 **jeden** ye·den
2 **dva** *dvuh*
3 **tři** *trzhi*
4 **čtyři** *chti·rzhi*
5 **pět** *pyet*
6 **šest** *shest*
7 **sedm** *se·dm*
8 **osm** *o·sm*
9 **devět** *de·vyet*
10 **deset** *de·set*

DISTINCTIVE SOUNDS

For the consonants, note that kh is pronounced like the ch in the Scottish loch (a throaty sound).

Question words

How?	Jak?	yak
What?	Co?	tso
When?	Kdy?	gdi
Where?	Kde?	gde
Who?	Kdo?	gdo
Why?	Proč?	proch

Common questions

To get by in Czech, mix and match these simple patterns with words of your choice:

When's (the next bus)?
V kolik jede *f ko·lik ye·de* (příští autobus)? *(przhee·shtyee ow·to·bus)*

Where's (the station)?
Kde je (nádraží)? *gde ye (na·dra·zhee)*

Where can I (buy a ticket)?
Kde (koupím yeez·den·ku)? *gde (koh·peem jízdenku)?*

How much is (a room)?
Kolik stojí (pokoj)? *ko·lik sto·yee (po·koy)*

Do you have (a map)?
Máte (mapu)? *ma·te (muh·pu)*

I need (a can opener).
Potřebuji (otvírák) *po·trzhe·bu·yi (ot·vee·rak na konzervy)*

WHO SPEAKS CZECH?

Czech (Čeština *chesh·tyi·nuh*) belongs to the western branch of the Slavic language family, with Slovak and Polish as its closest relatives. It has approximately 12 million speakers.

Around **12 million** people speak Czech as a native language

Czech is a minority language in countries such as Poland, Serbia and Ukraine

Poland
Czechia
Serbia

215

F. PROCHÁZKA 1902

STORYBOOK

Our writers delve deep into different aspects of life in Czechia

A history of Czechia in 15 places

For more than a thousand years Czechia hs stood at the heart of European affairs.

p218

Meet the Czechs

Under that blunt exterior, Czechs are friendly, generous people with a great sense of humour.

p222

The Battle Over Communist Buildings

Decades after the fall of communism, Czech society remains divided on its architectural legacy.

p224

Czech Humour: A Penchant for the Absurd

Czechs have a wonderfully irreverent sense of humour that infuses every aspect of day-to-day life.

p228

Natural-born Athletes

Sport plays a central role in Czech culture to an extent that visitors may find surprising.

p232

Statue at the entrance to Prague Castle (p48)
CHATMALI/SHUTTERSTOCK ©

A HISTORY OF PRAGUE & CZECHIA IN
15 PLACES

For more than a thousand years Bohemia and Moravia have stood at the heart of European affairs – both in good times and bad. Over the centuries, Prague has served at various times as Europe's leading city, while the territory of modern-day Czechia has found itself, reluctantly, at the middle of the continent's most destructive wars.

THE HISTORY OF Prague and Czechia starts with the dramatic rise of Great Moravia and the Bohemian Kingdom around the turn of the first millennium and then, moving forward, reads like a ride on a roller-coaster. For much of the 14th century, under Emperor Charles IV, Prague served as the seat of the Holy Roman Empire – in effect, the capital of Europe as it existed at that time.

A century later, much of Bohemia and Moravia were laid to waste by the religious strife of the Hussite wars. The pattern repeated itself in the 16th century, when, under Emperor Rudolf II, Prague found itself as the capital of the sprawling Habsburg Empire.

And then came the wanton devastation across Europe of the Thirty Years' War of the next century. Fast forward a couple of centuries and, in 1918, independent Czechoslovakia rose from the ashes of the old Austro-Hungarian Empire.

Just two decades later, the young country was tragically occupied by Nazi Germany. The horrors of World War II were followed by four decades of Soviet domination as part of the communist Eastern bloc. The peaceful anti-communist Velvet Revolution of 1989 allowed Czechia to start an optimistic new chapter as a parliamentary democracy and member of the European Union.

1. Dolní Věstonice
PALEOLITHIC PIECE OF ART

Incredibly, archaeological digs around this tiny village in southern Moravia have revealed evidence of one of the oldest human settlements ever discovered. A small grouping of mammoth hunters apparently lived here more than 25,000 years ago, during the Upper Palaeolithic period of the Stone Age.

The early inhabitants left an eye-popping abundance of ancient artwork, including the famed Venus of Věstonice, a startling ceramic figurine of a nude woman, with large breasts and wide hips.

For more on Dolní Věstonice, see page 188.

2. Vyšehrad (Prague)
FAIRY-TALE BEGINNING

Fittingly for a city that embraces so much mystery, the origins of Prague are shrouded in a fairy tale. Princess Libuše, the daughter of early ruler Krok, is said to have stood on a high hill one day in the 8th century

and foretold of a glorious city that would one day become Prague. Legend has it this hill may have been Vyšehrad, an abandoned fortress on a scenic outcropping south of Prague Castle (across the river), though there's sadly scant archaeological evidence to support the story.

For more on Vyšehrad, see page 100.

3. Brno
MORAVIA'S HISTORIC MOMENT

Moravia often plays second fiddle to larger Bohemia, but Czechia's eastern province was the seat of one of the earliest and most powerful empires of the early Middle Ages. The Great Moravian Empire, in the 8th and 9th centuries, stretched far beyond Moravia's current borders. Brno, along with Znojmo and Olomouc, was one of the early capitals. Attesting to the importance of Great Moravia, the early, celebrated missionaries Cyril and Methodius travelled here in 863 CE to spread both the Christian liturgy and their Glagolitic script, the oldest known Slavic alphabet.

For more on Brno, see page 178.

4. Old Town Square (Prague)
MARKETPLACE FOR CENTRAL EUROPE

Prague's Old Town Square has stood at the centre of the capital's commercial and urban activity since around the 10th century. Historically, the square benefitted from the city's position along major medi-

eval trading routes across Europe, and the proceeds earned here over the generations helped to fund the magnificent buildings you see around the square and throughout the historic core. These days, Staromák – the square's nickname – is lined by some of Prague's most important buildings and remains at the heart of city life.

For more on Old Town Square, see page 63.

5. Charles Bridge (Prague)
A 14TH-CENTURY SHOWPIECE

When construction of Prague's Charles Bridge began in 1357, the span was widely viewed as one of the engineering marvels of the known world. The starkly beautiful Gothic bridge, connecting the banks of the Vltava River, was seen as a fitting landmark for what was, under the rule of Holy Roman Emperor Charles IV, Europe's most important city. The baroque statues, which complete the bridge's aesthetic appeal, were not part of the original design, but added only a few centuries later.

For more on Charles Bridge, see page 54.

6. Kutná Hora
SOURCE OF SILVER WEALTH

The small, medieval town of Kutná Hora, east of Prague, incredibly once rivalled the capital in terms of wealth and importance. Enriched by the silver ore that ran through the surrounding hills, the town became the seat of the royal mint as early as the 14th century. The mines and mints here produced the silver groschen that circulated widely throughout Central Europe. Kutná Hora's ride ended by the 17th century, when the mines ran dry, though this silver legacy can be still seen in the surviving impressive churches and buildings.

For more on Kutná Hora, see page 163.

7. Prague Castle
SITE OF A TRAGIC DEFENESTRATION

Stately Prague Castle has been the heart of Czechia's storied history for more than 1000 years, though perhaps the castle's high point came at the turn of the 16th and 17th centuries, under the rule of Holy Roman Emperor Rudolf II. Rudolf's leadership brought widespread prosperity to

Bohemia but failed to resolve bitter disputes at the time between Protestants and Catholics. In 1618, two Catholic governors were pushed from one of the castle's high windows by Protestants. The 'defenestration' precipitated a brutal war across Europe that would last three decades.

For more on Prague Castle, see page 48.

8. Josefov (Prague)
JEWISH 'GOLDEN AGE'

Jews have lived on the territory of modern Czechia for centuries. Through the ages, Jewish settlements here have endured periods of hardship and persecution interspersed with decades of relative peace and prosperity. The 16th century is often considered to be a golden age for Prague's Jews, and the historic splendour of this time can still be seen in the surviving buildings of the city's former Jewish ghetto, Josefov, adjacent to the Old Town. Tour the synagogues and Old Jewish Cemetery to appreciate the community's size and influence from this period.

For more on Josefov, see page 65.

9. Slavkov u Brna
A SLAUGHTER OF EMPIRES

Slavkov (better known abroad as Austerlitz) and its surrounds, near Brno, were almost as significant in the Napoleonic Wars of the 19th century as the feared Frenchman himself. As the setting for the pivotal Battle of the Three Emperors, in 1805, it was here that Napoleon defeated the combined (and superior) forces of Austrian Emperor Ferdinand I and Russian Tsar Alexander I. The battle was later vividly described by Russian writer Leo Tolstoy in his War and Peace.

For more on Slavkov u Brna, see page 184.

10. Olomouc
FRANZ JOSEPH ASSUMES THE THRONE

Unlike much of the rest of Bohemia and Moravia, the stately college town of Olomouc served as a bastion of support for the ruling Habsburg family of the Austrian Empire for centuries. During the revolution of 1848, when the emerging middle classes across the empire revolted against their rulers, the Habsburgs fled here for their personal safety. Austrian Emperor

Franz Joseph I was even crowned emperor at Olomouc's Archbishop's Palace that year at the tender age of 18.

For more on Olomouc, see page 192.

11. Wenceslas Square (Prague)
BIRTH OF CZECHOSLOVAKIA

The cataclysm of World War I splintered the old Austro-Hungarian Empire into several smaller, independent states. These included a newly minted Czechoslovakia that brought together for the first time the Czech lands (the western provinces of Bohemia and Moravia) and Slovakia to the east. From near the top of Prague's Wenceslas Square, Czech historian Alois Jirásek read aloud the declaration of independence to cheering throngs on 28 October 1918. Though Czechoslovakia, as an entity, no longer exists, the date is still celebrated as a national holiday.

For more on Wenceslas Square, see page 72.

12. Terezín
HOLOCAUST FORTRESS

Terezín (also known as Theresienstadt; pictured below) began life in the 18th century as a garrison for Austrian soldiers. During World War II, occupying Nazi Germany transformed the fortress town into a concentration camp and weigh station for tens of thousands of Jewish prisoners who would later be

TENPO/SHUTTERSTOCK ©

Vila Tugendhat

sent off to be murdered at Auschwitz and other extermination camps. Around 35,000 men, women and children died here of hunger, disease or suicide before they could be transported. The town has been preserved much as it was during the war.

For more on Terezín, see page 107.

13. Plzeň
LIBERATED BY THE US ARMY

At the start of World War II, Bohemia and Moravia were occupied by Nazi Germany (Slovakia became an independent Nazi-puppet) and remained under German domination until the final days of World War II, in May 1945. Much of Czechoslovakia was liberated by the Soviet Red Army. The exception was the extreme western part of the country, around Plzeň, which was freed by units of the US Army, led by General George S Patton. The people of Plzeň have never forgotten and celebrate the liberation with a festival in early May.

For more on Plzeň, see page 132.

14. Národní Třída (Prague)
PEOPLE, POWER, REVOLUTION

Communist governments in Central and Eastern Europe fell like dominoes during the historic year of 1989, but none of the people-power revolutions that year captured the world's imagination quite like Czechoslovakia's peaceful Velvet Revolution. The demonstrations started on 17 November, when security forces violently put down a student protest on central Národní třída, one of the capital's main boulevards. Within six weeks, the communist government had been deposed and playwright-dissident Václav Havel installed as the country's first post-communist president.

For more on Národní třída, see page 72.

15. Vila Tugendhat (Brno)
DISSOLUTION OF CZECHOSLOVAKIA

Brno had a reputation in the 1920s as a centre for modern architecture, and the finest example can be seen in this family villa, designed by modern master Mies van der Rohe for Greta and Fritz Tugendhat in 1930. In 1992, as Czechoslovakia was heading toward a 'velvet' divorce, Czech prime minister Václav Klaus and his Slovak counterpart, Vladimir Mečiar, chose the Tugendhat's shady garden as the venue to hammer out the final details of the breakup. Entry to the villa (and garden) is by guided tour, booked in advance.

For more on Vila Tugendhat, see page 178.

MEET THE
CZECHS

Expect to be treated with suspicion, even distrust. But under that tough, blunt exterior, Czechs are friendly, generous people with a great sense of humour. Disclaimer: it does take a lot of time and beer to get there. IVA ROZE SKOCHOVÁ introduces her people

AN ITALIAN FRIEND recently returned from his first trip to Prague and he was perplexed. 'The city is incredibly beautiful. But why are the people so . . . grim?' he asked. To be fair, grim is one of the gentler verdicts I hear about my people.

Usually, it's 'rude' or 'miserable', or at the very least 'blunt'. And they have a point. Czechia consistently ranks low in surveys like 'the friendliest countries' or 'the most empathetic people in the world'. Many have tried, and failed, to import optimism and positive thinking into this region since communism crumbled in 1989. It's proven far more difficult than importing democracy and capitalism. Don't even try. Instead, try to find some amusement in the gloom. Yes, the beer helps.

Once you switch into the 'glass half empty' mode, beware – you might even enjoy it. Before you know it, you might be sitting in a local pub drinking your fifth plzeň, or Pilsner Urquell, with Honza or Jiří, commiserating about the tram being three minutes late.

If there's one quality that Czechs truly value, it's being on time. Annoyingly so. If you invite people over at 8pm, be ready for some to show up at 7.45, while other guests might be stressing out because they are running three minutes late. Probably because of the tram. The country happens to have an excellent public transport system, which, of course, doesn't stop the locals from complaining about it.

Complaining is a national sport, an ancient craft passed from generation to generation as a way to bond with thy neighbour. Bragging about how much you love your job or how talented your kids are is often met with an eye roll.

Smiles and lighthearted pleasantries don't come easily to the Czechs, so you might be fooled into thinking etiquette isn't important at all. And you might be wrong. It's surprisingly important here to have 'good manners'.

This can mean anything from taking your shoes off in someone's home and handling your cutlery properly to accepting copious amounts of unsolicited advice and predictions of calamity (your new business venture is naive and bound to fail) while offering up your seat to the elderly or pregnant.

Granted, the last thing you might need after a long day dealing with grumpy people is an eager teenager courteously springing up from his seat because they cast you as 'old enough to need to sit'. But hey, at least the tram arrived on time, am I right?

RELIGION

Czechia is one of the least religious countries in the world and getting more so with each new generation. Young Czech people are the least religious in Europe: 91% of 16- to 29-year-olds say they have no religion.

NEW-FOUND FREEDOMS

I grew up in the highlands in the middle of what used to be Czechoslovakia, sheltered from just about everything deemed dangerous: high winds, high fashion, Western music and most forms of freedom.

I was 12 years old when communism ended and that's when everything changed. Our history books at school were hastily replaced with updated ones. It wasn't mandatory to learn Russian anymore. Our Russian teachers became English teachers overnight, although they were just a couple chapters ahead of us. Most of us didn't know what to do with all this newfound freedom but we were hungry to travel and see new places. Especially places that had high winds and high fashion. I was 17 the first time I saw an ocean. Coming from a sheltered, landlocked place, this was a life-changing experience. I was hooked. Out of all the freedoms out there, the freedom to see an ocean is still my favourite.

223

THE BATTLE OVER COMMUNIST BUILDINGS

Is communist-era architecture worth preserving? Decades after the fall of communism, Czech society remains deeply divided on its architectural legacy

A HIGHLIGHT of any trip to Czechia is the chance to get up close and personal with some exquisitely preserved examples of European architecture through the ages. A trip here is not unlike attending a university seminar on historic architecture – but with the chance to drink beer as well.

Thanks to the fact that Prague and the rest of the country were spared significant war damage over the centuries, visitors are treated to a nearly unbroken line of architectural development.

The earliest surviving buildings – from the Romanesque period around the turn of the first millennium – seamlessly give way to the grand 13th- and 14th-century Gothic structures of Prague, like Prague Castle or the Old Town Hall.

Later centuries brought the symmetrical, Italian-influenced Renaissance and lavish, hypnotic baroque that was favoured by the Catholic Church and Habsburg monarchy. Czechia is also brimming with examples of those revivalist 'neo' styles –

such as 'Neo-Renaissance' and 'Neoclassical' – that were all the rage throughout the 19th century. Fans of sumptuous, early-20th-century art nouveau need look no further than Prague's Municipal House to get their fix. Cities like Brno and Zlín were hotbeds of 1920s' functionalism and early-Modern.

Brno's ground-breaking Vila Tugendhat predated by decades the massively popular 'mid-century modern' style that wouldn't come to much of the rest of the world until the 1950s and '60s. Czechs certainly understand the value of historic architecture and the necessity of preserving old buildings. That is, however, until you get to the legacy of buildings that were designed and built during the communist period from the late 1940s through the 1980s. That's where this consensus on preserving history starts to fray and opinions on aesthetics start to get heated.

More than three decades since the fall of communism, Czech society remains deeply divided on the architectural

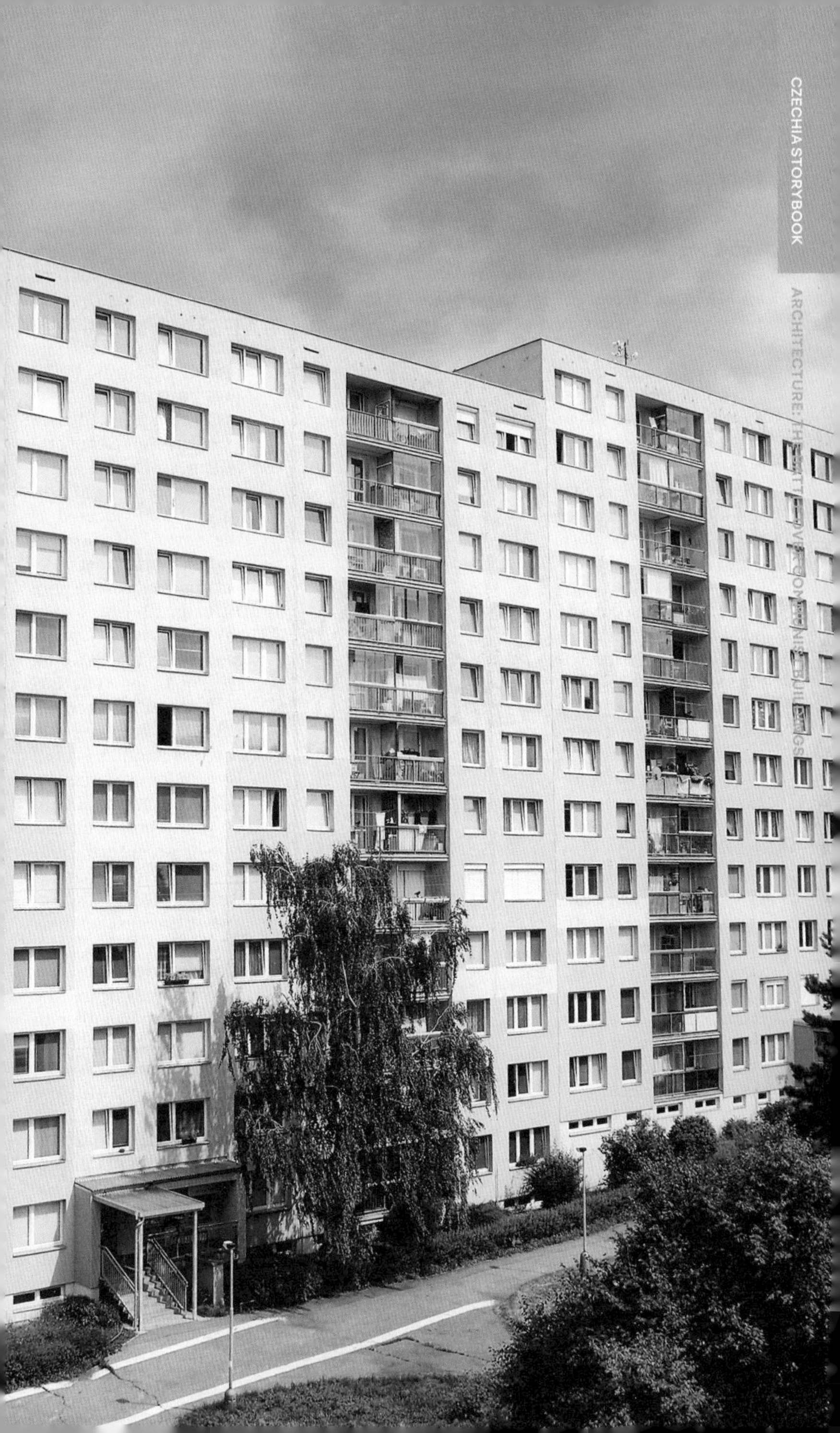

legacy of communism. Some people want to fix up and preserve the buildings for practical reasons and as a reminder of the country's recent history; others want to rip everything down and pretend communism never happened.

Know Your Brutalism

The earliest examples of communist-era architecture, from the late 1940s and 1950s, were built in the style of Socialist-Realism and imported directly from the Soviet Union. Socialist-Realist buildings tend to be grossly oversized and marked with mosaics and decorations that uphold the ideological line at the time of glorifying workers and peasants. One of the best-known Socialist-Realist buildings in Prague is the 1956 Hotel International (pictured) in the district of Dejvice, with its soaring towers, mosaics and impressive interiors. Olomouc's Socialist-Realist astronomical clock, built on the face of the town hall in 1955, provides a marked contrast to Prague's much-older astronomical clock. Instead of a parade of figurines from the Middle Ages, as in Prague, Olomouc's clock features a shockingly modern display of industrial workers and tradesmen.

In the 1970s, Czech architects took their cues from the West and crafted their own brand of communist-era brutalism – and this is the style Czechs most closely associate with communism. Brutalism takes its name from the French term for raw concrete (béton brut) and was extremely popular around the world (Boston's City Hall and London's Barbican Centre are good examples). Czech brutalism is similar to its Western cousins in that the buildings typically reject decorative elements and instead highlight less aesthetically pleasing aspects, such as the construction materials used to build it (often raw concrete or steel) or details like exposed pipes and ducts. The conceptual idea behind brutalism was to reveal the buildings' innards in order to make them more transparent. In reality, brutalist buildings are hard to love. Britain's King Charles III (then as Prince Charles) once famously called the buildings 'carbuncles'.

FABIANO WAEWELL/SHUTTERSTOCK © ARCHITECTS: VĚRA MACHONINOVÁ AND VLADIMÍR MACHONIN

Czechia is filled with excellent examples of brutalism. In Prague alone, both the prominent Kotva and Máj (located at the corner of Národní and Spálená streets) department stores are pure 1970s brutalism. Máj is said (charitably) to be modelled on Paris's Centre Pompidou. The former Hotel Intercontinental in Prague's Old Town is another brutalist gem (or eyesore). Hotel Thermal in Karlovy Vary – host venue for the city's international film festival – might well be the country's best-known brutalist building.

> **THE REAL BATTLE SEEMS TO HAVE LITTLE TO DO WITH THE QUALITY OF THE BUILDINGS THEMSELVES, BUT RATHER THE CONTINUAL TUG-OF-WAR CONCERNING THE LEGACY OF COMMUNISM ITSELF**

War over Memory

Like urban warfare, the battles over whether to preserve these buildings are often fought house-to-house. In 2019, the Kotva department store finally gained protected status from the Czech Ministry of Culture, ensuring it cannot be knocked down. That same year, a similar communist-era building in Prague, the brutalist Transgas complex in Vinohrady, was unceremoniously demolished as an eyesore. Czechia's cultural officials say they take several factors into consideration when deciding whether to grant a building protected status. These include things

Hotel Thermal (p120), Karlovy Vary

like how important or ground-breaking the structure was at the time it was built and how effectively it articulates a particular style.

The real battle seems to have little to do with the quality of the buildings themselves, but rather with the continual tug-of-war concerning the legacy of communism itself. Some three decades after the fall of communism, a significant proportion of Czech society understandably continues to see nothing redeeming about an authoritarian system that controlled their lives and limited their freedoms. For them, the buildings are constant reminders of a corrupt and immoral system.

Local architects designing today, they say, would be better off adopting the best of contemporary styles or turning the clock back to the last great Czech architectural iteration: functionalism from the 1920s.

On the other side, fans of preservation point out that fashions invariably change over time, and what one generation considers to be hideous can often be viewed by later generations as something beautiful (or at least interesting). After all, the baroque statues on the Charles Bridge were also once considered eyesores – the work of over-zealous Catholic overlords despoiling a dignified Gothic bridge.

These days, of course, it's exactly that tension between baroque and Gothic that gives the bridge its unique energy and beauty.

CZECH HUMOUR: A PENCHANT FOR THE ABSURD

While it might not immediately jump off the page to visitors, Czechs have a unique and wonderfully irreverent sense of humour that infuses every aspect of day-to-day life, writes Mark Baker

CZECH HUMOUR is hard to describe in a few words without resorting to generalisations, but the local wit has much in common with British humour – think Monty Python – in that it's dry, dark and drawn to absurdity. There's rarely any room for pathos, hypocrisy or overt sentimentality.

It's no coincidence that old British TV series, such as Monty Python's Flying Circus, remain wildly popular with local audiences. Sir Michael Palin, one of the members of the original Monty Python troupe, even once famously repaid the compliment, remarking that Czechia, among nations, may have the world's greatest sense of humour.

Speaking to British television in 2019, shortly after being knighted for service to culture, Palin said Czechs simply 'have a feeling that everything is up for laughter'. He said many countries have a 'laughter ceiling', meaning that some sensitive subjects remain off-limits. 'But not in the Czech Republic'.

This local appreciation for the absurd was on full display a few years ago in a TV poll where Czechs were asked to name the 'greatest' Czech person who'd ever lived.

Instead of selecting one of several deserving figures, such as Emperor Charles IV, Jan Hus, Tomáš Masaryk or Václav Havel, viewers instead overwhelmingly went with a fictional, comical everyman named Jára Cimrman, who had been created in the 1960s for a popular radio comedy. Carrying the farce a step further, Cimrman was later disqualified for the honour, because he had never actually 'lived'.

Lampooning the Empire

It's not clear just when and how Czechs developed this penchant for irreverence. Certainly, early Czech historical figures like Charles IV or the ever-stern Jan Hus weren't exactly famous for their great sense of humour. Czech wit really came into form during the late 19th and early 20th centuries, when the emerging Czech nation found itself trapped within an aging Austro-Hungarian Empire. The Habsburg monarchy, at the time already widely seen as a holdover from the Middle Ages, was rife with the kind of empty symbolism, hypocrisy and stale tradition that was ripe for lampooning.

In his 1921 comic classic, *The Good Soldier Švejk*, Czech author Jaroslav Hašek took full aim at the absurdities of life under the empire with his epic tale of a Czech Forrest Gump figure who manages to ride out the horrors of World War I through sheer stupidity (or perhaps through intelligence masquerading as stupidity?). While not many Czechs identify with Švejk – the novel's central character – they certainly recognise the dire (and ludicrous) situation the nation found itself in during that war, when Czechs were called on to defend to the death an archaic empire built largely on bombast. Hašek appeared to be saying that idiocy was the only rational response to the situation. Right from the book's first sentence, readers know they're in for a comic ride. It begins with an immortal line spoken by Švejk's cleaner, Mrs Muller. She remarks: 'And so they've killed our Ferdinand'. Here, she's referring to the tragic assassination in Sarajevo in 1914 of the Austrian Archduke Franz Ferdinand and his wife that sparked World War I and would drag the Czechs into war. Švejk responds with his characteristic cluelessness: 'Which Ferdinand, Mrs Muller? I know of two. One is a messenger at Prusa's, the chemist's, who once drank a bottle of hair oil there by mistake. And the other is Ferdinand Kokoška, who collects dog manure. Neither of them is any loss'.

Humour as a Tonic

Dark humour was certainly a necessary and healthy reaction to the difficult years of the Nazi occupation during World War II and of Soviet-imposed communism after the war. In the first decade of communism, during the 1950s, most of the jokes aimed at the system were forced underground and shared only between close friends and family members.

In one of his early books, fittingly titled *The Joke*, Czech author Milan Kundera writes of what could happen when a private joke went public. In the book, the main character, a young guy named Ludvik, feels rejected by his girlfriend, a devoted communist. In a fit of pique, he sends her a postcard emblazoned with a tongue-in-cheek reference to Marx and, in the process,

ends up changing his life forever. Echoing Marx's famous line that 'Religion is the opiate of the people', Ludvik writes jokingly that 'Optimism is the opiate of mankind! A healthy spirit stinks of stupidity! Long live Trotsky!' Things proceed poorly from there.

A brief political thaw and easing of censorship in the mid-1960s allowed, once again, for a fuller, public display of Czech humour. Film directors from the period, like Miloš Forman and Jiří Menzel, skilfully tiptoed around existing restrictions and crafted masterpieces like The Fireman's Ball (Hoří, má panenko), Loves of a Blonde (Lásky jedné plavovlásky) and Closely Watched Trains (Ostře sledované vlaky), which went on to win prizes around the world.

These films drew on classic, bawdy elements of Czech humour, the slapstick and appreciation of the absurd, while also telling stories that moved the heart and gently took the ruling communists to task. Forman's Loves of a Blonde, for example, takes place in a bleak factory town where lonely women work dull, endless shifts as shoemakers.

The factory director decides to try to improve morale by inviting over a group of Russian soldiers from a nearby base for a big party. Things, of course, don't go according to plan. The Russian soldiers are older than expected and many of them are married. In a classic comic scene from the film, one of the soldiers is so eager to rip off his wedding ring, that he pulls a bit too hard. The ring then rolls all the way across the dance floor and up to the shoes of one of the young women waiting to dance.

Joking Under Duress

Czechs' innate sense of comic creativity helped them immeasurably to cope with their darkest moment in modern history: the Soviet-led Warsaw Pact invasion of August 1968. The Kremlin had ordered tanks and troops over the border to put down a series of political and economic reforms that the Russians deemed too liberal. With the Czechoslovak Army confined to barracks, the general population did what they could to thwart the invaders. They painted over street signs and changed road-markers in order to confuse the Soviet tank drivers.

The period of 'normalisation' that followed the invasion put an end to the manic creativity of the 1960s, but elements of classic Czech humour thrived in the 1970s and '80s, and films from this period remain popular today. While directly criticising the Soviet Union was off-limits, film directors instead poked fun at social conventions of life in Czechoslovakia. One classic from the period, Run, Waiter, Run! (Vrchní, prchni!), starring comedic icons Josef Abrhám and Zdeněk Svěrák, follows a frustrated bookstore manager (Abrhám) who concocts a crazy scheme to earn money by masquerading as a pay waiter and pocketing people's tabs in restaurants.

Needless to say the deception lands him in hot water – most famously in a scene where Svěrák's character recognises him on the street and Abrhám comically modifies his voice to evade detection. The conceit is so ridiculous (a fundamental element of local humour that endures to this day), that it's laugh-out-loud funny.

SERGEY PHOTO/SHUTTERSTOCK ©

'THE CONCEIT IS SO RIDICULOUS THAT IT'S LAUGH-OUT-LOUD FUNNY.'

Wit and Wisdom of David Černý

Something of this signature Czech cheekiness – sharpened to make larger political or cultural points – can be seen around Prague today in the various installations of local artist David Černý. Černý gained fame in the years after the 1989 Velvet Revolution for painting over a sombre Soviet WWII war memorial in Prague – an old Russian tank – in a shocking shade of pink. With this thin coating of paint, Černý covered over generations of Soviet-era myth-making and machismo surrounding the war. Some people, naturally, complained the act was irreverent and sought to punish the artist, but most people simply, instinctively, laughed it off. The tank was suddenly transformed into a monument to Soviet hypocrisy.

Highlighting the absurdities of life under communism was a common early theme of Černý's, such as with his big bronze sculpture, Quo Vadis, which stands today in the garden of the German embassy in Malá Strana (sadly off limits to the public). The work depicts an old East German car, a Trabant, standing on four legs. It recalls the dramatic days of late 1989, when thousands of East Germans fled in their cars to Prague on their way to new lives in West Germany. Here, the artist mocks the old regime and calls out the obvious irony of people bolting communism in their own decrepit, communist-made vehicles.

Černý can be just as tough on Czech heroes and Czech history as on the country's former overlords. One of his most beloved works, Horse (Kůň), hangs from a ceiling in the Lucerna shopping passage, just off Wenceslas Square, for all to see. In this work, he's placed one of the country's patron saints, St Wenceslas, ludicrously seated astride an obviously dead horse (complete with tongue hanging out).

Černý pokes fun both at Czech history generally and the pomposity of Josef Václav Myslbek's grand statue of the same saint just a few meters away at the top of the square.

ONDREJ HAJEK/SHUTTERSTOCK ©

NATURAL-BORN ATHLETES

Czechs are not just inveterate sportspeople, but sport itself plays a central role in Czech culture to an extent that visitors may find surprising

CZECHS APPEAR to be natural-born athletes. Starting from a very young age, Czech children, through organised school trips, are introduced to activities like hiking and skiing. By the time a child has reached their early teens, they may have started to specialise in a particular sport like gymnastics, tennis, volleyball, football (soccer) or, especially, ice hockey. High school students who show promise in any of these sports, and several others, are invariably promoted to play in the various developmental leagues, supported by the biggest sports clubs and national associations.

This strong emphasis on sport and athletic achievement has its roots in the Czech national revival of the 19th century and widespread efforts across society at the time to support and build an independent Czech (as opposed to Austrian) identity within the ruling Austro-Hungarian Empire.

Bohemia's leading sporting association from that time, Sokol, was founded in 1862 with the twin aims of promoting the benefits of physical activity generally and fostering a budding Czech national identity

through athletic prowess and achievement.

After the country won its independence in 1918, Czechoslovak officials poured significant resources into the national Olympic team as a way of raising the young country's profile on the global stage. During the communist period, the authorities turned once again to sport – this time to a series of mass spectacles of synchronized gymnastics – known as Spartakiads – as a way of legitimising their rule and promoting national cohesiveness.

These Spartakiads were held at five-year intervals, from 1955 to 1985, at Prague's massive Strahov stadium (just west of the top station of the Petřín funicular railway). They were phenomenally popular (or at least well-attended); the Spartakiad in 1960, for example, involved 750,000 participants and was witnessed by more than two million spectators.

After the fall of communism in 1989, the Spartakiads were eventually abandoned (and Strahov stadium has since fallen into ruin), but sport remains central to the country's heart and identity. For proof, one need look no further than the way the country's

streets and pubs empty out whenever Czechia or individual Czech athletes compete in an important international competition, like the Olympic Games, the World Ice Hockey Championships or the football World Cup. The entire country remains glued to the TV, and national pride invariably rises or falls according to the result.

My Heart Belongs to Hockey

Czechs play and excel at many different sports, including cycling, kayaking, skiing, tennis, football and speed-skating (Martina Sáblíková is one of the best speed-skaters in Olympic history), but the nation's heart belongs to ice hockey. It's not entirely clear how Czechs settled on hockey as their national sport, but the experience of guiding a puck along a frozen pond in winter is universal for Czech kids – mostly boys but an increasing number of girls – growing up in a cold climate.

Czechoslovakia (and later Czechia) translated this love of hockey into genuine global success on the rink. Since the debut of the annual World Hockey Championships in 1920, the Czechoslovak and Czech men's teams have won gold no less than 12 times and taken home more than 40 medals. The Czech women's team hasn't enjoyed quite the same level of success, but the women's team took home a historic bronze at the 2022 Ice Hockey Women's World Championship in Denmark and look to have a bright future.

Czechia's successes are no doubt rooted in the competitive nature of the junior leagues all the way up to the country's premier league, the Extraliga, where perennial powers like HC Sparta Praha and HC Kometa Brno often battle it out for the top

TENNIS GREATS
MARTINA NAVRÁTILOVÁ WON 18 GRAND SLAM TENNIS SINGLES TITLES, INCLUDING A WHOPPING NINE VICTORIES AT WIMBLEDON

spot. Czech players are staples on the rosters of many teams in the North American National Hockey League (NHL). Past greats – still household names – include Jaromír Jágr (b 1972), who won the Stanley Cup with Pittsburgh in 1991 and '92. Dominik Hašek (b 1965), the 'Dominator', was once regarded as the world's best goaltender after winning a Stanley Cup with the Detroit Red Wings in 2001.

Ice hockey plays such an important role in the country's psyche that it's indelibly linked to the country's most important political and historical moments. At the 1969 World Ice Hockey Championship in Sweden, the Czechoslovak men's team stunningly defeated the Soviet Union twice during that tournament. The final victory, 4-3 on 28 March 1969, set off delirious riots on Prague's Wenceslas Square and all around the country. The championship came just seven months after the Soviet-led Warsaw Pact invaded Czechoslovakia to crush the country's budding political and economic reforms; emotions on all sides were running hot.

At the 1998 Winter Olympic Games in Nagano, Japan, the Czech men's team repeated that feat, beating the rival Russian Federation by a score of 1-0 to win the gold medal. The country erupted with joy and, once again, Wenceslas Square was flooded with revellers. Delirious fans climbed atop Myslbek's famous statue of St Wenceslas at the upper end of the square.

Masters of Tennis

If Czechs have a second-favourite sport, it would probably be tennis. Nearly every park or field of green has a tennis court nearby. Promising players are typically identified at a young age and steered into highly competitive local and regional tournaments as a launchpad for the international game.

Similar to hockey, Czechs have converted their love of the sport into phenomenal success on the world stage. Indeed, two of the sport's all-time greatest players, Czechs Ivan Lendl (b 1960) and Martina Navrátilová (b 1956), honed their craft here before moving on to global dominance. Lendl commanded the men's circuit for much of the 1980s, winning a total of 11 Grand Slam titles and participating in some 19 finals matches (a record only broken in recent years by Roger Federer). Navrátilová's feats are, if anything, even more impressive. In the late 1970s and throughout the 1980s, she won some 18 Grand Slam singles titles, including a whopping nine victories at Wimbledon, the last coming in 1990. At one point she won six Grand Slam singles titles in a row.

Czechs, particularly female players, continue to perform well in international matches. Two Czech players currently rank among the world's top players. Karolína Plíšková (b 1992), a former world number one, reached the finals at both the 2021 Wimbledon and 2016 US Open tournaments. Petra Kvitová (b 1990) won Wimbledon in 2011 and 2014, and currently hovers around number 20 in the world.

Planning an Active Holiday

Visitors to the country are warmly encouraged to share in Czechs' love of sport. Thousands of kilometres of marked hiking and cycling paths crisscross Bohemia and Moravia and invite endless exploration. Czechs' fondness for skiing has resulted in the country having several decent ski resorts, including at Špindlerův Mlýn in North Bohemia – arguably the best of the resorts. In terms of other participation sports, there are always tennis, golf and beach volleyball. Visitors can also try their hand (or foot) at nohejbal, a uniquely Czech fusion of football and tennis that was first played here in the 1920s.

Czechia is also an excellent destination for spectator sports. The professional ice hockey season runs from September to April and the quality of play is high. The top-league Extraliga's 14 teams are spread out among big cities throughout the country, including Prague, Brno, Olomouc, Karlovy Vary, České Budějovice and Plzeň. Tickets are affordable and often easy to snag mid-season (ticket availability tends to dry up during playoff time).

Attending a football match is also a fun way to spend time and gain insight into the local culture. Czechs' fondness for their national team waxes and wanes in step with how the team performs. The golden age for the men's team arguably came in the late 1990s and early 2000s. In 1996, the Czechs made it to the finals of the UEFA Euro tournament, before losing 2-1 to Germany in a nail-biter at Wembley Stadium. A few years later, in 2004, the national team went on a historic run and nearly won it all before being knocked out in the semi-finals by eventual champs, Greece. These days, the men's team hovers somewhere in the low-30s in the world rankings and doesn't garner nearly the attention it used to. The Czech women's team has improved in recent years but, at the time of writing, has not yet qualified for a major international tournament.

Despite the ups and downs of the national squad, Czechia's leading professional football league, the Fortuna Liga (First League), is highly competitive. In recent years, the 16-team league has been dominated by FC Viktoria Plzeň, though Prague's two main teams, AC Sparta Praha and SK Slavia Praha, usually make a credible showing. The season runs from August to May. As with ice hockey, tickets are affordable and pretty easy to get mid-season.

Of course, football is played at all levels all around the country. Often the best matches – and the best evenings out – are spent in smaller stadiums, holding a beer and cheering on the local heroes.

INDEX

A

accessible travel 211
accommodation 203, *see
also* individual locations
activities 28-9, 36, **38-9**,
see also individual
locations
air travel 200
animals 94, 180, 190, 196,
208, *see also* butterflies,
individual species
archaeological sites
& ruins, *see* historic
buildings & sites
Archduke Franz Ferdinand
d'Este 108
architecture 8-9, 16,
140-1, 224-7, *see also* art
galleries, *see* museums &
galleries
arts & cultural centres, *see
also* cinema, museums &
galleries, theatres
MeetFactory 96
Palác Akropolis 82
Paper Mill 133
Astronomical Clock 63

B

bars 17
Basilica of St George 51
Baťa, Tomáš 183
bathrooms 218
beer 17, 18-9
festivals 33, 132
bicycle travel, *see* cycling
boat tours 113, 138, 162
Bohemia, see also North
& east Bohemia, South &
West Bohemia
itineraries 24-5

Map Pages **000**

236

books 31
breweries 19,
Budvar 140, 141
Krumlov 138
Pilsner Urquell 132
Starobrno 178
Staropramen 96
U Fleku 78
bridges
Charles Bridge 54
Cloak Bridge 136
Lazebnický Bridge 136
Powder Bridge 53
Tyršův Bridge 161
Brno 26, 178-181, **179**
Old Town Hall 181
Třebíč 184
Beyond Brno 182-4
Brno Reservoir 178
budgeting 88
Budvar 18, 19, 140, 141
bus travel 200
business hours 213
butterflies 93

cable car 143
cannabis 192, 208
canoeing 36
car travel 144
castles & chateaux 9, 14-5,
see also palaces
Bečov nad
Teplou castle 131
Český Šternberk 167
Děčín Chateau 161
Dívčí Kámen Castle 139
Hluboká Chateau 141
Hrubý Rohozec
Chateau 151
Karlštejn Castle 23, 104
Kokořín Castle 111
Konopiště Château 108
Křivoklát Castle 110
Lednice Chateau 190
Litomyšl Chateau 168-9
Loket Castle 125
Mělník Château 109
Prague Castle 48
Průhonice Castle 111
Rožmberk Castle 139
Trosky castle 151
Valtice Castle 190

Villa Tugendhat 179
Vyšehrad Castle 100
cathedrals, *see* churches
& cathedrals
caving 36
cell phones 200
cemeteries
Mikulov Jewish
Cemetery 185
Old Jewish Cemetery 65
Olšany cemetery 81
Vyšehrad Cemetery 101
Černý, David 57
České Budějovice
140-1, 141
Český Krumlov 136-9, 137
Český Šternberk 167
Charles Bridge 8-9, 22, 54
chateaux, *see* castles &
chateaux
children, travel with 37, 204
Brno 180-1
iQLANDIA 148
Liberac 148
Prague Zoo 94
Chods, the 135
churches &
cathedrals 10-1, 52,
see also convents &
monasteries
Archbishop's Palace 193
Basilica of St George 51
Basilica of Sts Peter &
Paul 100
Cathedral of Assumption
of Our Lady & St John
the Baptist 165
Cathedral of St Barbora
164
Cathedral of St Moritz 193
Cathedral of Sts Peter &
Paul 180
Cathedral of St
Wenceslas 193
Chapel of St Jan
Sarkander 193
Chapel of St Wenceslas
50
Church of Our Lady
Before Týn 64
Church of Saint Ludmil 85
Church of St James
(Prague) 67

Church of St James 194
Church of St Nepomuk on
the Green Mountain 167
Church of the Holy
Spirit 194
Church of the Most Sacred
Heart of Our Lord 84
House at the Stone
Bell 64
Mariánské Lázně's
Quartet of Churches 128
Rotunda of Our Lady & St
Catherine 191
Sedlec Ossuary 164
St Nicholas Church 55, 64
St Vitus Cathedral 50
climate 28-9
climbing, *see* rock climbing
clothes 30
comedy aimed at 230-1
Communism 13, 67, 74, 224-7
comedy 228-31
convents & monasteries
Capuchin Monastery 178
Convent of St Agnes 66
Sedlec Monastery 164
Strahov Monastery 53
Teplá Monastery 131
Zlatá Koruna
Monastery 139
country code 213
cultural centres, *see* arts &
cultural centres
culture
festivals 135, 176
humour 228-31
religion 222-3
cycling 37, **39**
Vlatava River 79
Karlštejn Castle 113
Slavkovský Forest 131
Jizerské Mountains 153,
Mikulov Wine Trail 188
Czech Switzerland, the
156-9, **157**

Dancing House 75
dangers, *see* safe travel
Děčín 161
disabilities, travellers
with 211

drinking & nightlife 206-7
drinks, see beer, wine

 E

electricity 213
emergencies 213
environmental issues 90, 209
etiquette 30
events see festivals & events

 F

family travel see children, travel with
festivals & events 29
Benátská! festival 147
Český Krumlov International Music Festival 119
Chod festival 135
Christmas markets 119, 132
Colours of Ostrava 176
Gastronomic Festival of MD Rettigovat 33
Karlovy Vary International Film Festival 120
Karlštejnské vinobraní 187
Liberation Festival 132
Mělnické vinobraní 187
Mezipatra 210
Pálavské vinobraní 187
Pilsner Fest 132
Prague Burgerfest 33
Prague Festival of Micro-brewers 33
Prague Pride 210
Queer Ball 210
Riegrovka Live Music Festival 132
St Martin's Day 33, 187
TUTO Jídlo Food Festival 132
Vlčnov's Ride of the Kings 176
Znojmo Wine Festival 33, 177
films 31, 58
festivals 120, 210
fishing 37
food 32-5, 206
festivals 33, 132
football 83, 95
Franz Ferdinand d'Este, Archduke 108
funiculars 37, 48, 54-5, 59, 121-2

 G

galleries, see museums & galleries
gardens, see parks & gardens
gay travellers, see LGBTIQ+ travellers
Golden Lane 51
golf 37
Grandhotel Pupp 122

 H

Hašek, Dominik 234
Havel, Václav 13, 42, 72, 221
favourite cafe (Prague) 78
grandfather, designer of Lucerna Palace 74
namesake airport (Prague) 200
namesake square (Litomyšl) 169
overlooked in a TV poll 200
health 205
highlights 8-19
hiking 36-7, 39
Czech Hiking Club trails 159
Czech Switzerland, the 156-8
Elbe Sandstone Rocks Protected Area 160
Ferdinandova soutěska 158
Jetřichovice 157
Karlovy Vary Region 123
Kopec 158
Labské Pískovce 161
Malá Pravčická brána 158
Mariánské Lázně 130-1
seasons (northern mountains) 152-3
Slavkovský Forest 131
Suchá Kamenice 158
Valtice-Lednice 190
Žižkov 'Highline' 82
historic buildings & sites
Brick Gate & Casemates 102
České Budějovice 140-1
Chodsko 135
Colonnades 120-1
Dietrichstein Burial Vault 186
Gothic Cellars 102
Italian Court 165
Leopold Gate 102
Lidice Memorial 106
Knights' House 170
National Memorial on Vítkov Hill 80
National Memorial to the Heroes of the Heydrich Terror 77, 106
New Town Hall 77
Portmoneum 171
Rotunda of St Martin 100
Sacred Hill (Mikulov) 186
Slavkov u Brna 184
Telč's Historical Centre 194-5
Terezín 107
Troja Château 92
Villa Müller 92
Villa Winternitz 98
history
Brno 219
Charles Bridge 219
Dolní Věstonice 218
Josefov 220
Kutná Hora 219
Národní Třída 221
Old Town Square (Prague) 219
Plzeň (Pilsen) 221
Prague Castle 219
Slavkov u Brna 220
Terezín 220-1
Vila Tugendhat 221
Vyšehrad 218
Wenceslas Square 220
hockey 90
Holešovice 88-91
holidays 213
Holy Trinity Column 9
Hotel Jalta Nuclear Bunker 75

 I

Iron Curtain 13
internet access 200
itineraries 22-7, 23, 25, 27, see also individual regions

 J

Jágr, Jaromír 234
Ještěd 149
Jewish life 12, see also synagogues
John Lennon Wall 57

 K

Kafka, Franz 50-1, 65, 71
Karlovy Vary International Film Festival 118
Karlštejn 23
kayaking & canoeing 36
Kroměříž 26, 196-7, 197
Kutná Hora 163-5, 163
beyond Kutná Hora 166-7

 L

language 31, 214-5
Lendl, Ivan 235
Liberec 148-151, 149
beyond Liberec 152-5
LGBTIQ+ travellers 210
Litomyšl 168-71, 169

 M

Mariánské Lázně 127-9, 127
beyond Mariánské Lázně 130-1
markets, Christmas 119, 132
Mikulov 27, 185-191, 185
mobile phones 200
money 200
Moravia 173-197
itineraries 26-27, 176-7
navigation 174-5
travel seasons 174-5
mountaineering 37
mountains
Český ráj 152, 154-5
Jizerské 152
Klet' 139
Krkonoše 153
Krušné 125-6
safety 205
Pavlovské hills 187
Sněžka 153
Šumava 135
Municipal House 68
museums & galleries
Czech Museum of Music 56
Czech Silver Museum 164
DEPO2015 133
DOX Centre for Contemporary Art 91
Dvořák Museum 76
Franz Kafka Museum 56
Gallery of Central Bohemia 165
Hotel Jalta Nuclear Bunker 75
Karel Zeman Museum 58
Kroměříž' municipal museum 196
Kunsthalle 58
MeetFactory 96
Moravian Museum 181
Moser Glass Experience 123
Mucha Museum 75
Museum Kampa 57
Museum of Communism 74
Museum of Czech Cubism 69
Museum of Decorative Arts 66

Museum of North
  Bohemia 151
Museum of Romani
  Culture 181
Museum of South
  Bohemia 140
Museum of the Infant
  Jesus of Prague 56
Museum of the Senses 74
National Museum 73
National Technical
  Museum 89
Open-air Folk Museum 183
Prague Jewish
  Museum 65
Retro muzeum
  na Statku 181
Retro Muzeum Praha 67
Škoda Family
  Museum 133
South Bohemian Aleš
  Gallery 141
Špilberk Castle 181
Technical Museum 181
Trade Fair Palace 68, 88
Telč Technical
  Museum 195
Zetor Gallery 178
music 31
  classical 70
  festivals 119, 132, 147, 176
  jazz clubs 98
  live 82
  museums 56
  opera 78

Náplavka 78
National Memorial to the
  Heroes of the Heydrich
  Terror 77
national parks 36-9, 38
  Czech Switzerland
    National Park 143
  Saxon Switzerland 159
  Thayatal National Park 191
  Znojmo & the Podyjí 190
Navrátilova, Martina 235
New Town Hall 77
North & East Bohemia
  143-171, 144-5
  itineraries 24-5, 146-7
  navigation 144-5
  travel 144-5

Old Jewish Cemetery 11
Old Town Hall 63
Olomouc 26, 192-3, 193
opening hours 213
Ossuary at St James 178

palaces
  Archbishop's Palace,
    Kroměříž 196
  Lobkowicz Palace 51
  Lucerna Palace 74
  Schwarzenberg
    Palace 52
  Šternberg Palace 52
  Sychrov 151
  Wallenstein Palace 58
Palach, Jan 81
parks & gardens 60
  Kokořín Castle &
    Landscape Park 111
  Křivoklát Castle &
    Landscape Park 110
  Kroměříž Baroque
    Gardens 197
  Květná zahrada 197
  Podzámecká zahrada 197
  Prague Botanical
    Gardens 93
  Průhonice Castle &
    Park 111
  Rieger Gardens 84
  Stromovka Park 95
  Vyšehrad 103
people 222-223
Petřín Hill 59
Pilsner Urquell 18
planning
  Prague & Czechia basics
    30-31
  winter sports 212
Plíškova, Karolína 235
Porsche, Ferdinand 150
Powder Tower 69
Prague 42, 103, 44-5
  accommodation 61, 70,
    79, 83, 99
  activities 46-47
  beyond Prague 104-13
  Bubenec 92-95
  Dejvice 92-95
  drinking & nightlife 53, 59,
    70, 78, 82, 86, 90, 94, 96
  Holešovice 88-91, 89
  Hradčany 48-53, 49
  itineraries 22-3, 46-7
  Jewish Quarter 10, 11, 12, 65
  Karlín 80-83, 81
  Malá Strana 22, 54-61, 55
  navigation 44-5

Nové Město 72, 73
Nový Svĕte 53
Prague Castle 22,
  48-53, 49
  shopping 74, 90, 91, 94
  Smíchov 96-9, 97
  Staré Město 62-71, 63
  travel within Prague
    44-45
  Vinohrady 84-7, 85
  Vršovice 84-87, 85
  Vyšehrad 100-3, 101
  Žižkov 80-3, 81
Plzeň 132-3, 133
  beyond Plzeň 134-5
Prague Zoo 94
public holidays 213
pubs 17, 207

rafting 36
responsible travel 208
rivers
  Elbe 143
  Sázava River 166
  Vltava 70, 78, 140
rock climbing 37, 123, 155
running 37

safe travel 205
Schiele, Egon 137
skiing & snowboarding
  36-9, 212, 38-9
  Harrachov 153
  Jizerská 50 146
  Pec pod Sněžkou 153
  season (South & West
    Bohemia) 118
  Špindlerův Mlýn 153
Smetana, Bedřich 168
Smíchov embankment 97
snowboarding, see skiing &
  snowboarding
snowfall 28
solo travel 205
South & West Bohemia
  115-141, 116-17
  itineraries 24-5, 118-19, 25
  navigation 116-17
  travel 116-17
spa culture
  British Royal
    Connections 129
  Františkovy Lázně 126
  Karlovy Vary 120-1
  Mariánské Lázně's spa
    zone 128
  West Bohemian Spa
    Triangle 126
sports 232-5, see also
  football

squares & plazas
  Jiřího z Poděbrad 86
  náměstí (Mikulov) 186
  náměstí Přemysla
    Otakara II 141
  náměstí Zachariáše z
    Hradce 194
  Old Town Square
    (Prague) 62
  Olomouc's Piazzas 192
  Smetanovo náměstí 170
  Týn Courtyard 69
Staropramen 18-9, 96
statues
  Horní náměstí
    columns 192
  Jan Hus (Ladislav
    Šaloun) 62
  K (David Černý) 76
  Marian Column 62
  Plague Column 165
  Proudy (David Černý) 57
  Quo Vadis (David
    Černý) 57
  St John of Nepomuk 54
Švabinský, Max 196
swimming 36
synagogues 65
  Great Synagogue 132
  Old-New Synagogue 65
  Pinkas Synagogue 65
  Rear Synagogue 184

Telč 27, 194-5, 195
tennis 234-5
Terezín 23
theatres
  Estates Theatre 67
  Kasárna Karlín 82
  Municipal House 68
  National Theatre 76
  Palác Akropolis 82
  Rudolfinum 66
  State Opera 78
  Švandovo Divadlo 98
time zone 213
toilets 213
tours
  Brno underground 181
  Budvar Brewery 141
  carriage rides 138
  Crystal Valley 149
  Czech Switzerland,
    the 158
  Moravian wine 186
  Litomyšl, trips from 171
  Graphite Mine 138
  Krumlov Brewery 138
  Magic Herb Garden 138
  Telč underground 195
  travel to/from Prague &
    Czechia 200

Map Pages 000

travel within Prague &
  Czechia 201
Třebíč 184

Váchal, Josef 171
vegan travellers 33
vegetarian travellers 33
Velvet Revolution 13, 72
visas 200
Vyšehrad 23

walking 16, 36-7, **39**
walking tours
  Liberac 150-151
  Plzeň 132-3
  Prague pubs 99, **99**
water 213
weather 28-29
weights & measures 213
Wenceslas Square 72

wi-fi 200
wine
  Brod nad Dyjí 188
  festivals 33, 187
  Mělník 109
  Mikulov Wine Trail 188
  Moravia 176, 177, 185, 186
  National Wine Centre 190
  Pálava area 188
  Plzeň 133
  tours 177, 186, 188, 190
  Vinařské Centrum 188

Zlín 183
Znojmo 27

"Linking the south and west of Czechia (p115) are endless forests and mountains, an unbroken string of virtually uninhabited, thickly forested peaks and valleys."

MARC DI DUCA

"Spending an evening in the pub (p207) may be Czechia's quintessential experience. The pub is more than a bar and means more than the beer. It functions as the country's collective living room."

MARK BAKER

THIS BOOK

Design development
Marc Backwell

Content development
Mark Jones, Sandie Kestell, Anne Mason, Joana Taborda

Cartography development
Katerina Pavkova

Production development
Sandie Kestell, Fergal Condon

Series development leadership
Darren O'Connell, Piers Pickard, Chris Zeiher

Commissioning Editor
Daniel Bolger

Product Editor
Gary Quinn

Book Designer
Hannah Blackie

Cartographer
Katerina Pavkova

Coordinating Editor
Barbara Delissen

Assisting Editor
Kellie Langdon

Cover Researcher
Naomi Parker

Thanks Esteban Fernandez, Gwen Cotter, Charlotte Orr, Kathryn Rowan

LEFT: I. HAJEK/SHUTTERSTOCK ©
RIGHT: WESTEND61/GETTY IMAGES ©

MIX
Paper from responsible sources
FSC™ C021741
www.fsc.org

Paper in this book is certified against the Forest Stewardship Council™ standards. FSC™ promotes environmentally responsible, socially beneficial and economically viable management of the world's forests.

Published by Lonely Planet Global Limited
CRN 554153
13th edition - June 2023
ISBN 978 1 78701 6316
©Lonely Planet 2023 Photographs © as indicated 2023
10 9 8 7 6 5 4 3 2 1
Printed in China